four souls

Matt Kronberg
Mike Peterson

Jedd Medefind
Trey Sklar

W Publishing Group™

www.wpublishinggroup.com

A Division of Thomas Nelson, Inc.
www.ThomasNelson.com

Library of Congress Cataloging-in-Publication Data

4 souls / by Matt Kronberg ... [et al.].

    p. cm.

   ISBN 0-8499-1633-X

   1. Christian biography. 2. Kronberg, Matt, 1974—Journeys. 3. Medefind, Jedd, 1974—Journeys. 4. Peterson, Mike, 1974—Journeys. 5. Sklar, Richard, 1975—Journeys. I. Title: Four souls. II. Kronberg, Matt, 1974–

BR1700.3 .A14 2001

270.8'3'0922—dc21

[B]

                                   2001026272

Printed in the United States of America

01 02 03 04 05 PHX 7 6 5 4 3 2

Acknowledgments

We would like to extend our heartfelt gratitude to the many remarkable individuals from around the world who welcomed us into their homes and lives throughout our journey.

This book would not have been possible without the generous help and love of our dedicated wives, families, and friends. We are deeply grateful to you all. A special thanks to Dr. David Winter, Coach Jim Birschbach, Mr. Jason Hamm, and Senator Tim Leslie for believing in the vision behind this book and working with us as we seek to travel the most excellent road called "Epic Life."

"WHAT DO YOU HAVE THAT YOU DID NOT RECEIVE?"
1 CORINTHIANS 4:7

TO GOD BE THE GLORY

Contents

Preface vii

Introduction: First Seeds of an Adventure .ix

Part I: Mexico
1. 3,000 Miles in Ten Days 1

Part II: Guatemala
2. A Lesson in Generosity: Guatemala City, Guatemala 21
3. The Four Amigos! Together in Guatemala City 34
4. Into the Highlands: Uspantan, Guatemala 47
5. A Scathing Letter and Some Sweet Sorrow: Leaving Guatemala . .61

Part III: Russia and Beyond
6. The Wounded Bear: Moscow, Russia 71
7. The Secret Police: Orekhovo-Zuyevo, Russia 75
8. Scarred Hands and Iron Doors: Serpukhov, Russia 92
9. Village at the Edge of the World: Loly, Russia 102
10. Heart of the Gulag Region: Yemva, Russia 117
11. Waltzing through the West: From Moscow
    to the Mediterranean Sea 139

Part IV: Egypt
12. Land of the Pharaohs: Cairo, Egypt .153

Part V: South Africa
13. Beauty and Strife 171
14. The Mountain Kingdom: Maseru, Kingdom of the Lesotho . . .176
15. The Road to Durban 193

Part VI: India
16. Rajas, Rice, and Rickshaws 215
17. A Change of Plans: Chirala, India 238

18. Sisters of Charity: Calcutta, India 249

Part VII: Bangladesh
19. The End of Our Rope 261
20. 100,000 Rickshaws: Dhaka, Bangladesh 285

Part VIII: Thailand
21. From Mosquito Nets to Marble Tile: Bangkok, Thailand 301

Part IX: Vietnam
22. Notes from the Underground 329

Conclusion: The Adventure Begins 358

vi

Preface

there was definitely some fear. Hope as well. The two are always inter-twined in one way or another.

The four of us—Matt, Jedd, Mike, and Trey, all seniors at Westmont College in Santa Barbara, California—stood at one of those points in life where the future seemed to lay spread out before us like a boundless land-scape, heavy with both expectation and uncertainty.

We could not shake our feeling that the expected, "sensible" routes might not actually lead to the fullness and purpose we hoped for. Would life out there ultimately leave us weekend-waiting, vacation-dreaming, diversion-driven, and dissatisfied?

We knew we had to choose our own route, or else the expectations of others, along with the ruts of our culture, would make the decision for us. If we were serious about pursuing something more in life, we had to start *now*.

Grad schools pressed for decisions and job opportunities tugged at our shirt-sleeves, but a different idea also began to take shape: the prospect of traveling around the world working with local Christians for the better part of a year after we graduated.

Perhaps we heard the same voice calling us that has beckoned young people throughout the centuries, drawing them to board an explorer's ship, enlist in the cavalry, or join the wagon train heading west. We wanted more than just adventure, though. We wanted to discover something we called "epic life," the kind of living that would make each day worth waking up for. We desired to see our character grow stronger, our relationships deeper, and our vision of life clearer. Though we did not know exactly what epic life would look like or just how it should be defined, we simply knew we had to find it.

This story is about that quest, as best we can tell it, our discoveries alongside the bumps, bruised expectations, and jagged edges. Many of the questions we ask—and sometimes try to answer—are questions others have wrestled with as well: Is the "good life" really the best life? Who defines success? What will I value on my deathbed? How can I best serve God and my neighbor? What can I learn from people whose lives are radically different from my own? How can I learn to love my friends well, day after day and mile after mile?

We do not venture into these questions as theologians or philosophers, but as fellow explorers on a grand journey. Our hope is that the stories can be experienced by you in much the same way they were experienced by us: sometimes provoking, sometimes enlightening, sometimes confusing. If you are looking for a master plan for life, you will not find it here. You may end up with more to wrestle with than when you started. But if you are up for a journey, join us for the adventure of four souls in pursuit of real life. Our travels together just might get you moving in the direction you want to go.

Matt Kronberg   Jedd Medefind
Mike Peterson   Trey Sklar

California, 2001

Introduction

First Seeds of an Adventure

The little knots of Friends who turn their backs on the "World"
are those who really transform it.

—C. S. Lewis, *The Four Loves*

trey burst through the front door of our apartment.

"Sorry I'm late!" he called, slightly out of breath. His hair stuck out every which way, and his wire-rimmed glasses were slightly askew. He had been driving his Jeep with the top down, as usual.

Matt looked up from his philosophy text. "We're all ready. Let's get Mike and Jedd in here."

Mike came in through the back door, his surfboard under his arm.

"What's that smell?" Matt wrinkled his nose.

"Just fiberglass. I had to patch a ding in my board."

"If you don't mind, let it dry outside. You're going to get us all high."

A moment later, Jedd emerged from the closet he had converted into a study. It was humorous to see his tall body squeeze out of that small space. He shoved aside a pair of dirty socks and flopped down on the old orange couch between Trey and Matt.

Jedd looked at the other three. "So, tonight we decide."

Matt agreed. "Graduation is just a few months away. We're going to have to nail down our decisions about grad schools and job offers."

"I've already put down one deposit for law school and the next one is due soon," said Jedd.

Trey nodded. "The trip will fall by the wayside unless we commit to it now. As I see it, tonight we have to decide the question one way or another."

"Someone want to pray before we begin?" suggested Jedd.

"I'll do it," said Mike.

We bowed our heads as Mike requested God's guidance in our decision. Then, Jedd picked up again. "Okay, guys. I think we all feel the same. We've talked about the trip plenty. But now we're at the point where if it's going to happen, we have to totally plunge in and let our other options go."

"Let me say something real quick," said Trey. He could hardly hold himself back. Trey's energy and irrepressible optimism were probably the main reason we were still discussing the idea of such a venture at all. "See guys, we've got to think about the *purpose* of a trip like this. This vision we have isn't just about traveling. Everywhere we'd go, we'd live with the locals. We'd be working with them and learning from them. It'd be incredible! Even if there'd be some things that would be a little hard, it would shape us into the kind of men we want to be."

Mike smiled at Trey's enthusiasm. "Hey, I'm definitely in," he said. "The work I do with my concession business wraps up by October. If we can wait until then to leave, I'm committed." Mike worked in the family business, selling concessions at summer fairs. Recently, he had purchased the business from his grandfather, which committed him to operating concession stands at nearly a dozen fairs over the course of the summer.

Jedd offered his verdict next. "Well, you know law school was my plan. The more I think about it, though, the more I want to put it on hold. Once the wheels of grad school start turning and the loans build up, I'll probably never have another chance to do something like this. If Matt is in, too, I'll call UVA tomorrow and tell them to pull my application."

We were not sure what to expect as we turned toward Matt. His parents had expressed reservations about the trip, particularly regarding the safety of traveling in Third World countries.

"I've told you guys it's difficult for me to feel totally comfortable with something like this," he said, pausing momentarily as if still thinking it through. "I usually like to know exactly what I'm getting into before making any big decisions."

Trey groaned, but Matt continued. "I've been thinking, though, about what I want my life to be about. I really *do* want to be someone who steps out and takes risks, who grows deep with a few good friends, and learns how to better serve God and people in need. I really can't imagine a better way to do that than . . ."

"So you're in!" declared Trey.

"That's what I'm saying," affirmed Matt. He paused, then continued, "Grad school can wait. I don't really know what we are getting into, and I still have some doubts. But I'm excited, and right now I'd rather have this uncertainty than anything else."

We fell silent for a moment, feeling as if we had crossed a line in the sand. Expectations we had held for years were now officially shoved to the side. The only thing standing in their place was an idea, a somewhat vague idea, that was far-fetched and perhaps even impossible.

Trey wrote in his journal later that night.

 Trey's Reflections—January 28

We're all committed! I feel just about as excited as I've ever been. This trip idea is what I've always hoped for: a great adventure that will help lead me to be the man I want to be.

When I think of previous generations—even my father's years as a soldier in Vietnam—it seems that people faced such amazing challenges. For my generation of Americans, these kinds of trials have become rare. Like it or not, this is the generation of cushy circumstances—no World War, no Vietnam, no famine, and jobs available for just about anyone who is willing to work. On the surface, this is a blessing, but I believe our character is weaker.

Trials test character. In an extended difficult situation, you find out how long you can last on nothing but your deepest beliefs—and if you make it through, you come out stronger and ready for more. I hunger to be sharpened into a man who can be used by God. This trip around the world could do just that. I know it would involve some trials, but I'm willing to accept those for the benefit I see in it. If it can lead toward the kind of meaningful, purposeful life I hope to live, then it is worth anything I can put into it.

Getting It All Together . . .

To actually begin was thrilling . . . and also daunting. How would we ever organize an around-the-world trip? Discovering the right places to go would be a task much bigger than us. And what could we actually offer to the people with whom we would stay?

Our little apartment soon became the incubator for the specific plans for the trip. International phone calls, e-mails, and letters—often to people we had never met—began to open possibilities for living and working all around the globe.

The time we planned to spend in each country would be relatively brief—probably only one or two months. People who had spent years in overseas service warned us about the pitfalls into which "short-termers" often fall. Many rush into a place expecting to perform some heroic work in only a few days. As a result, they leave either disappointed or bloated with what they think they have accomplished. Although service projects and other work alongside the locals would be a central part of the trip, they would not be the foundation. Instead, we would set our vision based upon what we believed were the key aspects of *epic life*.

We expressed our priorities in the following mission statement:

> *To come to know and love Jesus Christ in a deeper and more meaningful way through loving and serving people throughout the world. To come to know and love each other in a deeper and more meaningful way. Finally, to share the love of Jesus through our actions and our words.*

The question of funding soon became significant. Though housing costs would be low, due to the fact that we planned to live and eat with the local people, there were still travel expenses. And our little savings accounts would not cover it all. Mike was strongly opposed to seeking outside support for the trip and our work. He hated asking for money, especially from people he knew. Mike had always been self-reliant, working long summer hours in the family concession business and starting a few of his own entrepreneurial ventures to pay his way through college.

"We'll earn as much as we can during the summer, but I don't think we can do it without raising some support," argued Trey.

"I don't like asking people for money, either," added Matt, "but I think there are some people out there who would be excited about being a part of this. I'm sure our churches would help some, too."

We realized right away that we did not all have equal fund-raising connections. If each of us had to be responsible for our own funds, it seemed likely that not all of us would be able to go. We would be a true team in all respects. Each of us brought certain talents and abilities to the group—access to funds was only one of these. The early Christians described in the book of Acts would serve as our model. Every cent brought in for the trip would be shared equally. Either we would raise enough money for all of us to go, or we wouldn't go at all.

Opportunities for places to work and live on the trip showed up in the most unexpected ways. Time after time, it seemed that one friend knew another who happened to know someone who just might want to put us to use. In the final weeks of school—after months of planning—a tentative route for our trip began to take shape.

We would start in Guatemala with Salomón and Mery Hernández, a Guatemalan couple committed to serving their poorer countrymen. We would help them construct a clinic from which they could help those otherwise not able to afford medical care. Since the soon-to-be-built clinic would need an ambulance, we planned to purchase a used one and drive it down through Mexico to Guatemala.

We intended to fly to Russia next. Since Trey's father worked in Moscow, we could stay with Trey's family for a few days before joining the work of a former world-class wrestler named Steve Barrett, who did service and evangelism throughout the former Soviet Union.

From Russia, we would pass briefly through Europe and Egypt on our way to southern Africa. We would teach English and other classes at the Mount Tabor school for village children in the Kingdom of the Lesotho.

Next would come India. In addition to spending some time with an Indian pastor and his family, we would volunteer at Mother Teresa's Home for the Sick and Dying in Calcutta.

From Calcutta, we would fly to Bangladesh, and join the work of Bangladesh Christian Service, a branch of the JESUS Film Project run by nationals.

After Bangladesh, we would assist in a microeconomic development project in Thailand operated by World Vision. Finally, we would smuggle Bibles to the underground church in Vietnam, and attempt to join the work of another World Vision group during our short time there. Before returning home, we would stay briefly with Matt's aunt and uncle in Shekou, China.

And Taking It on the Road

Graduation was bittersweet. We had never felt both so sad to leave a place and yet so excited about what lay ahead. Countless details would need to be worked out over the summer months—visas acquired, more contacts established, funds raised, train and boat schedules obtained, and much more. Since his father had served in the army, Trey grew up living all over the world. His international studies major in college—which included a semester studying in Zimbabwe—also contributed to his excellent sense of the world and travel. He was the natural for our logistical point man. Within a few weeks after graduation, he had already set up a makeshift office, complete with a phone hot line and Web page.

With little more than a month remaining, we still did not have an ambulance lined up to purchase and drive to Guatemala. A company that sold used ambulances continued to promise that one would become available, but as the departure date drew near, nothing had materialized. If we could not purchase an ambulance, we would need to buy plane tickets to Guatemala.

Just days before we planned to purchase the tickets, we received a phone call from a fellow Westmont alum, a young man who had spent time working with Salomón and Mery some years before and had come to believe deeply in their work. Hearing of our trip, he had decided to donate his 1993 Ford Ranger with a camper shell to their work in Guatemala.

We contacted Salomón to ask if he thought the truck would meet their need for an ambulance. He said it would work perfectly. Jedd and Mike would drive the truck down through Mexico. Matt and Trey would travel via plane, arriving in time to welcome them to Guatemala.

The only major dilemma remaining was funding. We had pooled our summer earnings in a single, shared account. Friends, family members, and our churches contributed significantly as well. Even so, we were more than $10,000 short of our projected budget as the day of departure approached.

Matt's face was uncharacteristically flushed when Trey informed him of the financial situation. Trey's prior reports on the success of our fund-raising had suggested a much more optimistic picture. "What do you mean, Trey? That is *all* we have in our account? I thought you said we already had most of the money we needed. After we pay for our plane tickets, we'll hardly have a cent left for the trip itself."

Trey was apologetic. "I thought we had more than we do. It's been really hard to get any information about our account the last few weeks. There's quite a few people who told me they're still planning to contribute, but I don't exactly feel comfortable reminding them."

"Well, what should we do? If we're still planning to go, we have to send in our check for the plane tickets tomorrow."

"It doesn't seem like a question to me. We're just going to need to jump and expect that the parachute is going to open. I think it will."

Phone calls to Mike and Jedd confirmed we would proceed as planned. We would depart with enough in the bank to get us through two months of the trip and trust that the rest would come through.

Matt's Reflections—September 29

I've been in few situations that require faith like this. Usually I set up my own safety nets—just in case things don't work out like I planned.

The place I'm in now is different. I don't have anything to fall back on. This trip can only succeed if God comes through for us on the money and everything else. If He does, it will be a great faith-building experience. If things don't work out . . . well . . . I guess it will be an adventure nonetheless.

I Mexico

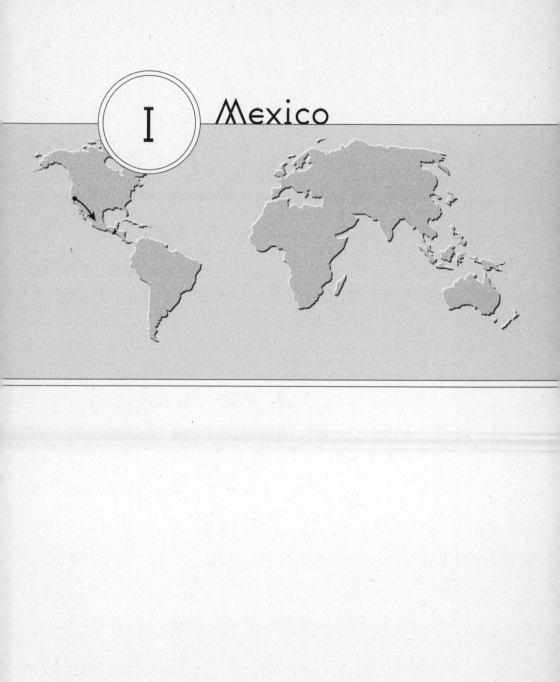

3,000 Miles in Ten Days

He either fears his fate too much,
Or his deserts are small,
That puts it not unto the touch
To win or lose it all.

—James Graham, Marquess of Montrose

the truck border station appeared strangely deserted. Just a few miles away, the main border station in Nogales passed hundreds of cars an hour through a half-dozen kiosks. This one did not even have a stop sign. Its fluorescent lights looked feeble beneath the jeweled stars that spattered the desert sky.

"You think this is really where we were supposed to go?" questioned Mike.

Jedd shrugged. "We followed the directions that guard gave us. I would have expected something a little bigger, though."

We had begun the day in California, Highway 8 carrying us east and south from San Diego to the edge of Mexico. We arrived at the border town of Nogales, Arizona, as the last traces of a watercolor sunset faded from the sky. Our first attempt to cross at Nogales's main border station had failed when one of the guards would not let us through.

1

"You've got too many boxes of medical supplies. You need to go to the *truck* border crossing," he insisted.

Now we were making a second go of it at the truck crossing, hoping we would not face any further complications. A uniformed man leaned back in a wooden chair in front of the office, chin on chest. Without raising his head, he waved us through with a flick of his hand.

Jedd waved back. "That was easier than I expected."

The highway ahead loomed lightless, save for a handful of cracked reflectors that offered back the glow from our headlights. We had not driven more than a few miles when a fluorescent blaze rose out of the darkness. Signs in Spanish and English indicated a stop was required.

"I guess I spoke too soon," said Jedd, a bit disappointed.

He turned into a pebble-strewn lot and parked next to a few other vehicles. Nearby stood a complex of several buildings—mostly concrete painted green. Inside what seemed to be the main building, several people were filling out papers, writing against the bare wall since there were no counters. A Mexican-American was arguing with one of the officials who would not let him take his daughter any farther into Mexico without written permission from her mother. The little girl sat quietly on a wooden chair, glancing around with large brown eyes.

It took forty-five minutes to wade through the paperwork and fees. We had to charge an amount equal to 20 percent of the truck's estimated value onto Mike's credit card, nearly $2,000. If the truck did not exit the country within a month, they would assume we had sold it and would collect the money as a tariff. If we left the country as we promised, we would get the entire amount back . . . hopefully.

As we pulled back onto the road, we noticed that at the far end of the complex stood a lone guard shack. We slowed as we approached. It was nearly midnight. Two men were smoking and talking inside.

"Do we have to stop again, Mike?"

"I don't know. Did you see any signs telling us we need to?"

"No."

"Well, let's go then."

Once past the shack, Jedd pushed down on the accelerator. He took one last look in the rearview mirror and saw two men come out of the shack and run toward a military Jeep parked nearby.

"Uh-oh, Mike, I think those guys are coming after us."

"Think we can outrun them?" said Mike dryly.

Jedd laughed. "Not in this truck."

We slowed, moved onto the shoulder, and turned around. As we pulled up alongside the guard station, the two men stepped out of their Jeep, yelling in Spanish and motioning to the area under a large awning that covered several long, green tables. We stopped next to the tables and got out. The man was still shouting, his speech so rapid we could understand very little of what was being said. Jedd gave Mike a rough translation: "He's mad at us."

Border Problems

After another string of angry Spanish, the shouter stormed away and reentered the guard shack. The other fellow, a younger man, stepped forward. His English wasn't bad. "You speak Spanish?"

"Only a little," said Mike.

"Okay, I will try English then. You see, that man, the captain, he is angry."

"What's the problem?"

"He wants to know why you tried to sneak past us."

"We weren't trying to sneak past you. We didn't know we were supposed to stop."

"Yes. You must stop. We put up the red light for you."

Mike was growing defensive. "I didn't see that. Did you, Jedd?"

"I didn't see anything that looked like we had to stop."

The guard glanced back at the shack before giving us orders. "You must go unload everything in your truck on those tables."

Mike was carefully laying his old surfboard on the table next to our backpacks when the captain emerged from the office. He went straight for the largest boxes, his face deadpan as he riffled through the medical supplies: cases of gauze, empty blood sample vials, aspirin, rubber gloves, and the like. Among the donated medical supplies there was even a box of three hundred Chap Sticks.

The junior guard spoke up again. "The captain wants to know what is all this."

Jedd responded in Spanish. "It is all medical supplies for the poor in Guatemala."

"Do you have permission for them?"

We showed them the papers we had acquired at the last station, but they were not satisfied. We had heard that a special permit might be required

3

to bring medical supplies into Mexico. Such permits, though, were to be acquired three months prior to entry, and our supplies had been donated to us only the previous month. We had decided to risk it, as most of the supplies were past their official "expiration date" and would just have gone to waste in the U.S. even though they were still usable.

The captain stomped off to his shack again. The guard's eyes narrowed as he turned back to us. "This is very bad. The captain says we are going to have to impound your truck."

"Impound our truck!" exclaimed Mike.

"Yes. And we will fine you three times the value of your medical supplies, which the captain says is $3,000. Your fine will be $9,000. When you pay it, you can get the truck back."

We looked at each other. The guard seemed to be waiting for something. We felt the first tinges of desperation. "Is there anything you could do to help us?"

The guard's face didn't flinch, but he smiled faintly. He opened his palms toward us and tilted his head to one side. "Yes, we are men of honor. Let me go talk to the captain. I will try to help you."

The captain was standing, arms crossed, next to the guard shack. Beneath his narrow mustache, a hand-rolled cigarette hung from thin lips.

The two men disappeared into the office. A minute later the guard returned. "I think I have been able to help," he announced with a magnanimous gesture. "This is a *very* bad situation, but I have told the captain you might not be able to pay the entire amount. How much of your fine can you pay?"

We exchanged glances, wondering what to suggest. It appeared that a game of good cop/bad cop was developing. Mike took a stab. "Forty dollars."

The guard snorted. "That will not be enough for the captain. Wait a minute." He returned to the office.

When he rejoined us, he had the look of a warm-hearted benefactor on his face. "The captain is still very upset, but I argued with him. All you will need to pay is $200."

"We are not wealthy. We are only going to help the poor in Guatemala. We just do not have enough money," replied Jedd.

The guard let out a sigh. "Just a minute. I will see if there is anything more I can do."

When he came back, he was shaking his head. "The captain says $40 is still not enough. You will need to come up with more."

We huddled for a moment. Finally, Mike offered, "We can give you $40 and this box of Chap Stick. That is the best we can do."

"I will see if that is enough."

After another brief conference with the captain, the guard announced that our proposal would be sufficient. "The only problem is," he said apologetically, "we will not be able to give you a receipt. We ran out yesterday."

We reloaded the truck quickly. As Mike reached into his pocket for the money, the guard blurted out, "Wait! Do not pay us here. Just drive down the road a little ways and put the box and the money by the side of the road."

He waved as we drove off down the road. Jedd glanced at Mike and shook his head. "Those jerks. I'm tempted to hit the gas and not look back."

Still within sight of the station, we pulled over. The box of Chap Stick was behind the driver's seat. As he placed the forty dollars in it, Jedd scooped a few handfuls of the tubes out onto the floor of the truck. Mike chuckled. "What's that for?"

"You never know when we might need some Chap Stick."

We set the box by the side of the road and hopped back into the truck. The blaze of the station, like a bad dream, faded as quickly as it had appeared. A few house lights twinkled on the horizon, timid reflections of the stars above. We drove on, our adrenaline slowly beginning to ebb.

Several minutes later, Jedd broke the silence. "I really don't know what to think about that, Mike. I just don't know."

"We didn't have much of a choice."

"We could have said, 'Go ahead and impound the truck if you want, but we won't give you a bribe . . .'"

"They said it was a *fine*."

"It was pretty clear what it was."

"They were the government officials, demanding a payment. We gave it."

"There's a lot of good officials out there who would probably like to root out this sort of thing. Then we go and . . ."

"Come on, you've got to deal with the face the government gives you. What do you do—tell 'em to go ahead and impound the truck?"

"I don't know. It's not clear-cut. What's the higher good—refusing to cooperate with corrupt officials, or just trying to get this stuff to people

5

who need it? I guess I feel all right about our motives. I just wonder if we should have done things differently."

"It seems pretty simple to me."

Mike's Reflections—October 9

I don't understand why Jedd is worried about what we did tonight. It seems he wrestles with his conscience so much. At times he reminds me of what I have read about the author Leo Tolstoy—always determined to do the right thing, yet sometimes tearing himself up as he wrestles over the questions of which path is best.

Maybe I should be worried about this bribe issue, but in all honesty I'm not. Corruption in many governments goes all the way to the top. Paying bribes is just part of the unwritten law down here. The locals understand that. As foreigners, I think we need to be flexible and, at times, work within their "system."

By 2:00 A.M., our conversation had run out, along with the last bits of our energy.

"I don't know how much longer I can keep my eyes open, Mike," said Jedd. "I thought for sure we'd come across a little hotel or something by now."

"Let's just take a dirt road a ways up and find a place to lay out our sleeping bags," suggested Mike.

A half-hour later, however, we still had not come across any promising side roads. Jedd pulled to the side of the highway and parked behind a thin patch of bushes. The truck would be only slightly visible from the road. We tossed our pads and sleeping bags on the ground and climbed in. Even the semitrucks, rumbling past ten yards away, could not keep us from sleep.

Southbound

The dawn's first light pried our eyes open. Traffic on the highway was picking up, and it was hopeless to try to go back to sleep.

"Mike, look at this," said Jedd, indicating the area around our bags.

Mike's puffy eyes surveyed the ground. Wads of toilet paper—some old, others fresh—lay everywhere.

"I think we just slept in the middle of a truckdriver poop stop."

"Wonderful."

After tossing the bags back in the truck, we downed a couple of bagels and got back on the highway. Three thousand miles of Mexican road lay ahead. If we were going to meet Matt, Trey, and Salomón at the border in ten days as we planned, we'd have to put in some long hours behind the wheel.

Jedd and Mike

7

Mike reached down and tried the radio. Nothing but mariachi. He popped in the truck's only tape instead—*Selena's Greatest Hits* in Spanish.

"I can't believe we didn't think of bringing any music for the drive," said Mike, shaking his head.

"Look at the bright side. We'll know every word of this Selena tape by the time we get to Guatemala."

Meanwhile, in Santa Barbara . . .

With less than a week before their flight to Guatemala, Trey and Matt still had to take care of dozens of last-minute details. Once on the road, communication with people in other countries would be extremely difficult.

The majority of our plans were well established, but the itinerary still had some gaps. Our Russian and Bangladeshi visa requests were still being processed. We had yet to find contacts for India and Vietnam. Our budget was still more than $10,000 short. These details and more would need to come together long after we were past the point of no return.

Deeper Still

Thick vines and ivies, accented by flowers of pink and purple, covered everything that had not been cultivated in the previous year or two. Nestled within the tropical valleys, rows of corn, fruit orchards, and expansive fields of sugarcane fought to hold on to the space they had won from the wild growth. The buzz of unseen insects filled the car when the windows were down.

Mike glanced over at Jedd. He seemed to be in thought after a conversation they had had earlier. "Still thinking about your mom?"

Jedd nodded. His mother had been diagnosed with breast cancer just a few months before. He thought about not leaving with the other guys, but she insisted that he go—he could fly home quickly enough if he was needed.

Mike reassured, "Your dad and your brothers will take good care of her."

"I know. It's just hard sometimes to think about not being there with them."

"Your family's really close."

"Yeah. I'm definitely going to miss my brothers and my parents."

Mike grinned, trying to lighten the conversation. "I've always said, you're the all-American boy."

Jedd smiled. When they had first arrived at Westmont, neither he nor Mike had thought much of each other. Mike's waist-length surfer hair and undershirt tank tops did not sit well with him. Jedd's near-perfect grades and athlete status did nothing to endear him to Mike, either. It took several years for them to realize they actually did enjoy each other despite their differences.

o o o

As our road rejoined the coast late in the day, orchards of coconut trees stretched along the shoreline as far as the eye could see. Banana trees had been planted between the taller coconut trees so that two expansive planes of greenery ran parallel to the ground. In the open spaces, palm-covered huts appeared amid the high grass.

"This place looks like Hawaii without the tourists," Jedd remarked.

"You've been to Hawaii?"

"No. It just looks like the pictures."

"Neither have I. I'd take a place like this over Hawaii for a vacation any day, though. No tourist traps or crowds. Just relaxing, eating tacos, and surfin'."

"Sounds nice. My family never took many travel vacations when I was growing up. I guess with my dad working as a ranger, we saw the whole summer as a vacation."

Jedd's father was a high school biology teacher, but in the summers, he worked as a horse patrol ranger in Yosemite National Park. Every year when school got out, the family headed up to their little two-room cabin in the mountains for three months.

"You guys really liked living in Yosemite, didn't you?"

Jedd smiled at the thought. "Seasonal rangers don't earn much more than minimum wage—they say they get paid in sunsets. It sure wasn't the money. My dad—we all—just loved being up there."

"That's great. I'll tell you one thing—I don't want to be the type of guy that doesn't do anything more than *survive* fifty weeks out of the year just so he can get to his two weeks of vacation."

"It's pretty sad how many people seem to live that way. I mean, not only the high-stress guys who hate everything except for their vacation time, but, you know . . . there just don't seem to be that many people out there living with the kind of purpose or joy I want to live with. There's so much halfhearted—"

"You mean, the way most people live seems to be less than epic life?"

Jedd nodded. "Part of me is afraid that's just the way it's going to be now that college is over. So many people graduate just praying they'll get well-paying jobs. What good are big paychecks if life is just ho-hum?"

Jedd continued, "Last summer I worked for Price-Waterhouse. The guy I was working for was billing at over $500 an hour. But I kept thinking, *Even if I make it to be twice as successful as this guy, I wouldn't necessarily be all that happy.*"

Mike nodded. "Yeah. You see so many people out there and you wonder, *Is that going to be me in ten years?*"

"I hope not."

"Yeah, but what's going to keep it from happening?"

"We're on this trip now. That's a good first step."

"Yeah, but how are we going to live out epic life when we get home at the end of it all? That's the most important question."

"I'm hoping we'll have figured that out by then."

"I hope so, too."

Jedd glanced out the window and took his foot off the accelerator. "You mind if we stop for a minute? I want to see if I can climb one of those coconut trees."

∘ ∘ ∘

The beauty stayed with us the following day, but large chunks of the road were missing in places, often opening into drops of a foot or more.

"How's your back doing, Mike?" asked Jedd. A slew of snowboarding accidents over the years had left Mike's back with a few odd kinks. Jedd knew that repeated ten-hour days seated in a truck must be agitating it a little.

Mike shrugged. "Not too bad." Jedd doubted Mike would admit it even if he was in pain.

Jedd swerved to avoid another large pothole. "These are the biggest holes we've seen yet."

"It's getting worse. I'm wondering if it's from the hurricane."

A few miles later, Jedd was forced to bring the truck to an abrupt stop. "I expected some bad roads, but I never expected this."

A large fissure, six feet deep, jagged across the highway.

"Man," Mike responded. He peered over the dash into the crevice for a moment, then suggested, "It looks like you might be able to get around up there."

Jedd managed to squeeze the truck between the cliff wall and the crack and continued. As we drew nearer to Acapulco, the destruction of the hurricane grew increasingly pronounced. More fissures, some more than twenty feet deep, split the road and forced major detours. Cement bridges had been torn apart and washed downstream. Cars lay where they had been crushed against houses, some covered almost completely by sand.

Groups worked here and there to clear the wreckage and begin the long rebuilding process. A few just sat, staring futilely at the wreckage that had been their homes.

The Mexican army had been called out to help. Some of the green-garbed men repaired roads or cleaned debris from the streets. Others worked alongside the locals to construct short-term shelters.

"The newspaper I saw this morning said Hurricane Paula killed more than two hundred people," remembered Mike.

"I can't imagine how these people feel."

"You get a sense by looking at their faces, don't you?"

Unable to pass through the center of Acapulco, we returned to a detour that led through the hills and back down to the highway on the far side of the city.

Once past Acapulco, we covered a hundred miles in less than three hours, only occasionally forced to circumvent major potholes and encountering fewer than a dozen cars. The day and our energy were on their way out when we came upon an unlikely sight. There appeared, out of nowhere, a vicious traffic jam—both lanes of the road, and even both shoulders, were blocked by lines of cars facing away from us as far we could see.

We pulled to a halt and sat speculating on what might be happening. It was several minutes later that Jedd commented, "You know, Mike, I don't see any people in any of these cars."

"You're right." We could not help but laugh. "Not much point in sitting here."

We hopped out to investigate. Sure enough, all of the cars ahead of us were empty. A hundred yards up the line, people were milling around.

As we approached, they greeted us in Spanish. "Good evening. You want to get across the river here?"

"Is it possible?" asked Jedd.

"Yes, but you will need to leave your car here. The ferry can take you across. The bridge was destroyed by the hurricane and will not be repaired for two weeks. When it is fixed, you can come back and get your car."

"There is no other way to get a car across?"

The man shook his head. "I'm sorry, no."

"Thanks for the advice, but we need to reach the Guatemalan border by Sunday."

"Then you will need to go around, back to Acapulco and then up toward Mexico City."

Federales

The road toward Mexico City rose steadily for several hours, taking us into the heart of the country. It was near the end of the rainy season, and the high, rounded hills were a vibrant, if tenuous, green. Late in the day we decided to take a shortcut and turned from the main highway onto a winding road that promised to cut hours from our route. The dizzying turns and jarring potholes brought us to the Mexico of yesteryear. Clay-brick homes dotted the countryside. Men in white cotton clothes tended to the sprawling cornfields that grew up and down the sides of even the steepest hills.

Descending into a lonely valley toward the end of the day, we were jolted back to modern times. Two sleek, black Suburbans—parked sideways—blocked the road. Men in dark aviator glasses stood in front of them, brandishing machine guns. Jedd's hand squeezed the steering wheel.

He looked back. We would not make it far if we tried to turn around.

"These guys look like professionals," said Mike.

"Yeah, professional whats?"

"That's just what I was wondering."

A tall, handsome man appeared to be the leader. He stepped to the driver's-side window and fired a series of words in Spanish. Mike indicated he did not quite understand. Jedd pieced together the gist of it: They were, or at least claimed to be, federal drug officers.

"Something seems a little off," said Mike in a hushed voice.

"It's out of our hands," Jedd whispered back.

The agents, if that is what they were, apparently thought it odd that gringos would be driving this far south in Mexico, and on such back roads. The "detour shortcut" explanation did not seem to satisfy. They launched into a search, tearing through everything we had brought and even spent a good ten minutes underneath the truck.

It appeared they had exhausted all the cracks and crevices of the vehicle when an officer approached us. Like the others, he did not speak English.

"What's in the bag?" he demanded, holding up a small paper sack that had been wrapped with masking tape several times. It looked like the classic *Miami Vice* package of drugs. We had never seen it before.

"That is *not* ours. We have never seen it before."

"We found it in the back of your truck." His tone permitted no arguing.

We knew we were being set up. We looked around. The hills were empty, not a house in sight. Night was fast approaching. Were they just trying to extort a large amount of money from us, or was it going to be worse than that?

The man pulled out a knife and slid it into the bag. Small green-brown seeds spilled out. "What is this?"

"We do not know!" Our sense of desperation was growing. Jedd set his jaw. "Where exactly did you find this bag?"

"In here." He indicated a cardboard box that another man brought forward. We could see similar bags packed within.

"That box did *not* come from our truck."

"Yes it did."

With few other options, we set to digging through the box as the men appeared to want us to do. Beneath the taped bags lay an odd collection of American goods: a shirt, blank tapes, a book on farming techniques . . . peanut butter?

Suddenly, Jedd broke into a broad grin. "Mike, I know what this is. It's the box my aunt packed for my cousin Jared, who I'm going to visit in Guatemala. I never had a chance to look in it. Those bags must be special varieties of seeds he wanted to try planting down there." Mike opened his eyes wide and let out a deep breath.

Jedd turned to the agents and explained as fast as he could. They detained us for another twenty minutes but seemed to accept our explanation. The first stars were popping out as the agents gave us leave and moved aside. One of the men even waved as we drove off.

Some time around midnight, we set up camp at the end of a dirt road. A heavy rain soaked through our sleeping bags by two. At three, we concluded there was not much use in trying to sleep in the truck's cab. We got back on the road, heading ever southward.

San Cristóbal

13

Surrounding the central plaza in the colonial city of San Cristóbal was a collection of outdoor cafés. Tourists and college students—both Mexican and European—talked over coffee or strolled the square. A band played music from the center of the plaza, and roaming musicians performed at its edges. Nearby stood a sixteenth-century cathedral and several mansions built during Spain's colonial reign. It was a strange juxtaposition, this old-world charm in the midst of jungle hills and primitive villages.

Mike pushed his empty plate away and placed his hands behind his head. "What a place, huh? I could live here."

"I was thinking the same thing. The cobblestones, the musicians, the cathedral over there, the strings of lights . . . it feels like Italy."

"Makes you want to be with the one you love."

Mike was the only one of us who had a girlfriend. He had been friends with Brittney since their freshman year but only as seniors did they begin to date. Mike insisted that marriage was still a long way off, but the once very single guy definitely had only one girl on his mind now.

Jedd returned to his prior thoughts. "Whenever I used to picture Mexico, I'd think of some border town like Tijuana. Here, there's a lot more beauty than I ever imagined."

"Everything seems so relaxed," added Mike. "People just seem to have *time*. In the evenings there's people hanging out together everywhere; guys just squatting and talking on the street corner."

"It's interesting. The people down here work so hard, but it also seems like once they've done the work they need to do, they just don't worry about doing anything more."

Mike laughed. "They probably think the workaholics up in the U.S. and in Mexico City are really stupid—working their butts off even when they've got more than enough to live on." He continued, "Of course, you've got to respect the industrious guys who make the American standard of living possible, but there's a lot to learn from the people here, too. It seems like their open schedule allows them to spend relational time we don't have much of in the States. So often, our goals of efficiency and achievement leave us without time for doing much for other people."

Jedd thought it interesting to hear Mike talk this way. Although he was outwardly low-key, the energy Mike poured into his small business ventures often totally consumed him. "I agree," Jedd followed. "How can a person help a friend or show hospitality when their time, money, and energy are always overextended? You've got to have a little something left at the end of the day or you won't have anything for others when the opportunity arises."

"Exactly!" Mike was getting a little worked up. "That's just what most Americans don't have! Hardly any of us live with any extra space in our lives. We push everything to the max, and often go beyond that. Credit card debt. Overbooked schedules. Car payments. Cell phones. When a friend needs help or a visitor could use some hospitality, we have little to spare."

"The disadvantages of living like they do down here are pretty apparent," Jedd responded. "Just look around at the shape most houses are in. Still, I bet there's more contentment in these guys squatting on the street corners with their amigos than in a lot of offices in America."

Jedd's Reflections—October 11

Most Christians would claim that what matters most is glorifying God, being happy and content, having good relationships and the like. It seems that in reality, though, we make most of our decisions based on what will bring us the most financial security, status, and whatever else society values, and only hope to glorify God and enjoy His gifts as a by-product.

I hope so much I can make my life decisions based on what really *matters. I guess that is what Jesus meant when He told us not to worry about the things most people desire, but to seek first His kingdom and let the rest take care of itself.*

Another beggar, the fifth of the evening, was working her way through the tables toward us.

"I bet she'll ask me," Jedd sighed. "They never ask you."

"You're just a beggar magnet," Mike teased.

As predicted, she held out a withered hand to Jedd. *"Por favor?"*

Jedd looked away for a moment before reaching into his pocket and pulling out a few coins. The woman acknowledged the gift with a nod and hobbled on.

"I've given to two and turned away three, all while eating a big sandwich. Here I'm filling myself up while they limp around hungry. What do you think, Mike; should I not eat?"

"I think you think about it too much. If you feel you should give, then give. If not, then don't. Just don't tear yourself up about it."

"Yeah. I know you're right. I just . . . well, I just don't know . . ."

Places You Shouldn't Go

Moving south again the next day, we drove deep into the surrounding hills on muddy roads. Not far from San Cristóbal, we came upon our first Indian town, a tourist affair complete with food stalls and a "museum" of local goods where weavers attempted to sell their wares.

As we traveled farther from San Cristóbal, the tourist atmosphere disappeared. Since visitors to the region rarely have access to vehicles of their own, they are generally restricted to the central tourist meccas serviced by the retired school buses that provide the only method of mass transit. The roads grew narrower as we forged deeper into the hills—more appropriate for burros than motorized vehicles.

A blend of pine forest and dense jungle blanketed the hills, occasionally broken by meadows full of white and purple flowers. Small groupings of mud-brick homes popped up here and there, always surrounded by cornfield quilts. Deep into the hills, our road suddenly emerged into a town that seemed to have been built around a strikingly large Catholic church. We stopped to look around.

"This place just seemed to come out of nowhere," remarked Jedd. "That huge church looks like it belongs in a city."

"Do you see the way people are looking at us? Like we're aliens or something. They sure aren't smiling like the last place."

As we entered the church through towering wooden doors, our eyes slowly adjusted to the near total darkness. Light trickled in from a row of small windows several stories above us. The air was thick and hazy and smelled of incense. Our footsteps echoed faintly as we walked forward on the cement floor, smooth and without pews all the way to the front. Near the middle of the vast vault of a church, a man was on his knees before a sea of candles. Among the candles were several clay statues formed in the shape of bulls. The man seemed to be bowing down to them, over and over again, murmuring a strange cadence.

"Maybe we shouldn't be here," whispered Jedd.

Mike shrugged. "It does seem a little . . ." Mike's words stuck in his mouth as he glanced behind him. A dozen men had silently followed us in, forming a half-circle that now stood between us and the door. Several had machetees in their hands.

"Where'd those guys come from?" Jedd breathed.

"I don't know. They must have sneaked in behind us."

The men's faces were hard, their dark eyes fixed upon us. Jedd glanced once more to the front of the church. His heart raced. He could not tell if an escape was possible from that direction.

"We'd better start moving toward the door," hissed Mike. "One way or another, we're going to be out of here in a minute. Let's try to do it for ourselves."

Heads down, we moved slowly toward the exit. Cold stares followed us, but the men did not move. We passed between them and reached the door.

Silently, the men filed out behind us. Several remained at the entrance to the church, apparently guarding it. Others followed at a distance as we walked to our truck. Jedd struggled with the key for a moment before getting the door open.

Jedd glanced in the rearview mirror as we drove out of town. The men stood, hands on hips, watching us until we were out of sight. "Man, what was going on back there?" he said.

"I have no idea. I wonder if they were trying to hide something."

"Or maybe had some bad history with outsiders."

"I'm glad we've still got all our body parts."

○ ○ ○

Border Run

Sunday morning traffic on the road leading to the border moved without any sense of urgency. We got a later start than we had hoped and could not help feeling some impatience with the old taxi trucks, their beds crammed with people, chugging along between residences and churches.

Matters became even more frustrating when we came to a small town having a market day, its main street a mass of carts and stalls, chickens and burros.

"I hope we can make it through here before too long," remarked Jedd with a bit of worry. "We're so close to the border now."

Mike nodded. "It could be pretty bad if we were late. I don't know what we'd do if we missed Salomón and the guys."

17

Buyers and sellers haggled all around us, trading corn, coffee beans, and cows. Some of the men were drunk, stumbling about with dumb, contented looks on their faces. Children, themselves intoxicated with the excitement of the day, chased one another through the crowd. Though the cars in front of us laid on their horns, the crowd didn't care. It took us ninety minutes to inch through the quarter-mile market.

○ ○ ○

Two hours behind schedule, we arrived at the border. It appeared nearly as chaotic as the market, with vendors and children, not to mention bureaucrats and soldiers in army-fatigue green. We parked and began walking into the tumult, not exactly sure what we were looking for. Groups of men and boys crowded around us.

"Change money? Change money?" "I help you cross border. Border cross not easy. I tell you who to bribe. Come with me."

Jedd turned to Mike. "I don't know what we are going to do here. On the phone, Salomón said to meet at the border at Tapachula but . . ."

"That's where we are, isn't it?"

"Yeah, but according to the guidebook, there are two different border crossings in this area. This one is my best guess, but I really don't know."

"And we're over two hours late. They may have gone to the other border already."

Jedd shook his head. "I have the feeling that these border guys could really work us over if we try to get across on our own."

"It looks like it will be a nightmare even if we do find Salomón."

"Let's just hope we do . . ."

II Guatemala

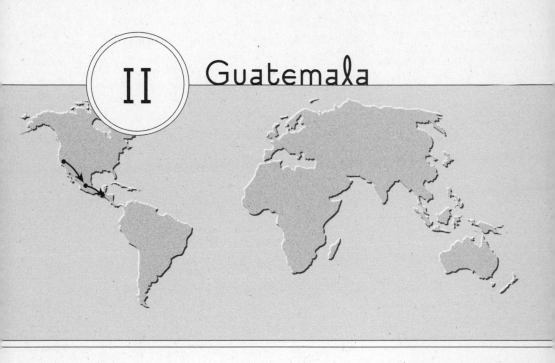

two

A Lesson in Generosity

Guatemala City, Guatemala

The Los Angeles evening was still warm, but the plane's cabin was cool and hushed. Waiting for takeoff, Matt flipped through the airline magazine and glanced over the safety information card. Trey occupied the seat next to him, poring over maps of Guatemala. Finally the 757 began to roll forward, building speed. With a shudder, the plane's front wheels loosed themselves from the runway.

"This is it! The trip is really starting!" Trey was glowing.

Matt's normally calm blue-gray eyes held a flicker of excitement. "It's hard to believe we're finally doing this."

"Are you nervous at all?"

Matt shrugged. "A little. Less than I thought I would be, though. It feels great to actually be doing what we've been talking about for so long."

"How do you think your family is doing with this?"

"Better than I expected. They're nervous about my getting sick. And the crazier places like Africa and Bangladesh. And our smuggling Bibles into Vietnam. Especially my mom. How about your family? I bet they're really looking forward to seeing you when you get to Russia."

"They are. And I'm looking forward to seeing them. I'm just . . ." A shadow seemed to cross Trey's face. "I'm afraid it may be difficult with my dad. From what I can tell from my end of the phone, things are getting worse between him and my mom. I just really hope there are no blowups while we're there."

Matt was not sure how to respond. "I don't know if you're worried about us guys being there, but if you are . . ."

"That's not the main thing. I know you guys are in this with me. You probably wouldn't see anything anyway. It's just . . ." Trey paused for a moment. "There's no point in dwelling on it. What's that book you brought?"

Matt accepted the change of subject without hesitation. "*Les Misérables*—Victor Hugo. I haven't started it yet."

"It's excellent. I read it a couple years ago. Did you see all those books Mike had with him when he left?"

"Yeah. Books, a surfboard, and nothing else. He's a contradiction. You'd think he's just a beach bum, and then you find him reading the *Wall Street Journal* or a thousand-page book by Dostoevsky."

"We'll be learning a lot together."

"That's one of the main reasons I decided to go."

"To learn together?"

"Not just facts and things about the world, but things about life—really learning how to love as friends, and how to serve people together. I don't think I've told you guys, but a year ago I prayed that God would give me some friends I could be close with for the rest of my life. I really see living together last year and this trip as the answer to that."

Trey laughed, but not in a mocking way. "That's great."

After a moment, Matt retrieved his journal from the overhead bin and began to write.

Matt's Reflections—October 13

It feels so good to actually be off. I can hardly imagine what lies ahead—so many adventures and experiences are just around the corner. It is hard for me not to have things planned out as much as I would like, but I realize it is good for me to know I'm not in control of things now. I've done as much thorough packing and planning as I can. Now, I'm just trying to look forward to what's ahead. I feel certain God is going to use this trip to shape and mold us more into the persons we were created to be. I don't know how it will happen, but I'm confident that on this trip we will become more like Jesus. I know this is where I am supposed to be.

Bienvenidos!

Trey stared out the window. Holes in the cloud cover allowed quick glimpses of the Guatemalan countryside. Dense vegetation seemed to coat every inch of the landscape. Here and there, small towns popped up among the fields. Not far beyond the end of the plane's wing, the tip of a volcano poked up above the clouds. A moment later, an opening in the clouds provided a window down upon an expanse of buildings and factories set in the shadow of several massive volcanic mountains.

"There's Guatemala City," said Trey. "The guidebook says the landing here is the second most treacherous in the world."

The plane banked sharply to the right and began descending at what felt like a ferocious rate. Matt's stomach slid halfway up to his mouth.

"This is great!" said Trey, turning from the window to glance at Matt.

Matt peered out the window at the valleys and volcanoes below. *So many unknowns,* he thought. He was thrilled to be going to Guatemala, but had little idea what to expect. Trey had traveled and even lived all around the world; Matt had spent most of his growing-up years in a quiet town in the Midwest. And while Trey's ebullient optimism often drew him to cliffs' edges, sometimes even off the side, he always seemed to land right side up. Matt, on the other hand, always wanted to clearly see firm ground

Mayan Ruins

before he took the next step. He was cautious, and sometimes overly prepared, never jumping without a careful look.

"Hmm, I wonder where Mike and Jedd are now," Trey continued. "They should be pretty deep into Mexico."

"I hope they're doing all right. They left a couple days before that hurricane hit Acapulco."

"They'll be fine. We'll have a few days with Salomón and Mery before going up to meet them at the border."

"Do you know if we're planning to start work on the clinic before they get here?"

"I don't see why we couldn't." Trey lurched forward as the wheels hit the runway. The plane shook violently as it braked, slowed, then stopped altogether. "Not a bad flight at all."

As we emerged into the terminal, weary businessmen and thankful homecomers swirled around us. Our eyes searched the crowd.

"*Bienvenidos, mis amigos!*" a booming voice captured our attention. Salomón grinned and wrapped us in the embrace of a welcoming uncle. Though in his sixties, his arms were strong and his thick hair a deep black.

"You remember my wife, Mery, of course?" he said in Spanish, leaning over and giving his wife a kiss. The bright flowers of her dress contrasted with the olive skin of a face that was wide and timeworn, and yet she was glowing with kindness. We had met Salomón and Mery only once before, when some American friends of theirs had helped them to travel north to speak in some California churches.

Salomón next turned to a slender American boy about our age.

"Joel has been staying with us for the last month. He's been a great help," said Salomón, allowing time for handshakes before leading off toward the baggage.

A few minutes later, we were loaded in the Isuzu Trooper that American friends had given to Salomón and Mery some years before. The city traffic was disorienting. The only rule seemed to be "Don't get hit." Cars swerved the wrong way down one-way streets. Buses whizzed by, horns blaring. It sounded like the inside of a pinball machine.

"We're glad you're down here, Joel. Matt and I are pretty rusty with our Spanish," said Trey.

"Salomón and Mery only speak a few words of English," explained Joel. "But if you talk slowly, they'll understand a lot of what you say."

"*Sí!* We learn from our gringo friend," shot Salomón over his shoulder.

"So where . . . *Watch out!*" Matt blurted as he slammed up against the door.

"Sorry, Matt." Salomón laughed, swerving out of the path of the on-coming traffic and back into his lane. "There was a big hole in the road."

"Driving is about the only thing in Guatemala that people like to do fast," explained Joel. "You learn to just close your eyes sometimes."

Guatemala City, in fact, was something like Monet's *Water Lilies*—beautiful from a distance, but blurred and confused up close. Situated on a vast plateau, the city is dwarfed by the magnificent volcanic peaks surrounding it. A few historic buildings crafted by the Spanish during the colonial era still stand in the town center. Across the entire plateau, a boundless urban octopus sprawls out and has even begun crawling up the sides of the volcanoes.

"What were you saying, Matt?" asked Joel.

"I was just wondering where we are going."

"Shelly's place. She's Salomón and Mery's daughter. We'll be staying here in the city until it's time to meet the other guys at the border. Salomón and Mery's home is up in the highlands, in Uspantan. We'll move up there once the guys arrive."

"Aren't we going to be working on building the medical clinic here in Guatemala City?"

"Unfortunately not. Salomón hasn't been able to secure all the necessary permits yet. Dealing with the bureaucracy down here can be a nightmare. They also still need to raise a decent amount of additional money before they can start. We probably won't be able to break ground for a few more months."

"So what will we be doing?"

"Salomón has several projects he needs help with in Uspantan. He'll show you when we get there."

The pink of a Dunkin' Donuts shop flashed by, looking somewhat out of place, similar to its siblings in the U.S., except that a uniformed man with a shotgun stood before the entrance.

Trey tapped the window. "Wow, they've even got hired guards at the donut shop? Where are the cops?"

Joel laughed. "Yeah, Guatemala City isn't exactly the safest place in the world."

As the group entered the apartment, Salomón spread his arms as wide as his smile and announced, "Our house is your house. What's mine is yours. Please, make yourselves comfortable." We had been welcomed into homes with similar words before, but never had we felt they were so sincerely meant.

o o o

As we cleared the table from our first breakfast, Salomón had announced, "We must go downtown today." He could not wait to begin showing us his country. A school bus painted with a rainbow of colors—apparently long since retired from its service in the U.S.—pulled up in front of the stop.

"This is it," explained Joel. The bus was packed. Passengers spilled out of the seats, aisles, and exit doors. Trey gave Salomón a questioning glance. He did not seem concerned. "There is plenty of room."

Matt could only fit half his body into the door. "Push!" encouraged Salomón. Matt somewhat timidly leaned into the wall of people ahead of him. With surprisingly little effort, the wall budged. A few more shoves cleared room for the others. The bus lurched forward and the crowd shook like a bucket of Jell-O.

"You think this is bad," called Joel over the din, "just hope we don't get robbed."

"You mean pickpocketed?" replied Matt. "I hear they're pretty bad here."

"No. I mean robbed at gunpoint. Salomón says that every day at least one or two buses get boarded and robbed."

"How?"

"I guess the most common way is for a couple guys to enter from the front of the bus and a couple from the back. Two of 'em guard the exits with machine guns while the others go through stripping valuables from everyone on the bus—wallets, purses, sunglasses . . . everything. If you refuse to give them something, they shoot. It's a simple procedure."

While Matt was mapping out what he would do if *bandidos* appeared at the exits, a man holding a trash bag got on the bus. He squeezed up beside Matt and seemed to be intentionally pushing the bag against Matt's side.

A few moments later, Matt felt something wriggle in his pocket. His hand sprang forward and closed over the wrist of a young Mayan woman. Her hand had been in his pocket. She quickly pulled away.

Matt moved the contents of his pocket into his shirt. He glanced at the woman but said nothing. Tangled hair spilled down in front of her face and over a filthy blouse. Her dark eyes stared at the ground, scared, yet somehow defiant. Compassion flooded over Matt's anger. How should he respond? He bit his lip and stared out the window.

That evening, after another hearty meal, Matt and Trey settled on the couch to read. Trey was deep in *Robinson Crusoe*. Matt had just begun *Les Misérables*. An episode from Victor Hugo's classic struck Matt as particularly poignant to his experience on the bus that day.

The book's protagonist, Jean Valjean, had just been released after decades in prison. As he roves the countryside, searching for a place to stay, he is turned away again and again. No one will receive an ex-con. Finally, an old priest takes him in. The priest welcomes Valjean not as a convict, but as a child of God and gives him hospitality worthy of a king.

Despite the priest's kindness, however, Valjean rises in the middle of the night, takes the priest's silver plates, and runs away. The police soon catch him and drag him back to the priest's door. But instead of berating the ungrateful thief, the priest cries out, "Ah, there you are! I am glad to see you. But I gave you the candlesticks also . . . Why did you not take them along with your plates?"

The police can do little more, and so they leave the man trembling before the gracious priest. Before letting Valjean go, the priest turns to his mantelpiece and takes down his silver candlesticks and places them in Valjean's shaking hands. Valjean is speechless. He has never known such kindness. The priest leans down and whispers one last thing to him. "Jean Valjean, my brother, you belong no longer to evil, but to good . . ."

The rest of the novel follows a transformed Valjean as he learns to pour out that same kindness and generosity upon everyone he encounters. A single act of selfless love has changed his life forever.

Matt thought intensely about the passage. The following day, he penned his thoughts in his journal.

Matt's Reflections—October 17

Yesterday, when the young Mayan woman tried to rob me, I wonder if I did the right thing. What would have happened if I had given her some money instead of making sure she didn't get anything? Reading the story of Jean Valjean in Les Misérables has really made me think. Perhaps a single act of love could have somehow changed her life.

I want my life to benefit others besides myself. I see that illogical acts of grace can change hearts, and I want to be able to demonstrate this love to others. But I don't know how to love in the way that changes lives. Jesus, give me the strength to live out Your teachings, that I might live my life in a way that will transform the lives of others.

We rose before the sun, excited to be heading to the border for our reunion with Mike and Jedd. The drive would take seven hours, and we had to be there by noon. Mery packed some food for breakfast.

"Are you ready, precious one?" Salomón asked when the car had been loaded.

"Everything is prepared." Mery smiled. "I think the boys will enjoy breakfast." They leaned close to each other for a moment, just brushing shoulders. Their affection was never overt, but very tangible, beautiful to see.

Salomón turned the ignition. The Trooper's engine coughed, but would not catch. Apparently, the device made to prevent thieves from starting the car had malfunctioned. Now it was preventing us from starting it. We were already running behind schedule, and we knew it was essential that we be on time. Salomón telephoned his son, Dr. Danny Hernández, to see if he could use his truck.

Danny was over with his truck in a flash. In the truck bed lay his bike, which he had brought to save us time in dropping him off. We watched, a bit amazed, as one of Guatemala's top surgeons, to save us a few minutes, peddled off through the morning mist on a bicycle.

 Trey's Reflections—October 19

The way Salomón and Mery's family functions seems to be totally unique. They do not hold on to what is theirs in the way that most people do. They hold their possessions loosely, as if they had just been entrusted to them temporarily. They do not insist on what is due them, even in regard to position. Within the family, whoever needs a particular asset most—whether car, house, money, or even time—is given it. They are hardly less open with those outside the family. I guess that is how Christian community is supposed to work. I love it!

"Gracias a Dios"

The drive to the border called for seven hours in the back of Danny's truck. Perhaps it was not the safest setup, but we could not complain, for the back of a pickup is a great place from which to experience new territory. Plantations raced by us on both sides of the roads, most dominated by rubber trees. An occasional banana or coffee plantation added some variety. The plantation borders have to be tended constantly to keep out the invading forces of the jungle. Even the roads seemed to be under constant attack, broken branches and vines filling the highway, giving the impression that only the continual traffic kept the growth from taking over.

Guatemalan Countryside

As the miles rolled by, we talked about the previous days and the things we had learned. Guatemala City had been interesting, but we were far more impressed by what we had seen in the Hernández family itself. We were beginning to understand that the way they lived was not quite like any we had encountered before. The centerpiece of their existence was loving others in the name of Jesus. Over Mery's delicious meals, stuck in traffic, or just hanging out in the evenings, we began to hear the stories of what such a life involved:

Salomón and Mery were driving down a dirt road through the highlands. The foliage on the edges was especially dense. Mery could tell Salomón was nervous by the way he tapped his fingers against his machete. Friends had warned them not to take this route today. There had been a lot of guerrilla warfare in this area in the past several months. They knew, though, that the mountain village to which they were driving badly needed the medical supplies they were bringing.

Around a sharp curve, three men with machine guns were blocking the road. Salomón slammed on the brakes, bringing the Trooper to a sliding halt.

29

Salomón froze. "Mery, please pray."

They opened their eyes to a man tapping the barrel of his machine gun against the window. Salomón rolled it down and greeted them with as much aplomb as he could muster. "Hola, mis ámigos. What may I do for you?"

"Little old man, you will do as I say," the guerrilla leader ordered in Spanish. Salomón nodded in agreement as the men climbed into the backseat.

"Take us to Nebaj. We must get there quickly. Now!"

Throughout the rest of the drive, the guerrillas spoke no Spanish. They conversed only in the local Mayan dialect, Quiché.

"After we arrive," the leader said, "we will kill the little man and have fun with his wife. We will be able to make good use of this truck."

Salomón winced slightly, trying not to reveal that he understood their words. Virtually no Guatemalans of Hispanic descent know Quiché. They would not dream of stooping so low as to study the "language of the poor." But Salomón had. He felt he could not fully serve the Mayans without knowing their language.

Just as Salomón was maneuvering through a streamlet, the Trooper stalled. Unbeknownst to the guerrillas, Salomón had used a mechanism installed to prevent car theft to cut off the gas. He turned the ignition, but the engine would not catch.

"Little man, what is wrong? Start it! Now!"

"Nothing is happening. May I get out and see what is wrong?"

"No, try again."

After several more attempts, the guerrillas' well of patience was nearly dry. Salomón remained calm. "Maybe we need gasoline. My wife can run into the nearest town to get some. I will stay here with you." The guerrillas had little choice but to oblige.

Mery raced through the jungle, fearing for her husband's life. She made it to the town in only a few minutes. Breathing hard she begged the first town official she found to aid her. But the man would not help. Neither would anyone else in the town. They felt sorry for her, but even the police were afraid to face the guerrillas. If they did, they might just end up with their throats cut in the not-too-distant future. Mery began to despair. All she could do was pray.

Things were tense back at the truck as well. The soldiers fingered their triggers and glanced around nervously. Just then, another guerrilla *appeared out of the jungle and greeted them. The men explained how they had hijacked the truck and were planning to kill Salomón once they reached their destination.*

"Kill this man?" asked the new arrival.

"Yes, the little man who is driving."

"I know this man. You should not kill him. He has fed many of my friends when they had no food. He will help anyone, no matter who they are. If you are hungry, he will feed you, too."

Mery soon returned, preferring danger at her husband's side to the safety of the town. She came upon a surprising sight. The guerrillas had volunteered to try push-starting the truck and, with Salomón quietly switching on the gas, it worked. They greeted her as she approached. Smiling and a bit confused, she climbed into the cab next to Salomón. "The Lord protected us," he whispered to her. The guerrillas waved as Salomón and Mery drove off the way they had come.

Reunion in No Man's Land

The mileage signs on the side of the highway suggested we were going to be more than an hour late to the border. Salomón did not seem visibly concerned. He pulled out into the opposite lane and passed a row of cars. A semi, announcing itself with several horn blasts, forced Salomón back into our own lane. "You know," said Matt, "I love being out here on such a beautiful day, but riding in the back is making me a little nervous."

Trey just smiled. "It'll be great to have Mike and Jedd here. I can't wait for them to get to see Guatemala and spend some more time with Salomón and Mery."

"Yeah, it's hard to believe we've been here less than a week. I feel like we've been friends with Don Salomón and Doña Mery forever."

"Well, remember that we did spend a little time with them when they came to the States last year to deal with Salomón's heart problem."

"That's true, but it was different then. It's so amazing to see Salomón and Mery in their own element. I don't think you can experience the whole of Don Salomón in America. Here he just boils over with confidence. His spirit seems to touch everyone he meets—even the guards at the supermarket."

"And Mery, she has such a servant's spirit and always seems totally content and full of joy. In the States she's just a quiet presence. Here you can tell Salomón would be lost without her. It's amazing to see them in action."

"If we pay attention, we'll learn a lot about how to love people from them and their family."

Being so late to the border, it seemed there was a strong chance of missing Mike and Jedd. It had been several days since we had talked with them. What if they thought they had mistaken the day or time or place of meeting? With our late start and Mike and Jedd's remarkable ability to get lost, some real problems seemed likely.

"I hope they have the sense to wait for us," said Trey.

"Yeah, me, too. Why don't we say a quick prayer for them." We bowed our heads. "Lord, I ask that You guide Mike and Jedd safely to the border. And even though we are going to be late, I also ask that we both arrive at the border at the same time. Please bring us together without complication. Jesus, we ask these things in Your name. Amen."

° ° °

The clock read two o'clock as we crested a hill and looked down on the border. A line of cars extended back from a mob of vendors, travelers, soldiers, and bureaucrats who whirled around a series of concrete buildings. Salomón had no interest in driving into that quagmire, so he parked and we went the last half-mile on foot.

The guards at the gate paid little attention as we walked by. In doing so, we passed out of Guatemala, but not yet into Mexico. The narrow swath of land in between is claimed by neither country. The tumult of "no man's land" churned around us. On our left stood a ramshackle collection of hotels and eateries. Apparently, they had sprung up to accommodate those unable to negotiate the perils of a not-always-by-the-books border stop in a timely fashion.

Matt peered at his watch. "We're over two hours late. I don't see how . . ."

Trey cut him off. "Look! There they are! Hey, Mike, Jedd!"

The two did not seem to hear. Both looked a bit confused.

"Jedd! Mike! Over here!"

A shared grin broke across the pair's face as they spotted Matt and Trey. We made our way toward each other through the crowd.

"You guys made it!" beamed Trey, wrapping the cross-country drivers in a hug.

"How long have you guys been here, Trey?"

"Just arrived."

"Amazing! Both of us got here almost exactly two hours and fifteen minutes late!"

Matt shook his head, thinking to himself, *Why am I always surprised when prayer is answered in specific ways?*

"*Bienvenidos, mis amigos, bienvenidos!*" cried out Salomón, greeting Mike and Jedd with hugs of his own. "Is everything well? You look fine. Are you tired?"

"We're feeling great, Don Salomón," Jedd replied.

"Good. Then we will get a hotel and then begin our work."

"Our work?"

Mike gave a wry grin. "I think he means getting the truck through the border."

three

The Four Amigos!
Together in Guatemala City

When checking into one of the little border-side hotels, we noticed its courtyard was littered with rows of vehicles.

"A lot of people are staying here," remarked Matt.

Salomón shook his head. "No. Most of these cars belong to *former* guests of the hotel. Their owners are gone, but their cars are stuck here in limbo. The owners were not able to supply a 'gift' large enough to expedite the necessary border paperwork."

It was beginning to become clear why Salomón referred to the border crossing as "work." We imagined the medical supplies in the back of the truck would only add to the difficulty. Since the truck was registered in Mike's name, he accompanied Salomón to the main border office to begin the process of securing the necessary permits. A gap in the cement walls suggested that a door had once existed. Through the opening, Mike could see a labyrinth of cubicles and desks. They were more than adequately staffed by "friendly civil servants." A sound like a flock of hummingbirds rose from the dozens of fans that whirred from the bureaucrats' desks. The relative importance of a given official seemed to be reflected in the size of his fan.

Unfortunately, they provided little relief from the heat. Pearls of sweat gleamed on Mike's brow and slid down his temples onto his glistening cheeks. The collar of his T-shirt was already soaked. Hesitantly, he handed the truck's registration and his passport over the front desk.

The hefty official heaved himself up from his chair, waddled back to a similar-looking man who sat behind a slightly larger desk, and handed him the passport. The bureaucrat glanced back at the pair who had just placed themselves at his mercy. Mike could not hear what the men were saying, but he could see their jowls flapping up and down.

A third counterpart was soon brought in, from a desk with a big fan. *This guy will take care of stuff*, thought Mike. But it was just the beginning. The trio disappeared into a side office. When they emerged a few minutes later, it appeared they had left the passport in the office. Mike's face began to flush. *What are these jokers doing?* A glance at Salomón quieted him, though. He was smiling the same as when they had entered, waiting patiently.

A beanpole of a man approached. "We will be working on your paperwork as fast as we can. Unfortunately, we are *verrrry* busy this week and it may take a *lonnnng* time. We also may have some problems getting the necessary paperwork. There will probably be some significant fees and perhaps some other complications."

Mike clinched his teeth and let out a long breath through his nose. *These guys are going to try to squeeze every penny out of this they can,* he thought. Salomón just nodded as the man continued. He was used to it. The process continued for twenty-four hours. Salomón kept his pleasant composure the entire time, all the while wrangling like a hardball lawyer for the lowest possible "fees." By the end of it all, we had paid $75 for a permit emblazoned with the words, "This permit shall cost ten quetzals" ($2). A receipt saying we had paid $100 in import taxes for the medical supplies had cost only $25. It could have been a lot worse.

Hernández Hospitality

As the border station disappeared behind us, Mery offered a prayer of thanks. In Salomón and Mery's view, making it through the border in only

Medical Supplies

twenty-four hours was a miracle. We had hardly said "Amen," however, when we were once again stopping at another guard shack.

"Please take a bottle for your head," Salmón cheerfully told the officer, handing him a container of aspirin from the medical supplies the man was inspecting.

"Thank you," the official said, indicating we were free to leave.

"That man will be able to use the aspirin as much as anyone," Salomón explained, "the important thing is that it gets to the hands of people who need it."

It was well after dark when we arrived back at Shelly's apartment. A guard greeted us at the entrance to the parking lot. "Three cars were stolen from the lot last night," he informed Salomón. "The guard who was supposed to be here was in another lot."

"Welcome to Guatemala City," joked Matt.

Carrying the medical supplies and Mike's and Jedd's gear, we plodded up the stairs and through the apartment building's long corridors. Through an open door we caught a glimpse of a stooped woman pounding dough between her hands into the Guatemalan staple: tortillas.

"*Bienvenidos!*" cried Salomón once again as we entered the apartment.

Mike looked from room to room, a bit puzzled. "Wait a second. If Matt and I are in that room, and you two are in the living room with Joel, and Salomón and Mery in the back one, where is Shelly going to sleep?"

"Oh, she is just going to move in with her sister's family while we are here," replied Don Salomón, understanding the question.

And so it was that Jedd and Mike got their first introduction to Hernández hospitality. That someone would move out of their own home so that there would be more room for the guests was beyond our conception of what hospitality could include. To the Hernández family, it seemed the natural thing to do. As if that sacrifice was not enough, Shelly came by every morning and night to make us breakfast and dinner. She voluntarily fought the Guatemalan traffic, just so that we could have home-cooked meals. What mystified us most of all was that we did not feel like intruding guests.

It began to dawn upon us that this was our first exposure to hospitality in its purest form. True service never reminds the recipient that they are being served. That is why it seemed so different with the Hernández family. They actually made us feel as if we were doing *them* a favor by staying in their home. This was something we had hardly ever experienced, even in the most hospitable, well-wishing homes in America.

 Mike's Reflections—October 24

As the days go by, I'm beginning to see that the amazing hospitality we're experiencing here comes as much from Salomón and Mery's outlook on life as from their desire to be welcoming. As Americans, we are results oriented. Our goal in life is to get things done. No matter how hospitable we may desire to be, all acts of serving distract us from getting things done, and thus take on the feeling of a burden. The people we serve usually know that they are, in some ways at least, a distraction from the "important things." This leaves the host unable to take full delight in giving and the guest unable to fully enjoy the hospitality.

But we never feel like we're a burden to the Hernández family. In a sense, it is like we are helping them accomplish their goals, rather than impeding them. Their goal is not to "get things done," but to show love to others. I feel I can enjoy everything that they give us infinitely more because of the simple fact that they enjoy giving it.

We had hoped to move on to Uspantan within a couple of days after Mike and Jedd's arrival in Guatemala, but it was not to be. Before we could leave Guatemala City, we had to take care of the paperwork transferring official ownership of the truck from Mike to Salomón. This placed our fate, once again, in the hands of Guatemalan bureaucrats. The border was only an appetizer for the feast of frustration that awaited us in the bureaucratic mazes of Guatemala City. Each department, branch, division, and subdivision had its own distinct title and purported function. They all, however, shared a single specialty: squeezing "gifts" out of every person unfortunate enough to need their services.

The conversation formula worked something like this:

Miserable Document-Needing Wretch: "Have you processed the paperwork I turned in last month? You told me you'd try to have it done in a week. I really need it soon."

Sympathetic Official: "Listen, my friend, I have been so very busy. We are all very busy here. I promise you, I will do it as soon as I possibly can. Perhaps later this week . . ."

This exchange will be repeated as often as the Miserable Document-Needing Wretch cares to visit the Sympathetic Official's office without bringing him a "gift." Once an appropriate gift is provided, the paperwork will materialize within fifteen minutes to three days, depending on the giver's generosity.

It is said that the Guatemalan government is excessively corrupt even by Latin American standards. The corruption has become so endemic to the culture that whole industries have grown up around it. In fact, Guatemala has an entire class of working professionals (*tramitadores*) who exist solely to help people figure out the size of the bribes they must pay different officials to get the paperwork they need. Although sometimes these *tramitadores* aid in illegal activities, the majority of the bribes they facilitate are necessary just to get an administrator to perform his official function. Those who do not play by the "rules of the game" most assuredly will see their requests doomed to eternal paperwork purgatory.

Day after day, Mike and Salomón (and whoever cared to join the fun) returned to the downtown offices to check on the progress of the request. The first officials they encountered insisted it was necessary that Mike's passport accompany the stack of other forms along their journey. This added a tinge of fear to Mike's annoyance. There was even a stretch of several days when every official in the office denied knowing where it was.

While these wheels of progress were slowly grinding, we were able to help Salomón and Danny with a few small projects in Guatemala City. A lot of the time, though, we spent at Shelly's, talking and reading. We enjoyed the relaxation, and the evenings were filled with rich conversation with Salomón and Mery. Even so, it was frustrating to feel that we were doing so little of anything "productive." We wanted to "get on" with the work up in Uspantan.

Salomón and Mery and Shelly never showed a sign of sharing our feelings, though. For them, life was life. There was no such thing as an interruption. As they saw it, whatever the circumstances, whatever the required task, if it is done with love and a thankful heart, it is profitable.

Trey's Reflections—October 27

Salomón and Mery always seem to live completely in each particular moment. Often, I feel as though I must have a long-term plan. They make plans, of course, but so much of their life seems to be spur-of-the-moment. They make the most of each moment while they are actually living it. They do not spend their time planning to live as much as actually living. They don't need to worry about the future, because they are always giving the present moment as a gift to God.

In contrast, one of my favorite quotes from the French philosopher Blaise Pascal describes the way I, too, often live:

> We never keep to the present. We . . . anticipate the future as if we found it too slow in coming and were trying to hurry it up, or we recall the past as if to stay its too rapid flight. We are so unwise that we wander about in times that do not belong to us, and do not think of the only one that does; so vain that we dream of times that are not and blindly flee the only one that is . . . [We] think of how we are going to arrange things over which we have no control for a time we can never be sure of reaching.
>   . . . Thus we never actually live, but hope to live, and since we are always planning how to be happy, it is inevitable that we should never be so. (Pascal, *Pensées*, Number 172)

I do not want to live this way. I see so clearly that living more completely in the present brings greater joy to our days and allows us to experience them more fully. More important, I think Christ called us to such an outlook: "Do not worry about tomorrow, for tomorrow will worry about itself. Each day has enough trouble of its own." Although Jesus had a deep sense of eternity and eternal values, He was always totally involved in the reality of each moment. His energy—mental, physical, and spiritual—was spent primarily on the present. Even on the cross, while His thoughts could have been in countless less painful places, He was able to give His full attention to a thief hanging at His side.

I'm excited to be learning about how to live in the present. It feels *strange but very fulfilling to be with people who are doing so. Each moment is full and rich. Truly, they are living "life to the full"!*

Whispers of the Past

The day had come for our departure to Uspantan in the Guatemalan highlands. Mike's passport was still floating around in some bureaucrat's office, but there was little more any of us could do for the time being. We could only hope and pray things would straighten out by the time we had to leave the country.

Down the road, lines of apartments, shops, and warehouses quickly gave way to steep, pine-covered hills. Cornfields surrounded the homey, unkempt villages that popped up here and there. The blaring of traffic was replaced by the rush of wind and lowing of cows. We breathed deeply of the air. It tasted sweet. We stopped in the town of Quiché for lunch. Following the meal, Salomón announced a visit to some nearby Mayan ruins.

Jedd leaned over to Mike, "Didn't Salomón say this was supposed to be an eight-hour drive today?"

"Yeah, but he doesn't seem to be in any hurry."

"It's such a different mentality. Just about anytime I've got a drive like this, my only thought is to get where I'm going."

"I like living this way."

"Me, too. Salomón and Mery pretty much model the words from Jim Elliot I've always liked: 'Wherever you are, be all there.' I wrote that one in my Bible, but I can't say that I live it that often. My mind is usually a mile ahead of where I am."

The ruins at Quiché did not look like much, sitting atop a lonely hill amid the trees and weeds. There had been some archaeological work on the site, but little effort to restore anything. Rocky mounds, once a room, a passageway, or protective wall lay in broken piles, slowly being eaten by wind, rain, and lichen. It filled us with wonder to learn that in the fifteenth century, this place had been among the greatest cities in North America. Its strong walls had contained twenty-three palaces and numerous temples. Several neighboring hilltops had had separate defensive citadels of their own. This fortress served as the capital of the Quiché people, mightiest of the Mayan tribes. By the middle of the fifteenth century, the Quiché had carved out an impressive empire in what are now the Guatemalan highlands. They dominated vast amounts of lands and subjugated a million people under their fearsome rule.

Just as the mighty Quiché vanquished their neighbors, however, so they were brought to their knees by the Spanish conquistadors. In 1523, a force said to consist of only 320 Spaniards and 200 Mexican warriors overcame a Quiché army of 30,000 in the lower highlands. The Quiché, not yet willing to accept defeat, invited the Spanish to this place, hoping to trap and destroy them. Instead, the Spanish took the fortress and destroyed it completely. It remains today as it was left by the Spanish, its temples and towers never rebuilt.

We were intrigued to learn how dominant, even imperialistic, the Quiché had been. People today often seem to assume that conquest and domination in the New World began with the Spanish. History textbooks often imply that the conquistadors stumbled upon—and then ravaged—utopia. No doubt, they did perpetrate great evils, but even the worst of them were simply playing by the rules of the same game the Mayans had been playing for centuries: survival of the fittest. Vicious rivalries, bloody conquests, and absolute domination were part and parcel of the Mayan civilization from its earliest recorded history.

A faint breeze whispered through the pines above us. Mingled with it, we could almost hear echoes of Mayan pomp, religious ceremony, sporting events, lavish celebration, and fiery combat. The grass-covered stones answered back, "All things, great and small, shall come to such an end."

Jedd's Reflections—October 29

In a place like this, it is so easy to see the vanity of the things we often value so highly. No doubt, the Mayans who lived here were proud of their mighty city, of their conquests and the victories they had won. Each of them struggled for position and wealth and honor in their own ways, just as we do today in boardrooms, athletic contests, and even Christian organizations. Their conquerors, the Spanish, did the same. But looking at all they valued so highly now, reduced to grass-covered rubble, you almost have to laugh at how meaningless so many of their worries and pursuits were. I pray that I will not spend my energies on things that will someday be as worthless as these piles of stone. May I spend my life on the things that are lasting—most important loving others and growing in relationship with Christ.

Salomón led us down a trail that descended through thick brush, dropped sharply, and then disappeared into the hillside. We were walking toward a black hole that gaped like an empty eye socket.

"Before we leave, I have one more thing to show you," Salomón said, indicating for us to follow.

At the cave's mouth, the remains of an abandoned fire smoldered. A faint breeze picked up some ashes and tossed them into the air, along with chicken feathers that lay clumped here and there. Many colors of wax, some old, some new, issued from little alcoves in the cave like frozen rivers. "They have been doing sacrifices here recently," Salomón explained. "These tunnels are regarded as sacred places by the Mayans. Practice of Mayan religion was banned by the Spanish, but the *brujos*, the priests, have never stopped performing their rites here."

"What do they sacrifice?"

"Chickens, mostly, but there are rumors . . ."

∘ ∘ ∘

Trey and Mike
in the Guatemalan Jungle

We had been back on the road for two hours when Salomón decided to take an excursion into the colorful colonial town of Chichicastenango. Strings hung with bright, triangular flags—usually emblazoned with the name of some American soft drink—crisscrossed above the cobblestone streets. Near the center of town, a vast labyrinth of vending stalls exerted its own gravity on locals and tourists alike. There were very few of the latter, however, and the vendors were eager to pawn their less practical goods on us: straw dolls, handmade slingshots, and colorful purses. Above the market rose a massive colonial church, standing in bright white contrast to the garbled colors around it. Salomón pointed to a sunken spot before the church from which smoke issued. "They offer sacrifices here also."

We were surprised. "Isn't this a Catholic church?"

"Yes, but much of the local pagan religion has been assimilated into its practices. It has been this way since the Catholics first proselytized here. When they were trying to convert the Indians, they presented many of their saints as similar to the Mayan gods. Each saint had his or her own sphere of power and influence, just like a god. The people could pray to the gods the same as they did before; only now they were praying to specific saints, rather than to a vague 'god of the river' or 'god of the air.'"

We entered the church. The hum of murmured prayers seemed to come from the walls. The air was hazy, sticky, and sweet. Along with paintings of the life of Christ and several crucifixes, the sides were lined with shrines to various saints. A menagerie of colors and candles, flowers and symbols, surrounded each saint doll. In front of every display was a place for kneeling and a box for contributions to the particular saint. Several men and women bowed before the displays in supplication.

43

A guidebook helped us piece together some of the history of the place. The original church was built in this location on the site of a Mayan altar. As Salomón had told us, priests allowed the Mayans to mix many of their traditional religious practices with Catholicism. In the early 1700s, the local priest even invited the Indians to move their pagan altars from the hills and establish them inside the church. We could see niches of the church where men and women prayed to their ancestors and carried out rituals with candles, rose petals, and even an alcoholic beverage called *chicha*. "They are trying to get special blessings—healthy babies, safe travel, a good marriage, fertile ground, or recovery from illness," Salomón whispered.

The most ornate display in the church was that of the Virgin Mary, the mother of Jesus. Blue eyes gazed from a mannequin face, her arms outstretched. Piles of pink feathers and plastic flowers clothed and surrounded the doll. The stand before her was full of lit candles, each representing the contribution and prayer of a pious supplicant.

Trey leaned over to Matt. "What do you think of this?"

"I don't know. It almost seems like idol worship."

"Like something out of the Old Testament."

Once back on the road, we discussed what we had seen. It left us a bit uneasy. Later in our travels, we would see other shrines built around similar, brightly dressed dolls, also surrounded with flowers and candles; but that would be in the Hare Krishna temple in Durban, the Hindu shrines in Calcutta, and the Buddhist temples in Thailand. We had not expected to encounter anything like this in a church.

Matt's Reflections—October 29

At least as far back as biblical times, it seems that people often preferred to pray to a physical object, instead of simply praying to the unseen God. I don't understand all the reasons for it, but God specifically ordered the Israelites not to make any likeness of any created thing, or to bow down to or worship any such image.

As far as I could tell, what we saw in the church today seemed to be breaking that command. At least as the guidebook and Salomón explained it, prayer and rituals in front of the right images have been presented to the people as magical formulas for getting things they need.

This is so different from the picture of prayer Jesus presented. He taught that prayer is not a formula to appease God or manipulate Him to do what we want. Rather, prayer is an opportunity to communicate with our Father. God wants to be close to us and to hear from us what our thoughts and needs are. Prayer that is anything other than genuine communication with God would seem to be so much less than what He desires.

The sun was setting as we descended into the riverside town of Sacapulas. "We will eat dinner in a little *comedor* on the far side of the river," declared Salomón.

Near the small, colonial church, an old ceiba tree spread its massive limbs over the central plaza. Although not large, the town of Sacapulas achieved some degree of importance from the valuable salt that has been produced in beds beside the river since pre-Spanish times.

Salomón and Mery played a role in Sacapulas's history as well. On February 4, 1976, a major earthquake rocked the nation of Guatemala. When the dust settled, 23,000 were dead, 77,000 were seriously injured, and a million found themselves homeless. The quake had also destroyed

Salomón and Mery's home in Uspantan. The next day, they pieced together a temporary shelter. Once their makeshift dwelling—literally nothing more than sticks and plastic—was over their heads, they turned their attention to those around them. Instead of rebuilding their own home, they began to help their neighbors rebuild *their* homes. As is the pattern of Salomón and Mery's lives, they considered the needs of others as no less important than their own.

"Our children were no longer babies," Salomón explained to us, "but many of our neighbors had little ones. They needed houses much more than we did."

Mery smiled humbly. "It was difficult to cook outside for all the meals, but I had help from our daughters. It was a happy time, too . . ."

Not until six months later did they turn their attention to rebuilding their own home. They were not even close to finishing, however, when a church in America sent them a large sum of money to help with rebuilding projects.

Many of Salomón's friends could not believe his good fortune. "Use the money to finish your own house and save the rest. This is your chance to get rich," they advised. Such practices were not entirely uncommon.

Instead, Salomón used the money to acquire a cement block-making machine and supplies. They located their rebuilding operation in Sacapulas. The evangelical church in Sacapulas and more than a hundred homes in the town stand today because of their work.

Jedd's Reflections—October 29

I was able to ask Salomón a question I've always wondered about as we were driving. I know God commands us to love others. The problem is, love is not exactly a choice. We can choose to do good deeds, but that is not all there is to love. First Corinthians 13 says that we can do all kinds of good deeds and still not have love. Love, then, must at least partly involve feelings. Love is not just doing the right things for people; it must also involve a desire for the other's good. The question is, How are we supposed to fulfill that command—how do we get that desire?

Salomón's answer was very straightforward. He said, "Our love comes from Jesus. He is the vine, we are the branches. If we are firmly rooted in relationship with Him, His life will flow into all parts of ourselves—our

45

mind, body, heart, everything." He warned that this takes commitment. It requires regular, daily time with Christ in His Word and in prayer. The fruit of love will be the natural product.

I pray that I may seek this rootedness in Him, not just a greater religiousity, but a true intimacy with Christ. It seems nothing else will produce the love and character in me that I desire.

We had been bumping over a rough, lightless road for several hours when the glow of a town appeared at the end of a valley.

"That is Uspantan," announced Salomón, a contented sound in his voice, "we are almost home."

Just before reaching the first houses, we pulled to the side of the road next to a fenced pasture. As Joel climbed from the Trooper, he explained, "At every homecoming, Salomón and Mery stop here to thank the Lord for a safe journey."

The darkness felt soft and velvety. A night bird whistled nearby. We joined together in a prayer of gratitude, then drove into the sleeping *pueblo*. On the far edge of town stood a two-story house at the end of Uspantan's main street.

"This is it!" declared Salomón.

We unloaded while Mery made a snack. Salomón showed us around and led us upstairs to our rooms. The place was a bit ramshackle and oddly put together, the product of many additions and "improvements" made by less-than-expert workmen (some of them visitors from the U.S.). But although nothing fancy by American standards, the house was comfortable, spacious, and felt like home.

"It sure seems quiet," Trey remarked later that night as he turned out the lights. After the gunshots, traffic, and whistles of the Guatemala City night, sleep in the mountain town was as peaceful as any we had known.

four

Into the Highlands

Uspantan, Guatemala

We woke feeling utterly refreshed. One by one, we stepped out onto the porch which ran the length of the house and overlooked Uspantan. Encircling the town were verdant hills, covered with pine trees and splotched everywhere by brilliant wildflowers. Rectangular cornfields were sewn into the slopes at odd angles. A roof-scape quilt stretched out below us all the way to the colonial church on the far side of town. Each roof had a texture all its own—weather-scarred wood, Spanish tiles encrusted with lichen, and many shades of rusted metal. Here and there, a tall bunch of cornstalks from a backyard garden poked up through the roofs to eye level.

Women and their daughters went about their daily tasks, many with enormous baskets balanced precariously on their heads. All were dressed in the tribal colors of the Uspantan region: turquoise, pastel green, and gray. Since ancient times, the women of each tribal group in Guatemala have worn distinct colors and patterns, rich and vibrant. The designs are not only for aesthetics. Those familiar with the language of the ornamentation can immediately discern the wearer's particular social role, superstitions, marital status, and occupation.

Men in less impressive outfits—white cotton clothing and broad-brimmed hats—crossed below us as well, always with a machete strapped to their sides. Many carried barely manageable piles of chopped wood, holding them on their backs with a cloth wrapped across their foreheads and back around the load.

Jedd's Reflections—October 30

The life of these people is not easy. Nearly all, especially the women, labor in a manner most Americans would find difficult to bear. All but the youngest have been ravaged by atrocities of war almost too terrible to recount. Salomón told us this morning about a boy who saw his parents killed, his dumb brother tortured, and his house burned to the ground. Yet with the memories of more than thirty years of civil war and all the other challenges they continue to face, the people plod on. It is hard to discern if the stalwart calm of their faces is actually true contentment, but it appears so, and I cannot help but sense a certain tranquillity in this lovely, slow-moving place.

After a grand, Mery-cooked breakfast, Salomón led us out into the property behind their house. With the help of friends in America, Salomón and Mery had been able to purchase several acres of land, and, as with all of their assets, they were using it to meet the needs of others, planting fruit trees and malanga plants from which hungry neighbors were welcome to help themselves. One of the bulbous malanga roots could feed a person for several days.

"Our big project while you're here is rebuilding that pond," said Salomón, pointing to what seemed to be nothing more than a large expanse of mud. On closer inspection, we saw it was lined with cement, but covered with moss and crumbled in several places.

"We used to use the pond as a model for teaching Mayans how to start their own fish hatcheries so they could feed their families. After instructing them here, we would provide them with seed fish to begin their own project. It was difficult, though. No matter what we said, they always ate the seed fish before they reproduced. Ultimately, we decided our energies were better used in other ways."

Matt asked, "So are you going to try to do the same thing again?"

"I think this time we will just have the fish available for people who really need them. Inviting someone to fish on your property is at least better than just providing a handout."

We spent the next two days removing several tons of mud, one shovelful at a time, before beginning repairs on the walls and laying pipes for flow of fresh water. Our muscles were sore, but it felt great to be working. Salomón labored alongside us from start to finish, and Mery frequently sent down refreshments.

Jedd and Trey were working side by side when they began discussing whether or not it was really efficient to work as we were. The labor was such that anyone could have done it. On a pure efficiency scale, it would have been much better to work in the U.S., and then send the money down to Salomón and Mery. With just one day's salary from any one of us, they could have hired a small army for a week.

Jedd set down his bucket for a moment. "You know, it's a little discouraging when you think about it that way. We could be doing a lot more for people down here by working somewhere else."

"Yeah, but I don't think that's how we should look at it. The relationships, our own growth through the experience, the knowledge we can share with people at home. It's all part of the package. I don't think God is all that concerned about efficiency, at least as we define it."

"What about the parable Jesus told about the talents? The master affirmed his servants based on how effectively they had used what they had been given."

Trey paused for a moment as he took another bucket of mud from Jedd. "Of course we're supposed to make the most of what we have. But when we give ourselves completely to God, He is probably going to use us in ways that don't seem exactly efficient to us. Think of Moses spending forty years tending sheep in the desert or even Jesus spending most of His life making furniture. The main issue is just to let God have His way."

Mike chimed in, "God doesn't need our money or anything else we have. He has no problem providing for Himself. I think the main thing He wants is for us to release both our time and our money to His will."

"Well, I agree." Jedd nodded. "Although you know it's not always easy for me to see things that way. I want maximum efficiency. I'll tell you, though, I really do like this work—using up our physical body, making it tired, and earning our rest."

We could not help thinking of a verse from Ecclesiastes: "The sleep of a laborer is sweet, whether he eats little or much, but the abundance of a rich man permits him no sleep" (5:12).

∘ ∘ ∘

As we had when we were living together at Westmont, the four of us met every night to read a chapter of the Bible and discuss it, followed by a time we called "Confession and Reconciliation." The purpose of Confession and Reconciliation was simply to share struggles we were facing and to work through any frustrations we might have with each other. James 5:16 states, "Therefore *confess* your sins *to each other . . .*" (emphasis added). Despite this directive, in recent years few non-Catholic Christians have made a habit of confessing their sins to others. As the days went by, we found that the practice, like all of God's directions for life, offered practical, real-world benefits—particularly in regard to increasing our sense of accountability. When we knew we would eventually have to confess our mistakes, it caused us to evaluate our decisions more closely. It also brought a deeper openness and honesty to our relationships with one another. Finally, confession helped us know how best to encourage and pray for one another in areas where we struggled. The truth is that we just cannot do it alone. God meant for us to live out our faith in community. We need one another, but we cannot fully receive the help of others until we are honest with them, and ourselves, about our shortcomings.

The second part, reconciliation, was a practical application of Christ's instruction "Do not let the sun go down while you are still angry." It gave us an opportunity to be forthright about frustrations and concerns we had with each other. It was a safe forum for getting things off our chests.

A wise, but less-than-optimistic, friend warned us before we left that we would probably not make it through the trip without a major falling-out. He even thought it more likely than not that at least one of us would return home before the trip was over. Looking back, we can see that, if we had not been committed to nightly reconciliation and confession, he probably would have been right. Because of our commitment, however, our conflicts never became destructive in the ways they otherwise probably would have. As Proverbs says, "Wounds from a friend can be trusted." When we can humble ourselves enough to indeed *trust* the "wounds" given us by those who truly love us, we will never be caught for long in stagnant backwaters. Spurred by the admonishments of our friends, we will be ever growing into the person Christ called us to be. After our time of confession and reconciliation, we would always close by praying together, committing ourselves anew to God and asking His involvement in every aspect of our trip.

Day of the Dead

That night, our sleep was invaded by distant sounds: singing, fireworks, and shouting. At 3:30, right beneath our window, a loud string of firecrackers ripped through the night. Before its echo could die, a mariachi band struck up a tune, pulling us most of the way to wakefulness. They were celebrating Allhallows Eve, Latin style. The following day, November 1, was *el Día de los Muertos*, the Day of the Dead, a time throughout Latin America to remember and honor loved ones now gone.

On the morning of November first, Salomón and Mery drove us to the town of Nebaj where Jedd's cousin, Jared, worked with a Christian aid organization. Jared and his wife were waiting for us in their small but cheery home not far from the center of town. They greeted us all warmly and wrapped Jedd in cousinly hugs.

"Did you guys see the festivities coming up?"

We nodded. "In all the little villages along the way, everyone was out in their finest. The cemeteries are packed."

"Yep. *El Día de los Muertos*. You want to visit the one here?"

Nebaj actually had two cemeteries. The one for the rich was filled with gaudily colored cement crypts, painted baby blue, bright red, and aqua green, some as big as a house. The other

Cemetery

51

cemetery, on the opposite side of the road, held resting places for the poor—only wooden crosses topped the mounds, sometimes painted, sometimes just one stick bound to another. Most of the town celebrated in the poor cemetery, men wearing their cotton outfits, scrubbed to gleaming white for the holiday, women gowned in long skirts and blouses woven with a kaleidoscope of geometric forms.

All around us, celebrants mixed funeral with Mardi Gras. Many prayed earnestly, lighting candles and delivering food to a grave or covering it with flowers. The air was thick with incense. Some people talked softly while kids ran hither and thither with kites, laughing, pushing, and shoving. For small fees, roving *musicantes* plucked guitars and scratched violins for the dearly departed. Other people drank the local alcoholic beverage, *kuxha*, made from the fermentation of wheat flour and sugarcane juice. They stumbled between the crosses or lay sprawled out in a stupor on unused lots.

"What do you think of this?" Jedd asked of his cousin.

"I don't know exactly what to think. When I ask them why they do it, they just reply, 'It's tradition.' Some just want to honor their ancestors, but a lot of the motivation comes from fear."

Salomón had similar thoughts. "The Mayans have always been very careful to satisfy the dead. When a person dies, they leave a cup of water on the table for the spirit for nine days. Then, they believe the spirit leaves, but it comes back on the Day of the Dead to gather with the other spirits and to be close to the living. This is all just one of the Mayans' many pagan practices.

"Some are Christians, though. For them it should be different. If we read the Bible, we should know that we cannot do anything for the dead. It is false religion that encourages people to try."

Reminders of a Bloody Past

We were on our way into the hills for a picnic when Salomón suddenly pulled the truck over to the side of the road. "Come, there is something I want to show you," he said, a hint of solemnity in his voice. We piled out of the truck bed and followed him up a short path. His face did not hold its usual smile. We stood silently, waiting for what he would say.

"Do you see those two crosses on the edge of the canyon?"

Fifteen yards from the road stood two large, rough-hewn crosses of wood.

"This is a very sad place for all those in Uspantan. The crosses are here to commemorate the many senseless deaths of the civil war." He paused for a moment, as if considering the weight of his memories, then continued, "At the peak of the fighting, this canyon served as a mass grave for those the government killed. The soldiers would wait in ambush for the guerrillas to come out of the hills to buy supplies in the market. Once captured, they were brought here and executed.

"The thing you have to understand about guerrilla warfare is that there are no uniformed soldiers. Any peasant is a possible enemy of the state. The soldiers killed many innocent people on rumor or whim. At times, the bodies would pile up so high that there was not room for any more. Then the army would soak the corpses in gasoline and torch them to make room for more. Those were horrible times. Both the guerrillas and the soldiers did unthinkable things. Many times the victims were the poor farmers who were just trying to eke out an existence. They didn't care about the war, but the war took them anyway.

"Every time I walked down this road, the stench was a reminder of the nightmare we were living with. The sky above was often black with buzzards seeking a few beakfuls of flesh. Dogs fed here as well. It was not unexpected, the day after a mass execution, to see one in town gnawing on a bloody arm or foot."

Salomón shook his head slowly. He seemed to see the scene before him as it had been. We stood by silently, trying to process the terrible things that had happened in the very spot we now stood.

Time for Truth

In town that afternoon, Salomón suggested we pick up the machete cases we had ordered from a local leatherworker.

"Did you know that the man who makes them is the uncle of Rigoberta Menchú?"

"The Guatemalan woman who won the Nobel Peace Prize?" asked Trey.

Salomón nodded. "She was born here in Uspantan."

"So is she the local hero of the town?" Mike asked.

"Not exactly. Many of the people of Uspantan do not see her as a hero. Some, I think, are jealous of her success. A lot of people, however, see her as a hypocrite: She criticized the government's treatment of the poor, in the process becoming rich, but then doing nothing to help the people of

53

her hometown. Her uncle, for example, hasn't seen a penny from her even though his family struggles to feed themselves. She paid a visit in a helicopter once, but that is about it. I know she's very popular internationally but, unfortunately, many Guatemalans, even the Mayans, don't have respect for her."

"But aren't they grateful for the fact that she brought the world's attention to what was going on in Guatemala?"

"That's a difficult issue," he said. "Most of the people feel like she didn't really know what was going on. She hadn't lived in Uspantan since she was a little girl, and many of the things she wrote were secondhand, or, even worse, some would contend, fabricated. A lot of people feel that she got rich and famous off of their suffering."

Mike's Reflections—November 3

It's kind of crazy that people in America view Rigoberta Menchú so differently than they do here. She did at least some good for the people, but they don't seem to appreciate her much. It is interesting to see the difference between how people view someone that helped them from afar, versus how they view someone who came alongside and served them with their own hands, like Salomón and Mery. Christ's model for us is definitely the latter. As it says in Philippians, "Who, being in very nature God, . . . made himself nothing, taking the very nature of a servant . . ."

After this trip, I know I won't be content to just send checks from a distance. That is valuable, too, but there is no substitute for coming close to people and serving them with all that you are.

• • •

Jedd's Reflections—November 1–6

I've enjoyed my time with Jared over the past few days, but it's given me a lot to think about. Church this Sunday was troubling. We saw all the things Jared had warned me are so common: blaring music from blown speakers; a pastor shouting, often in condemnation of other brands of Protestantism or those in his own group who weren't up to specs; women turning on and off the tear faucets in their eyes, apparently on demand.

The next day we visited a pastor in a nearby village. The man was young, about our age. His dark eyes were thoughtful and kind. Yet it seemed the only vision he had for his church was a bigger building and more musical instruments. Even when pressed, the issue of spiritual growth and discipleship did not figure in. Jared says that many of the pastors he has spent time with find it difficult to see things any other way.

It seems much of the Protestant church here is so consumed with externals. For the individual, it is the more obvious shows of piety. For the pastors, it is the way their buildings and services look and the size of their congregations. So few seem to be focused on Jesus and a relationship with Him.

I imagine this is what creates the divisions within the church here. There are eleven different Evangelical churches in the town of Nebaj alone. Christ and the New Testament writers emphasized unity so strongly. Yet unity is impossible when our focus is on anything besides Jesus alone.

Jared feels other frustrations as well. He came here hoping to improve people's lives. Yet he often has doubts as to his purpose and effectiveness. He tells me—only half jokingly—that when he's asked to submit a "Positive Impact Story" for his organization's newsletter, he wonders if he should make something up or just tell them he can't think of any.

I know it isn't that bad. I can see that he is accomplishing some things. But still, there are literally dozens of aid groups here in Guatemala, many just in this town. And despite the unceasing flow of dollars and man-hours, it is hard to discern if the people are really becoming any better off. Some human suffering has been relieved, but it seems that the expectations of the populace end up rising more than conditions. The net effect is discontent. This eats at Jared because he so desperately wants to help bring these people better, happier lives.

[Jared's wife] Jody is less of a crusader in these matters. She cares about the conditions, but isn't as enmeshed in the large projects. A big part of her focus is just building relationships and becoming involved in people's lives. But although she is less accomplishment-oriented, Jared says he thinks she may end up accomplishing more here than him.

Salomón and Mery have a similar way of doing things. Even the big projects they do are totally rooted in relationship with the people they are serving. I'm beginning to see that successful ministry—even basic relief work—must always be built, first and foremost, within the context of relationship.

The Mayans

The next morning, Salomón asked us if we would like to visit with some of his Mayan friends who lived in the nearby hills. We jumped at the opportunity, hoping to look into the lives of the local people, not as prying tourists, but as visiting friends. As always, we climbed into the bed of the Hernández pickup truck and bounced our way down the rutted dirt roads of Uspantan. The laid-back Latin culture was taking hold of us. Even Matt—who at first had been wary of riding unsecured in a truck bed—now thoroughly enjoyed the ride. Today, he even stood with the others, as we had often seen the locals do, arms resting atop the roof of the cab. We struggled not to fall as Salomón dodged brightly-clad women who seemed to glow in the foggy morning. Every now and then, the truck would come to a stop and a few of Salomón's friends would climb in, gratefully accepting the offered lift.

After a jolting twenty minutes, Salomón pulled off the road and hopped out, leading us up a path shrouded in mist. Foliage, lining the sides of the trail, released dewdrops that clung to our pant legs. As the path entered a small cornfield, green turned to gold. Salomón examined one of the stalks. "The Mayans are totally dependent on the corn crop. If it fails, the family could starve. We have been trying to teach them to plant other crops as well, so they will not be so devastated if the corn fails. But it is hard to get them to follow through."

Between the last of the golden stalks we saw a small shanty, smoke sifting out through the cracks in its rough board walls. Although all Mayans do their cooking indoors on an open fire, none of the homes have chimneys. They simply allow the smoke to find its way out through chinks. As we entered, we found this method to be less than advisable. The home choked of wood smoke.

"If there really is a danger from secondhand smoke, this is it," Mike whispered to Matt.

A crude wooden bench in the corner served as the dirt floor's only accent. Cautiously we ducked beneath the low-hanging rafters, trying not to disturb the corn that hung drying from the ceiling.

Salomón called out a greeting to the woman of the house. She offered a shy smile, revealing stained, crooked teeth. Quickly, her humble eyes returned to the floor. The little children gravitated toward us, gazing inquisitively at the pale-skinned giants. In the corner near the smoldering fire, a young teenage girl rocked a baby in her arms. A slight pitter-patter resonated through the roof, suggesting that the mist had turned to rain. Water ran down through a gap in the shingles, but no one seemed to notice.

"These people are my good friends," said Salomón. "When I first met this woman, her husband had a severe drinking problem and was neglecting his family. After years of prayer, he finally turned to put his faith in Christ. The rest of his family soon followed. Now he does his best to care for them. Their life is hard, but we help out a little when their corn runs low."

Outside, someone sloshed up the muddy path toward the door. He entered, but quickly took a step back before a smile crept onto his face. It was Juan, the father of the family. He bowed faintly, acknowledging Salomón as if he were an angel. This seemed to be a common reaction of those we encountered during our time in Guatemala.

In Guatemala there are two distinct societies, the Ladinos and the Mayans. Technically, a Ladino is any-one with mixed European and Indian blood. Broadly, the term *Ladino* is used to refer to anyone who embraces a Western style of life. As in other Latin American countries, the higher the percentage of European blood, generally speaking, the higher one's level in society. In contrast, most Mayans live today in much the same fashion as they have for centuries. As uneducated subsistence farmers, they are looked down upon by Ladinos. The friction between these two groups was a major undercurrent in Guatemala's civil war.

The Salomón Hernández family has worked to heal these wounds one family at a time. They believe following Christ in this situation means serving people considered worthless by the higher classes. When serving as pastor of the local Methodist church, Salomón invited the local Mayans into the fold. But the existing congregation did not want the "bad-smelling" Indians invading their church. When Salomón would not back down, he was told, "Go with your Indians; we don't want them." The elders decreed that Salomón was pastor no more.

But he and Mery were

The Village of Uspantan
(View from Don Salomón and Doña Mery's Front Porch)

undeterred. They left the church, seeking to live by Jesus' teachings rather than the cultural norms of the church. It was plain to see their decision had a profound effect upon a great many lives, including those we were seeing today.

Juan and Salomón talked quietly in the corner of the room. We gathered from Juan's gestures that he had been consulting Salomón about his roof. Apparently, it had been leaking for quite some time. Without a word, Salomón hoisted his agile sixty-year-old body onto the roof, moved a few tiles around, and *voila!* No more leak. It did not take a rocket scientist to do what he did, but the family would have lived with the rain indefinitely had Salomón not visited.

The incredible patience exercised by Salomón and Mery in their service amazed us. They are dedicated to helping a people who has never learned how to learn. Their fish hatchery project failed because the people ate the seed fish. The mattress they brought this family last year was sitting in the middle of the pasture a week after they had given it to them. The vitamins they brought for the children often went unused, though the kids needed them desperately.

At some of the stories we heard we could hardly help but laugh. We will never forget the story of the couple who came to Salomón for birth control. They already had eight kids and could not afford to feed any more. Salomón prescribed some birth control pills with strict directions on their use. To his dismay, the woman returned three months later beginning to show.

"What happened?" Salomón exclaimed "Haven't you been taking the pills I prescribed?"

The woman affirmed that she had. After some prying, however, she acknowledged they had made one slight alteration: "I didn't like taking them, so my husband has been taking them instead."

Mike's Reflections—November 9

It amazes me how Salomón and Mery can continue to serve without getting angry at the people they are trying to serve. I certainly think I would have long ago.

Dostoevsky observed, "The idea of loving one's neighbor is possible only as an abstraction: it may be conceivable to love one's fellow man at a distance, but it is almost never possible to love him at close quarters." This statement is truer than we'd like to admit. I've known a lot of supposed humanitarians who go out to do all kinds of good, but end up despising the people they came to serve.

It seems so clear that the only thing enabling Salomón and Mery to avoid that sort of frustration is their relationship with Christ. Despite all the exasperating situations, the Hernández family somehow continues to give love. It is a love that is not based on the qualifications of its recipients, or even on their ability to receive it well. Salomón and Mery love because Christ first loved them. They are intent on pleasing Him, not just on "doing good." Most important, as they walk with Him, He gives them love for the people they are serving. And since they love the people they are serving, even though they may get frustrated at times, they are no more likely to give up on them than is a parent whose child is having a hard time learning to walk.

59

Principles of Amor

After dinner that night, we sipped tea and talked. Jedd, who had caught a glimpse of Salomón taking Mery's hand under the table, said he could not help but smile; they seemed to cherish each other so deeply.

"How is it that your marriage is so strong?" Jedd asked Salomón.

"Because I cannot live without her," he replied with a grin. Mery seemed to blush a bit. "It is true. So much of what we do together is thanks to Mery."

Despite the clear male headship of the Hernández family, it was easy to see that Mery's quiet strength and servantlike heart was, in many ways, the growing soil of their ministry.

Salomón turned to Mery. "Tell the boys about our nightly commitment."

Mery nodded. "Since we were first married, we have come together every night before we go to bed and held

Salomón Kissing Mery

hands. We look in each other's eyes and ask forgiveness for whatever we have done to wrong the other that day. Then we ask if there is anything we have done to offend the other, so that we can ask forgiveness for that, too."

"How did you know to start doing that?"

"No one told us. It is a biblical principle: 'Do not let the sun go down on your anger.'"

It was humbling to realize that for their whole lives, Salomón and Mery had been living out the principle of nightly reconciliation and confession we were only beginning to discover. We were particularly struck by the fact that a Latino man, steeped in the machismo tradition, would humble himself enough to ask forgiveness of his wife. It was just another example of how Salomón and Mery set the patterns of their lives by Jesus' instructions rather than by their culture.

We also saw that, although each had their own strengths and very distinct role, they were truly a team. They had attended seminary together, and then nursing school. Later, they studied the Quiché language together. As they carried out their shared vision for ministry, Mery aided the women and children while Salomón worked with the men.

"Salomón chose me because he planned to be a pastor and work within the church," Mery explained. "He noticed me working with the children, leading Sunday school, and helping with many things in my church. He knew we could be a team."

"But Mery wasn't so sure about me at first," Salomón interjected.

"No, when Salomón asked me out, I had some doubts. I told him to pray about it for three months, and then come back. Three months to the day, he was back on my doorstep."

We all laughed.

Salomón shook his head. "So she said, 'Okay, we can date, but first you must talk to my father.' My knees were shaking, but I did it." He squeezed Mery's leg. "It was worth it. I'd do it again a thousand times."

A Scathing Letter and
Some Sweet Sorrow

Leaving Guatemala

When the time came to leave the Uspantan countryside, we felt a hint of melancholy. Its quiet streets and lovely hills had wedged themselves deep in our hearts. The long drive back to the city was wet and mud-spattered, the prospect of our departure making the gloom even heavier. Here and there, though, a sunburst broke through the sullen clouds, bathing the scene in warmth and light.

"Mind if I ask another question, Don Salomón?" said Mike. We had been mining his and Mery's wisdom most of the trip down the mountain. "How do you know who to serve? I mean, there are so many needs here in Guatemala. How do you choose which ones you will meet?"

Salomón glanced at Mike in the rearview mirror. "That's a difficult question, Miguel. I used to worry about it a lot. The way I see it now, though, is this: Jesus called us to love our neighbors, and that is what we must try to do. The people around us, the people God puts in our path, those are the people whose needs we are to meet."

"So do you go out seeking these people?"

"In the past we did more, but not so much now. People know we are available to help them. They come to us. If you offer yourself to God, He will open your eyes to the needs all around you."

The Ethics of Bribery

Back at Shelly's apartment, a fax waited for us from Westmont College. According to the message, we had set off a big debate at our alma mater. Before the trip began, we had agreed to send articles about our trip every few weeks to Westmont's school newspaper, the *Horizon*. The first to appear in the paper described Jedd and Mike's drive through Mexico, including their incident at the Mexican-American border. The following week's edition of the newspaper carried a stinging letter to the editor:

> Last week the Horizon *printed a letter from "The International Missions Team." The team recounted their exciting adventures running borders and bribing officials. They were carrying illegal goods described in the letter as "medical supplies . . . donated only recently," which, "because of time constraints, had not been preregistered with Mexican authorities." Consequently, they were stopped at the border and told they couldn't take $3,000 worth of medical supplies into the country. How inconvenient for Christ's workers.*
>
> *So the International Missions Team found another border station and snuck through. This was entirely illegal. When they later got stopped and their smuggling was discovered, they bribed the officials. They laughed as they drove off, "expressing doubts as to whether those fees would end up in the Mexican treasury." What silly, corrupt officials, accepting bribes like that. Apparently, only accepting bribes is wrong: giving bribes is acceptable, especially if done in God's name.*
>
> *Last year, [a Westmont group that does service work in Mexico] ran the border with trailer loads of food and medical supplies. This was also in defiance of Mexico's laws, but later in chapel, [our chaplain] was ecstatic as he recounted how they twisted the laws to their liking and smuggled tons of food and medicine into Mexico.*

This is wrong.

Mexico has laws, and those laws are to be respected when one is in Mexico. The fact that you are a Christian, that you are a missions worker, that you are working toward what you think is God's plan does not exempt you from anything. Christ told us to respect and follow the laws of the land, that temporal authorities were placed there by God. "Render unto Caesar" means paying respect as well as taxes.

There is a dangerous feeling of superiority which can breed in missions work, and it is this that tells us that it is acceptable to break laws and ignore the wishes of those to whom we are proselytizing. But it is simply not acceptable to infantilize our "targets." It is arrogant, it is offensive, and it is sometimes even illegal. Perhaps if the International Missions Team realized this they would cease to be the International Criminals Team.

63

Controversy bloomed, with questions of smuggling, fees, bribes, and bureaucracy becoming hot topics in Westmont's dining hall, dorms, and coffee shops. Debates sprang up in classrooms, and an evening forum was held to allow open discussion of the issue.

Our feelings were mixed. Despite the criticisms of some, we felt secure in the fact that our motivation from the beginning had simply been to get medical supplies to people who needed them. We also felt some indignation. What right had our critics to sit there in their dorm rooms pointing an accusing finger at us? After all, we were not profiting from any of this. We were just doing the best we could to help our Christian family in Latin America.

As our defensive, somewhat knee-jerk reaction wore off, however, we returned to what Mike and Jedd had wondered even in the midst of the exchange that night in Mexico: Maybe we had been wrong. We did believe we had good reasons for our actions, but there were good reasons for questioning them as well. Our critics were simply raising important issues that ought to have been raised. If we were to strike back at them, seeking only to defend ourselves, it would have been nothing more than an attempt to avoid the difficult reality that we ourselves simply did not know if what we had done was best. Trying, as best we could, to be honest and not overly defensive, we responded with a letter to the editor of our own:

Friends at Westmont,

We are challenged and encouraged by your struggle over the issue of bribes in foreign countries. Many of the things you are discussing mirror our own thoughts and questions. For the Christian, when to diverge from the laws of the land is a challenging question.

Having grown up in a nation where laws are generally reasonable and just, we have little direct contact with many of the subtleties of this issue. The Christians who live in lands where laws impede, and even make impossible, acts of love and service have a much fuller understanding of the issues involved. It is difficult for us even to conceive of authorities who demand bribes to carry out their appointed functions, or bureaucratic desks where requests will never be considered unless accompanied by a "gift." Even so, we can still wrestle over these questions in theory and through the Word of God.

One could say that there is a continuum between those laws that clearly must be obeyed, such as those against murder, and those that must be broken, such as one mandating the death of Jews. At some point between the black and white, however, is the realm where we must struggle to discern the will of God.

Should we, like Rahab, lie to authorities to protect noble spies? Should we, like Daniel, brazenly display disobedience before an open window when laws limit our religious freedom? Should we, like the disciples on the Sabbath, disobey the law of our society if it conflicts with the spirit of God's law? Should we, like [a group that went south of the border last year], smuggle much-needed medical supplies into Mexico? Should we, as we actually did, have given a demanded "fee" to authorities who would otherwise have taken our car, even though they wrongly sought to profit from a law intended to keep people from importing unregistered medical supplies into Mexican markets, while we were bringing the supplies through to Guatemala? The answers are not easy. Crucial issues of the spirit of the law (both Christ's and society's) only add to the complexity.

We do not have pat answers. We know we must seek to honor earthly powers. We also know that such authority is not the highest authority. In regards to our own past choices, we join you in wrestling over the question of what was best. While perhaps [the young man who wrote the original criticism] misunderstood what actually happened at the border, we share his desire to seek truth.

Looking forward to our planned smuggling of Bibles into Vietnam, we must consider similar questions. Until the answers can be known for certain, we encourage you all to continue seeking . . .

Sincerely,
Matt, Mike, Jedd, and Trey

A Well-Watered Garden

Before leaving Guatemala, we were able to enjoy one last meal with the extended *familia Hernández*. Once again, the long table was covered with

65

mouth-watering dishes. Matt looked around the table. A granddaughter sat smiling on Salomón's lap. Shelly and her sister-in-law were deep in conversation. Another of Salomón's daughters had begun to clear the table. Mery talked with two of her small grandsons, while a third stole another helping of dessert. Dr. Danny laughed at something his brother-in-law had said.

It is amazing, Matt thought. *This family has such tender concern for the poor, and yet, they can enjoy life so fully as well.*

Jedd Sends a Niño Skyward

Matt's Reflections—November 11

Sometimes, when I'm around the poor, I have a hard time not feeling guilty for all that I have. But at the same time that I feel guilty, I have a hard time being generous because I doubt that the money I'm giving away will be used wisely. I think my problem is that I see the money that I have as my money, not money that has been entrusted to me by God. The Hernándezes, on the other hand, seem to really believe that the money they have is not theirs but God's. And they live this out! Seeing their generosity astounds me. They give away so much, yet they don't seem uptight at all about the chances that sometimes they might be taken advantage of. They are more generous with others than with themselves, but even in that, they are able to take so much pleasure in the good things God has given them.

There is probably a poor man out on the street right at this moment. Maybe tomorrow Salomón will give him the shirt right off his back. But that is not his calling right now. His calling right now is to enjoy an evening with his family. It is beautiful to see how God does expect real sacrifice, but He gives real joy as well. I'm beginning to understand that the two come together. You can't separate them. I hope I can embrace them both.

° ° °

66

At the airport's departure gate, in a flurry of pictures and hugs, we bid good-bye to the family.

Trey shook his head, "I don't know if I've ever been so sad to say good-bye to anyone. I feel such a strong sense of the family of God . . . they really *are* our family."

Matt nodded. "I know what you mean. The hardest part of this whole trip may be saying good-bye."

As the plane shot heavenward, we took a last glimpse of Guatemala before the volcanoes, jungles, chaotic streets, and soldiers were swallowed by clouds. Our flight would take us to Miami, where we would spend a one-day layover, hosted by a friend of a friend of a friend, before moving on to Russia.

The book of Isaiah promises, "If you spend yourselves in behalf of the hungry and satisfy the needs of the oppressed, then your light will rise in the darkness, and your night will become like the noonday. The LORD will guide you always; he will satisfy your needs in a sun-scorched land and will

Adios at the Airport

strengthen your frame. You will be like a well-watered garden, like a spring whose waters never fail" (58:10–11).

For perhaps the first time in our lives, we had been able to observe— even live with for a time—people who truly spent themselves "in behalf of the hungry" and satisfied "the needs of the oppressed."

God seemed to be keeping His end of the bargain as well. While Salomón and Mery focused on meetings the needs of others, God had been faithful to take care of theirs. Anyone could see that they were, most certainly, "like a well-watered garden, like a spring whose waters never fail."

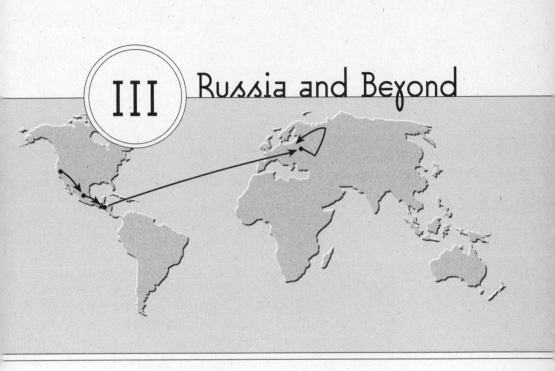

III Russia and Beyond

Trey, Jedd, Mike, and Matt in Moscow's Red Square

six

The Wounded Bear

Moscow, Russia

In the kingdom of hope, there is no winter.

—RUSSIAN PROVERB

Moscow's international airport could not have been more different from Miami's. Gone were the gleaming buildings and the bright Florida sun, the palm trees, warm air, and shorts-clad tourists. In Moscow, a heavy gray pallor had settled over all, from the stone-colored terminal and the dour attendants to the leafless trees and sullen sky above. As we walked into the terminal, the word *cave* came to mind. Funding for carpet and lighting must have been viewed by the Soviet planners during the Communist years as unnecessary extravagance for the workers' paradise.

Trey stepped up to the passport control booth. *"Zdrastvuitiye!"* he greeted the lady sitting behind the desk.

She offered no reply, but grasped his documents and stared at his face as if it was a rotten plum. Satisfied there was some resemblance between the photo on the passport and the man before her, she stamped the book and waved him through. Trey caught sight of his mother, Mary, jostling for position along the low fence just outside of the terminal.

"Can you grab my backpack?" he said to Jedd, already moving off toward her.

As the rest of us emerged from passport control, Trey waited, standing next to his mother, his arm over her shoulder. Mary's blue eyes—much like her son's—were glowing.

"It's great to have you here," she said, welcoming each of us in turn with a motherly hug.

"You're looking great, Mary," said Jedd. It was true; her vivacity and petite frame suggested she was quite a bit younger than her fifty-something years.

She tilted her head and winked. "I guess the ice-cold weather here preserves you pretty well."

The multilane road leading to central Moscow was deep in slush. Row after row of identical drab apartments filled the skyline with two-hundred-foot-high boxes of gray concrete that had been built during the Communist years to house the masses. It is often joked that the Soviet government saved money by hiring only one architect to design all their buildings. From one end of the former Soviet Union to the other, and even into the former Eastern Bloc countries, a traveler will find countless replicas of the same towering cement-block apartments.

Most of inner Moscow, however, was built before the Revolution of 1917. So, as our road wound closer to the center of the city, the dreary apartments gave way to magnificent buildings crafted in the nineteenth century or before. Finally, we tumbled from our vehicle into a snow-filled alley in back of a building that fronted on Moscow's famous Petrovka Street. Bags in tow, we squeezed through a battered door on the ground level and lumbered up four flights of stairs to the top floor. Mary opened the heavy oak door and a second, metal-plated one just inside the first.

"This is home as long as you're here, boys," she exclaimed, ushering us from the dreary stairwell into a warm room that smelled of cookies.

 Trey's Reflections—November 15

It feels great to be back in Russia! Each time I visit my family, I feel like I appreciate this place more. Every aspect of Russia is deep and

strange to me, yet also inviting. I can't wait to plunge further into this mysterious land with the guys.

We had originally planned to spend two days with the Sklars in Moscow before traveling south to the Republic of Dagestan, but a recent outbreak of civil unrest in Dagestan's capital city caused us to change our plans. Under our revised itinerary, we would spend our first weeks in two cities near Moscow, then travel to Russia's far north for the final three weeks before Christmas. Our contact, Athletes in Action missionary Steve Barrett, would be contacting friends of his in the areas to which we would travel; the locals would work to set up opportunities for us to speak about our travels—and Christ—in schools, hospitals, retirement homes, and the like. Apparently, Americans were enough of a novelty outside of Moscow to gain a hearing in most any location.

That first evening, Moscow beckoned and we could not resist. Though we had gone twenty-four hours with almost no sleep, we bundled up and headed outside, hiking down the sidewalk, through the piled snow, with icy patches crackling beneath our boots. We examined bread shops, banks, and the many-pillared Bolshoi Theater. An immense statue of Karl Marx stood in the middle of a large plaza, looking down with disapproval at a nearby Western-style mall. Men and women bustled past bright shop windows. In the sky, a high, wispy fog was turned ghostly yellow by the city lights.

A pair of Russian girls flowed past in long, fur coats, one glancing at Jedd long enough to offer him a faint smile.

"Must be the beard, Jedd. It makes you even more irresistible than ever," quipped Mike.

Jedd shook his head. "I thought Russian women were supposed to be hairy-faced. It seems like every girl I've seen tonight is gorgeous."

"They are," affirmed Trey. "I don't know how that stereotype got started, but it couldn't be more wrong."

"Must have been Cold War propaganda from the U.S. government," joked Mike. "They were afraid all the guys would defect if they knew the truth."

"What a contrast with the men," Matt added. "Most of them seem to have the same haircut and wear nothing but black and gray."

"It's true," Trey agreed. "I wonder if that comes from growing up under a police state like the U.S.S.R. where being noticed was a fearful thing."

At the end of Petrovka Street, we entered a three-story, red-brick gate-house.

"What's this?" asked Matt.

"You'll see," replied Trey in a hushed voice.

We passed through the gatehouse and came out onto a vast plate of cobbled stone. Glowing walls hemmed us in on all sides. To the left, the intricate facade of what looked like a nineteenth-century department store extended on for more than a hundred yards; on the right, the turreted walls of the Kremlin rose high into the foggy night. Directly ahead, the multi-colored onion domes of St. Basil's Cathedral blazed out of the mist. We were standing in the immortal Red Square.

The hammer-and-sickle flag no longer flew above the Kremlin, but atop a massive clock tower, an immense Communist star—each arm five feet long and made of solid rubies—turned the shredded clouds around it bloody. Mystery flowed from the granite-hewn mausoleum where Lenin's corpse lay. Distant echoes of rumbling tanks and goose-stepping soldiers from the past blended with the sounds of enchanted visitors and strolling lovers.

Mike's half-whisper broke the silence. "I remember seeing the Soviet military parade through this place on TV when I was little. I always thought about what I'd do if they attacked."

"Part of me hoped they would," Jedd said, nodding. "A little boy's fantasy. I thought it'd be great to take to the hills and fight for America."

Mike smiled faintly. "Yeah, like in that movie *Red Dawn*."

○ ○ ○

We explored Moscow for another hour before a combination of cold and sleepiness finally began to penetrate the excitement.

"I think I'd say I'm just about ready for a nice, warm bed," announced Matt.

"Are you sure?" asked Trey with a bit of disappointment. "How about we turn back in another half-hour?"

"I'm getting pretty tired, too, Trey," affirmed Mike.

"Okay," Trey agreed. "But we'll take the long way back."

The Kremlin Wall

seven

The Secret Police
Orekhovo-Zuyevo, Russia

dozens of tracks extended before us across the station. Snow fell slowly that morning, leaving a light dusting on the train platform. Mike pushed his hands deep in his pockets.

"What time is Steve supposed to be here?" he asked, knowing the answer.

"He's a little late," said Trey. "Steve's Mr. High Energy, but he always seems to be a few minutes behind."

Steve Barrett, the director of Athletes in Action of Moscow, would be traveling with us out to the nearby city of Orekhovo-Zuyevo. Christian friends of his who lived in the town had arranged for us to spend the week speaking in schools, orphanages, and other locations. Steve would get us situated and spend the first few days with us before returning to Moscow.

"It takes the body a little while to adjust from Central America to Moscow," said Mike, a slight shiver in his voice.

Matt dragged his backpack over next to Trey. "Were you ever able to find out if our bank account has received any more donations?" he asked.

Trey shook his head. "I know it's stupid, but I forgot to check when we were in Florida. Now it's going to be difficult to do it from Moscow."

Matt seemed a little annoyed. "Jedd, what did you say your calculations came out to?"

"We've used up just about all of the funds we had in our account when we left. Unless more donations have come in, we could be very close to broke."

Trey was rescued from having to respond as a stocky man in a black pea-coat strode toward us across the platform. "I think that's Steve," he said.

The man's hat stretched low across his brow. His chiseled face was covered with three days of stubble, looking more like a member of the Mafia than a missionary. Back in his college days, Steve was an NCAA national champion wrestler for Oklahoma. He would have competed in the Olympics in 1980 had the U.S. not boycotted the Moscow games. It was ironic that Moscow is now his home.

In addition to a weightlifting regimen, Steve often runs stairs, up and down the twenty flights in his apartment complex. Some of his Muscovite neighbors think he is a bit crazy.

Steve allowed for a quick round of introductions, then asked, "You guys've got everything you need?"

We nodded.

"Long underwear?"

"I've got mine," said Matt.

"Good. Keep that stuff on and you'll be fine."

Exotic #274

We reached Orekhovo-Zuyevo by early afternoon. The sun was already low in the sky. The city appeared much like the dozens of other small cities that encircle Moscow. We had passed through several on the two-hour train ride out. Most flew by the windows as little more than a blur of gray and white. At the occasional stops, the dull colors came into focus: a smattering of nondescript factories; white snow on buildings and brown sludge in the streets; some individual homes built early in the century, and always at least a few of the huge concrete-box apartment buildings.

Steve hailed a taxi and we loaded it up with our luggage. We would walk the mile or so to the central part of town to Orekhovo-Zuyevo's only hotel. Hotel 274 did not look like much from the outside. Wooden bars covered small, dingy windows. As with the exterior, the interior paint falling from the walls was a faded pea green. Behind a green desk in the corner sat an immense lady dressed in a slightly darker shade of pea green.

As we entered, she glared suspiciously. There was no doubt who was queen of this castle. Steve approached in respectful silence.

"What do you want?" Only her lips moved. Her eyes and facial expression remained remarkably fixed.

"Two rooms, please."

She shook her head slowly, leading with her chin. We had heard that the role of a hotel desk clerk in Communist days was not to facilitate stays for guests, but to ensure that none but the "right" sort of people stayed; at Hotel 274, apparently nothing had changed. For several minutes, Steve and Pea Green debated—her presenting trumped-up reasons why we could not stay and him refuting each faulty argument.

"Give me the passports and visas," she finally demanded, apparently yielding.

After scrutinizing them for several more minutes, a hint of a smile crossed her face. "You cannot stay here," she sniveled. "The authorities in Moscow have not authorized you to stay in this city."

Steve was correct in protesting that our multientry visas, procured by friends of the Sklars in the Russian government, did not require special authorization to stay in cities outside of Moscow. She would hear none of it. Two hours, several phone calls, and half a dozen attempts to contact the local authorities produced no change. We were stuck. It appeared that we might be forced to return to Moscow.

"I can't believe this lady," Trey muttered.

Matt—rarely one for sarcasm—laughed quietly in disbelief. "The only thing worse than a corrupt Third World bureaucracy that takes bribes is a corrupt Third World bureaucracy that doesn't."

"Let me call the guy who has been trying to set up speaking stuff for you guys. If he doesn't have any ideas, we may have to cancel," said Steve.

When he returned from the phone booth, Steve's face was hopeful. "He's putting the word out among the locals. I doubt any of them have big places, but Russian believers always surprise me."

Twenty minutes later, the man Steve had called drove up in front of the hotel. He embraced Steve, greeted us, and then related that a Christian woman had volunteered to move out of her apartment for us and we could use it as long as we were in town.

Matt glanced at Steve with some concern. "You sure about this?"

"Believers here see things differently. She wants to do this. If she didn't, she wouldn't have offered."

It was the second time someone had moved out of their home for our sake.

The apartment was small—a kitchen, dining room, and closetlike bedroom—but it fit our needs wonderfully. Our hostess was a middle-aged woman with graying hair and big, childlike eyes. She helped us move in and then disappeared before we had a chance to thank her.

o o o

We spent much of the following days at several orphanages for young children. The ladies in charge would gather the children for our Bible stories. Afterward, the affection-starved youngsters delighted in romping and wrestling or just sitting in our laps, often three or four at a time.

In the evenings after dinner, we often remained around the table for hours, drawing stories out of Steve. As he spoke, his face reflected the extraordinary twists and turns of each narrative, his sky-blue eyes bulging as he reached the story's climax. The tales of his work throughout the former Soviet Union proved fascinating: wrestling contests against savage men in the mountains south of Russia whose disdain became respect after he managed to pin their champion; visits to the peoples of Ossetia, whose entire "Christian" faith consists of eating a lamb and getting drunk once each year in a holy copse of trees; the Olympic gold medalist wrestler whom Steve hid from organized crime bosses for several months after the man accepted Christ and decided to change his ways.

Steve recounted a time when he had shown the *JESUS* film to a group of men in the Caucasus Mountains. One man watched with rapt interest. When the film ended, he watched it a second time, absolutely enthralled. After it was over, the man sat deep in thought. Finally, he announced to Steve that he wished he could follow Christ, but would not be able to because he ran a gas station.

Steve allowed us to ask the obvious. "A gas station?"

"The man couldn't become a Christian because he ran a gas station," Steve repeated with a smile.

We waited for him to continue.

"In the Caucasus Mountains, the gas stations are all tied to the Mafia. You can't run one down there without being tied into a lot of shady dealings. If the guy decided to follow Jesus, he knew he'd have to get out. And he couldn't just sell the station. He'd have to be on the next train to Siberia, or the last thing he'd hear would be the sound of his brains flying out the back of his head."

"Man," Matt muttered under his breath.

Jedd mused, "It is easy for me to think that I would follow Jesus in any situation, but I wonder how I'd come out if the first decision I had to make for Christ was something like that."

"That was a tough decision," followed Steve, "tougher than we know—leaving family, friends, job, everything. And it all had to be decided right when he first encountered Jesus, just like it did in the story of the rich young ruler. But when it comes down to it, that's a decision we all have to make. We tend to think that being a nice, churchy person is at least halfway there. But Jesus didn't want any disciples who weren't in 100 percent. It was all or nothing."

"So you'd say that someone who wasn't completely sold out isn't saved?" Mike questioned.

Steve responded thoughtfully, "I don't know, Mike. In the end, it's up to God to decide exactly who has committed their life to Him. I'm thankful to know that even the greatest saints failed at times. Just think of Peter.

"But I do know that Christ demanded that those who follow Him follow with everything, even if that involved fumbling and bumbling along the path. We'll all make mistakes, but it all comes down to the root-level question: Do I want to give Him my all or not?"

Trey probed further. "Some people seem to have to decide everything at the beginning: all or nothing right off the bat. Others have a lifetime to think about it."

Steve rubbed his jaw as he thought for a moment. "Yeah, some people do have more time than others. But ultimately, they have to choose also. That's how it is for most of us. We may not face the big decision right at first, but the truth is, by the time we reach the decision point, the choice has probably already been made. All the little, day-to-day decisions we make shape who we are. When we come to the big crossroads, we will just continue in the way we are already moving."

"What was it like for you?" asked Mike.

"I accepted Jesus when I was young, and most of the way it's been smaller, easier decisions. In the little things, was Jesus the master or was I? I hit my big 'follow me' decision when God called me to leave my farm in Missouri and take my family to Russia. When I was younger, I had done some work in Eastern Europe, but as an adult, I was pretty content out on my farm. I had a wife, three young daughters, not much money, and I didn't know a lick of Russian. But there was no getting around the fact that God wanted me here."

"So you went?"

"Yep. There've been some rough spots along the way, but I'd do it again a hundred times. When you know you're living for something eternal every day, even the worst isn't too bad. Anyway, I knew I would probably have been more comfortable at home, but I'd never be satisfied with farming if God wanted something different for me."

At Home with Aunt Lucy

The woman who had lent us the apartment was not the only face of warm hospitality in Orekhovo-Zuyevo. A big second (and we do mean BIG) was a rotund elderly lady who everyone called Aunt Lucy. Aunt Lucy outweighed many an NFL lineman. Her dark eyes twinkled fiercely in her broad face, and only when stopping to catch her breath was she not in motion. As she had every morning during our stay, Aunt Lucy entered the apartment before dawn and set a kettle and the breakfast victuals on the stove to warm.

Then—much earlier than we had requested the night before—she crashed like a Gestapo raid into the room where we slumbered. Angry

Hanging out with Aunt Lucy

Slavic tones boomed off the walls. Steve did not open his eyes, but hissed translations to us as she rolled on and on, her hands on her hips, jowls bouncing up and down.

"You're guilty of many unforgivable offenses," he explained. "You sleep too long, you fail to jump to your feet upon waking, and you generally resemble old women."

Just when we were sure she was about to begin beating us with a rolling pin, Aunt Lucy broke into laughter so jolly we could not help wondering if she was related to Father Christmas. Matt and Jedd sat up halfway, not sure how to respond. When we finally began to smile ourselves, she once again set her jaw and resumed her tirade . . . only to burst into yet another round of raucous laughter. Once assured we were awake, Aunt Lucy returned to the kitchen, leaving us to pull on our many layers of clothing and gather at the table before her food—chunks of fatty sausage laid on heavily buttered pasta. Lucy stood over us as we ate, ready to whisk a not-quite-finished bowl from under our nose, pile on more pasta, up to the brim, and then push the filled bowl back in front of its owner. She would not be satisfied until we had eaten all she had cooked.

81

Breakfast finally done, strong chai downed, and heavy jackets donned, Steve and the four of us shuffled out the door to the day's work. Aunt Lucy clogged traffic in the little coatroom as we passed by, harshly admonishing us to put on our caps and zip up our jackets. Before returning to her own home, she would wash the dishes and straighten the house. We could hear her voice launch into a Russian hymn the moment the door shut behind us.

"We'll be at an *internot* today," said Steve. "That's an orphanage for older kids—junior high and high school."

"You think it'll be pretty much the same as the other places we've been—speaking and then just hanging out?" Jedd asked.

"There's a lot of kids. You'll probably speak to a few different groups. They'll probably want to play you in some sports, too."

"I could use the exercise," remarked Jedd. "I love Aunt Lucy, but sausage and white pasta isn't exactly the breakfast of champions."

"Just keep doing your push-ups," said Trey. Throughout the trip thus far, Jedd had remained faithful to his regimen of push-ups, pull-ups, and other exercises, often with his backpack on.

Jedd bent down and scooped a mound of snow with his mitten. As he walked, he shaped the crystals into a sphere, then pitched it over Matt's head toward Mike.

"Nice shot," said Trey.

A moment later, a return snowball crashed into Jedd's Russian cap.

"Hey, you about knocked my head off." Jedd turned his head parallel to the ground and tried to pick snow out of his ear.

Mike grinned and offered something of an apology. He turned back to Trey, taking on a more sober tone. "Did you have a chance to talk with your mom about how things are going with your dad?"

"Not as much as I wanted to. When I brought it up, she seemed a little strained and said we should talk about it when we had more time. We just didn't have a chance. She's trying to be strong, but I can tell it's been pretty rough."

"From what I can see, she's being incredibly strong."

"She always is, but it seems like things are getting worse. I was telling Jedd that I want to try to spend some time in Moscow to be with the family for a few days next week. Is that okay with you?"

"Of course. Let me know if we can . . ."

Another snowball broke against Mike's shoulder, spraying Trey with snow as well. Trey offered Mike a "we can talk about it later" smile.

○ ○ ○

The boys at the other side of the soccer field appeared to be between nine and thirteen, the biggest one hardly reaching Trey's shoulder. We had talked with several groups in the internot, telling about our travels and life in America as well as our faith in Christ. As Steve predicted, at the end of our last talk, the challenge had come from a straw-haired boy in a ragged coat: Will you play us in a game of soccer?

Matt sprinted toward the ball, reaching it before his ten-year-old opponent. He had not dribbled the ball twice, however, when he landed on his back with the wind knocked out of him. Beneath a thin layer of recent snow, the ground was more like a hockey rink than a soccer field. The little fellow had snagged the ball and taken off down

Soccer Game with Local Orphanage

the field. Jedd—a little out of control—collided with the boy and both tumbled. Jedd made it to his feet first, but a boy in old red sweats stole it from him and headed off in the other direction. Moments later, a thin spring-loaded leg fired the ball past Mike's hands.

"Come on, fellas!" shouted Jedd. "That was pitiful."

We improved a bit as the game went on, but not by much. What the kids lacked in height, they made up in skill. After an hour of ice-rink soccer, we were exhausted.

The outcome particularly disappointed Jedd. "It's pretty sad we couldn't even half their score," he said, shaking his head as we walked off the field.

○ ○ ○

Steve headed back to Moscow that afternoon. We would continue to visit schools and orphanages on our own, with a student from Moscow named Elena translating for us. Steve would return one morning later in the week to join us for a speaking engagement at a nearby military base.

"We're on for nine-thirty on Thursday, so meet me there around nine. I'll explain the details then," promised Steve. "It's an OMON base, so the security will probably be tight. Just have Elena explain who you are—they'll be expecting you. By the way, I'll be bringing my Russian teammate Victor out with me. You'll like him. Great guy. He used to be in the navy."

Costs of Discipleship

After a full day of speaking and sports, Aunt Lucy's dinner of beet-laced borscht, mounds of bleached pasta, and hot dogs looked very appetizing. Halfway through the meal, friends of Aunt Lucy stopped by for an unexpected visit. Lucy found two extra chairs and plates, and we squeezed shoulder to shoulder around the table. The man was a Baptist pastor from a neighboring town, his bushy gray eyebrows matching his stiff suit, his wife's jet-black hair pulled back tight in a bun. They greeted us politely but said little during dinner.

As the chai tea and candies were brought out, it became apparent that the pastor did desire to speak with us. With Elena translating, he quizzed us on our backgrounds, families, and denominations. He had not heard of Calvary Chapel, Covenant, or even Presbyterian before. His eyebrows

83

seemed to lower with apprehension, but he ultimately appeared satisfied with Trey's description: "They're a lot like Baptists." We could not quite tell whether he was just curious, or if he was probing to see if we were sincere in our faith; probably a little of both. No doubt a pastor who served in Communist times took care to be initially inquisitive with those who presented themselves as Christian brothers. After a time, we were able to ask questions of our own.

"You've been a pastor all your life?" inquired Matt.

"Since I was a young man," he said. "My job was at the factory, but my real work was teaching at the church that met in a home near our apartment."

"Do you have children?" Mike asked.

"One," his wife said, almost inaudibly.

We waited for her to continue, but she said no more. We wondered if it was a sad thing in Russia to have only one child.

Jedd spoke up. "What was it like to be a pastor before Communism ended?" The pastor's eyes rested on the table for a moment after Elena had explained the question.

He glanced at each of us before replying quietly. "There are books now written about it, but we lived it." After a moment of silence, the pastor looked up at us again. "I don't want to bore you," he apologized.

"No, please, we want to hear what you have to say," assured Trey.

"I don't want to bore you, but it is true," he repeated. "We have had our share of troubles. Often the KGB came crashing into our gatherings. They'd smash tables and break chairs and yell at everybody. They would write down the names of every person there and take away our few Bibles and hymnals."

"Did they hurt you physically?" asked Matt softly.

"I was lucky. They did little harm to my body. I know other pastors who lost fingers and worse. Some were taken and never came back. Usually they would bring me to the station and question me and yell at me for hours. Then they would let me go, warning me that they'd send me to Siberia if I kept preaching. It was she who was once hurt badly." He nodded toward his wife. She offered her same soft, sad smile. "She was very pregnant at a time when our church was raided. They pushed her down and someone kicked her. It caused our child to be crippled."

We could only stare at the table.

The pastor seemed ready to move on to another topic. The conversation was interesting, but images of clandestine services, angry soldiers, and pregnant women continued to spin through our heads. They remained with us that night in our sleep.

o o o

The following evening after Lucy had gone home, we sat around the table discussing the day's events.

"I'm really enjoying our times at the orphanages," remarked Trey.

"The soccer games are great," said Mike. "Everywhere we go, they want to challenge us. They feel like they're on top of the world if they beat the Americans."

"They always do," stated Jedd flatly.

Matt said, "It's hard to know how to talk to the kids here. It's so much easier to connect with people when you understand their culture."

"Right," agreed Mike. "You think, what do I have to say to a Russian orphan? Our lives are just so totally different."

"I think the way we're doing it is the best we can do—just trying to be real," said Trey. "Tell 'em about our lives and some of the things we've seen and what faith in Christ can be."

Matt nodded. "It's a good lesson for me. Speaking in places like this cuts out the illusions I sometimes have that I'm going to change people's lives with the right words. If there's going to be any real impact, God is going to have to do it. You always know that in theory, but here it kind of hits you over the head."

"What about tomorrow morning?" said Mike. "How did Steve set this up for us to speak to Ministry of Interior troops anyway?"

"I have no idea," said Trey, shaking his head. "You guys know what OMON is? It's the special federal police of the Ministry of Internal Affairs. The KGB was split into several divisions after the fall of Communism. OMON is the part that works inside Russia, like the FBI in America. As I understand it, they're really feared. I've seen some of the OMON troops in Moscow. They usually wear all black with only a single Ministry of the Interior patch."

"How do you know all this stuff, Trey?" Jedd mused. Trey just smiled.

Matt's thoughts wandered. "I wonder what these guys were doing when we were kids, during the Cold War. If they were KGB officers in the Communist years, who knows what kind of terrible things they've done."

"Maybe we'll find out tomorrow," said Mike, his eyes wide with mock fear.

"I'm starting to get a little tired," said Trey. "You guys mind if we do our evening Bible study now?"

During our reconciliation and confession time, Mike wanted to talk.

"Jedd, there's something I've been wanting to bring up with you," said Mike. He seemed a bit wary, unsure how to proceed. Jedd reassured him with an I-can-take-a-hit smile.

"It seems to me that, in games and other little contests and stuff, you lose your focus sometimes. You get too competitive. You care so much if your team wins."

Jedd nodded. "I know that I was that way when I was younger. You've seen this recently?"

"Well, I've seen it a lot of the times we've had competitions. I'm especially thinking—in some of the soccer games. We've been playing against junior highers, but I can tell you're always just dying to win."

"Of course I want to win. Why not?" replied Jedd with a questioning, slightly irritated smile.

"It's not that. It's just . . . I mean, what's our purpose for being here? Like today, I could tell you were getting frustrated with Trey when he wasn't up to speed. I was out of breath, too, and I knew you weren't happy with me, either. You shouted several times . . ."

Jedd cut in, "I only shouted at my own mistakes."

"Maybe. It was just the whole attitude, though. It seemed to me like you even got kind of rough with the kids. Why was the little game so important? We might even make a bigger impression on the kids when they beat us."

"I disagree, Mike. I know at that age I wouldn't have had much respect for lame foreigners if they came to America and played a sport like they didn't care. Why should we ever give anything something less than our best shot?"

"We shouldn't, but 'the best' isn't always in winning a game or declaring some sort of victory. I admire that about you, Jedd, how you never settle for a halfhearted effort. It's great how you always want to seek the best, but I think that sometimes you've got to be more careful in defining what the best really is."

The discussion continued late into the night. Jedd tried to be open to the criticism, but could not help being defensive. Reasonable conversation gave way to frustrated argument, then returned to discussion, only to get bogged down once again in debate.

The words Jedd shared before going to bed were terse but genuine. "This stuff is hard to hear, but I do appreciate your bringing it up, Mike. I've got some thinking to do."

Jedd's Reflections—November 19

I feel painfully reminded tonight of how far I am from the man I want to be. The more I think about it, the more I realize that many of the things I enjoy and value most—athletics and weightlifting, reading for knowledge, intellectual discussion—all good in themselves, find their motivation in me with a desire to be seen as great.

I know it is not the facade of greatness I seek to achieve. If everyone in the world thought that I was great, but I knew that I was not, I would only be disgusted. I desire to be good, wise, and loving through and through. But even this is still all about me, and I am so often concerned about others' perceptions of me. How do I rescue what is best in these desires while cutting out what is so self-centered and self-serving? Please help me, Lord!

Victor the Captain

In the morning, we said little to each other as we stumbled around the apartment, pulling on our clothes.

"You just put on my sweater, Mike," stated Matt flatly.

"Oh. Sorry."

Gray light trickled through the windows. It was as overcast outside as it was in our heads, and a breakfast of rubbery hot dogs and buckwheat did little to help rouse us.

The OMON base assembly hall was empty when we arrived. Our footsteps echoed loudly as we walked between the rows of empty seats. By 9:25, we were getting nervous. Steve and his partner, Victor, had still not arrived. Had the speaking engagement slipped Steve's mind? What had he told the OMON commander this presentation was supposed to be about, anyway? Did the officers even know we are Christians?

At precisely 9:30, a group of sharply dressed cadets filed into the room and filled the front four rows. The only sound came from the squeaking of their boots. The officer turned from across the room and looked at us, his voice deep and hard. Our translator turned to us.

"He wants to know if you're ready."

Jedd swallowed hard and opened his mouth to reply. Just then the auditorium door swung open. A wiry Russian entered, followed by a smaller man in a black peacoat. It was Steve and Victor. Relief washed over us as they strode across the room. Victor spoke with the OMON officer while Steve explained the situation to us. We were to be only part of the presentation. Jedd would share briefly, but Steve and Victor would cover the rest.

The cadets appeared curious enough as Jedd spoke about the United States and his faith in Jesus. An American was enough of a novelty to be interesting. Victor, however, held a different sort of interest. He had been a high-ranking military man himself, one of the youngest submarine commanders in the history of the Russian navy. Steve translated for us as Victor paced back and forth behind the podium, laying out the story of his life.

"I know what it is like to be in your place," he began. "The navy was the place of my service to our country. As a young officer, I felt great pride in my work and in my position. Men like Napoleon, Peter the Great, and Admiral Lord Nelson were my heroes. My life's aim was glory—for Mother Russia, and maybe even more than that, glory for myself. I gave all I had to my pursuit of power and prestige.

"Success came quickly. I rose through the ranks. My life was very sweet to me. All the things I sought after fell into my hands: a high level in society, influence and importance, the praise and privilege given to top officers. I believed in myself 100 percent and trusted completely in my own strength.

"But one day, everything changed." Victor stopped his pacing and stationed himself in front of the podium. "I was in the Barents Sea. My submarine came upon an overturned boat. In the icy water, the capsized men struggled to reach us. We worked desperately to save them, but everything we did seemed to fail. One after another sank before our eyes. And I, the great and infallible, most brave and smart commander of the submarine, could not do anything to save them."

He paused and looked at the floor; it seemed as if the scene were being played out before him again. Many of the cadets' faces—up to this point hard as flint—reflected a hint of the emotion we could see in Victor. His eyes swept over the soldiers, seeming to stare deep into each of them.

Finally, he began again. "Something happened that day in my head and in my heart. I saw my own helplessness. I saw how false it was that I could imagine to put all my trust in my capabilities, significance, and greatness. I had armed myself with my victories in athletics, my successes in the naval service, and my high titles and responsibilities. It fell apart in one minute. From that day on, life began to lose its interest. Joy and accomplishment no longer interested me and sadness didn't affect me. Everything around me was vanity and weariness of spirit. I decided to quit the navy and move to Moscow.

"It was there that something happened to change my life. I met some Christians. They didn't have any titles or positions. I had grown up hearing my teachers make fun of them in school. But there was something in them that I couldn't ignore. I looked inside myself and thought a lot about the purpose of life. I began to see that my new friends were worthy of my trust. I saw that they were sincere in their love.

"Several months passed before I understood the verse one of my new friends had read to me from Revelation 3:20—'Behold, I stand at the door and knock. If anyone hears my voice and opens the door, I will come in to him and dine with him, and he with me.' I decided to let the One I knew was knocking at the door of my heart come in. The whole purpose of my life changed at that moment. I knew the search for power and position and prestige would no longer be my god. I would serve Jesus.

"Now, I am giving myself more to Him every day. The question I ask each of you is: What is it that you are giving your life to?"

Silence held the room for a long moment. Steve returned to the front to join Victor. Together, they explained what it meant to become a Christian and invited any of the cadets who might be interested to pray with them to give their lives to Christ. When Steve finished his prayer, the lead officer barked an order, and the group filed out. We stood by the door, offering the soldiers copies of a paperback that contained both the Gospel of John and the book *More Than a Carpenter*. Most were at least interested enough to receive a free book. A handful stayed behind. They wanted to learn more from

Victor, Steve, a Secret Police Jeep, and the Guys

Victor about what the decision they had just made would mean for their lives.

∘ ∘ ∘

Sunday morning we went to church with Elena and Aunt Lucy. The local Baptists gathered in an old theater, dark and worn. As we settled into the pull-down seats, the people seated around us turned to welcome us. After a few announcements and Aunt Lucy's introduction of us, there was music, the Slavic hymns sounding rich and deep and sad—much like the history of Russia.

Halfway through the sermon, Elena leaned over. "I can't believe what this pastor is saying. He is preaching on why women cannot wear pants."

Matt couldn't help but smile, noticing Elena's jeans.

Elena had her head tilted, listening carefully. "Ahh. He just said that there are some exceptions."

"Oh, great." Elena turned to us again. "It is okay for women to wear pants if they are picking mushrooms and . . ." She paused for a moment to hear more. "And if a woman has nothing else to wear except a short skirt, she probably should wear pants."

We surveyed the audience. They listened intently, heads nodding from time to time.

Elena observed for a few minutes before turning to us again. "You will be glad to know that black is not the only acceptable color to wear. We can also wear gray."

"This guy's a real libertine," joked Mike.

The pastor rolled on, laying out specifics on acceptable and unacceptable activities and attire. No dancing, of course, and no makeup. A wedding ring might be okay, but other jewelry was out. Men should not engage in exercise or sports, which they should shun as "vain."

We really did not know what to make of it. Surrounding us were people who had kept the flames of faith alive through darkest night. They had withstood the worst that evil could unleash. Furthermore, they were not—for the most part—dour, crotchety individuals. In fact, most of the people we had spent time with were extremely loving and kind. But somehow, in his zeal to be "not of the world," it seemed that the pastor had allowed externals and cultural patterns to become a primary focal point of his teachings.

After church and a final Lucy-cooked meal, we hurried out to the train station to catch the one o'clock to Moscow. Crowds were returning to the city after the weekend, and we were forced to stand most of the way. Like our fellow passengers, we talked little. Matt and Jedd read. Mike stared out the window, thoughts inward.

Mike's Reflections—November 23

I just don't know what to make of what we saw this morning. I definitely don't want to criticize the church here—I know all that they've gone through. Even so, it frustrates me that this pastor would focus so heavily on external issues.

He talked much more this morning about women not wearing makeup or pants than about becoming like Jesus.

Of course there are different expressions of Christian faith in every culture. In a more traditional culture like Russia has outside of its big cities, maybe it is appropriate for Christian women to take steps I would consider unnecessary for the sake of modesty.

But it definitely seems to me that this pastor has gone way too far. Wouldn't it be far better just to focus on the person and teaching of Jesus and let the smaller details be just details?

91

eight

Scarred Hands and Iron Doors

Serpukhov, Russia

Steve had seen us off at the Moscow train station, where he introduced us to a seventeen-year-old boy named Sasha, our guide and translator for the week. We liked Sasha immediately, his earnest eyes peering out of a puffy face; frizzy, sand-colored hair; a thickly lined denim jacket giving him a slightly rounded appearance. A two-hour train ride brought us to the town of Serpukhov, where we were met at the station by Pastor Eugene, a thin man in his sixties whose lithe body stood erect as an old pine. After introductions—translated by Sasha—Eugene led off across town with a long, aggressive stride.

Days with Pastor Eugene

"It is good to have you here," he said, not slowing his gate. "Steve told me on the phone about your work last week in Orekhovo-Zuyevo."

"Will we be doing the same things here—speaking in schools and inter- nots?" asked Jedd.

Eugene nodded. "When I'm not doing my pastor work, I like to spend time with kids in the orphanages and hospitals. Their lives are difficult, and they're always happy when I come. I know they will be very excited to see you and hear what you have to say."

We passed several rows of cement apartment buildings before Eugene turned into the entrance of one. Unlocking a door on the second floor, he announced, "This is for you. A young family from the church moved in with their parents so you could stay here." The apartment's main room had enough floor space for all of us to sleep comfortably. There was also a small kitchen and a bathroom. It was tiny, but would suit our needs per- fectly. We stood quietly, soaking in another dousing of hospitality.

"Please, tell them how thankful we are," said Matt sincerely.

Eugene smiled nonchalantly. "They were glad to do it."

93

o . o o

Heavy scars marked the backs of Eugene's hands. They did not pre- vent him from playing with the kids when he would join us at the schools, but they were a reminder, carved in flesh, of a Christian's lot under a Communist regime. Over lunch during a break between two orphanages, we asked if he would share his story with us. He nodded, setting down a slice of the bologna he was about to put in his mouth.

"When I was only three years old," he began, "Stalin had my father shot because he was a Christian. Without him, it was very hard for us to meet our needs. My mother worked in a factory, but we didn't always have enough. My older brother died of malnutrition. I got work at a tool factory to help support my mother and younger brother.

"When I was fifteen, the KGB caught me listening to a Christian radio program on Voice of America. The penalty for that was ten years in prison, but since I was a minor, they kept me in prison for only a

Pastor Eugene and Serpukhov Snowman

few months. When they let me go, they warned me to never listen to that foolishness again.

"But after I got out of prison, I kept on listening, even though I knew they had me under surveillance. Then one day, the KGB showed up at my tool factory. They took me in a room and tried to force me to sign a paper that said the Baptists I knew gathered together to sacrifice children and eat them. Of course, I wouldn't sign it, so they threw me in prison again. They kept me in a cell with a murderer. I was terrified. Every night, when I went to bed, I wondered, *Is this man going to kill me while I sleep?* But I will tell you, during that time, I felt God closer to me than ever in my life.

"When I was released, they moved me to another factory. I worked on an assembly line, picking up tiny parts and putting them in the right boxes. Perhaps it sounds strange, but I repeated the same little task so many times over the decades that my hands became permanently deformed. Last year, some Americans I've never met paid for me to have surgery to fix my fingers." Eugene demonstrated, wiggling his digits in front of us. "Now I can use my hands again." We smiled at his display of dexterity, but Eugene's story had left a heaviness on our hearts.

"Our road is so easy," sighed Trey.

"Have you ever been married, Eugene?" Matt asked.

"Yes, but this, too, is a sad story. My wife was a secretary in the Communist Party. When I became an elder in the Baptist church, the KGB came to her with an offer. They said, 'Either you leave your husband or you will lose your job here.' As you see now, she chose to keep her job."

○ ○ ○

Several days of speaking and sports had left us feeling grubby. Because our apartment had no shower, Eugene suggested a trip to the *banya* as the cure for our woes.

"The banya," said Eugene when we got there, pointing to a towering wooden structure. "I promise we will all be made very clean and fresh."

"A lot of Russians outside of Moscow don't have their own bath," explained Sasha. "The banya is where they get clean."

"How often do they come here?" questioned Matt.

"Usually once every week or two." Seeing our surprise, Sasha said, "You think that is not very much? I have heard that some people visit the banya only once in a winter."

Near the entrance, Eugene stopped at a stall to buy a bouquet of thin birch branches. We glanced at one another questioningly. Were the branches to be a part of our Russian bathing experience?

In the banya's dingy changing room, we abandoned our bulky clothing. Eugene led us toward what looked like a magical mirror through which naked Russian men were appearing and vanishing. As we walked into the hazy steam room, the roar of rushing water surrounded us. Jedd surveyed our surroundings.

"Its like we're in a Roman bath. Look at the craftsmanship that went into the vaulted ceiling and the arches over the doors."

"Yeah, but all those rows of piping and showerheads cluttered it up with plenty of Communist efficiency," Mike said with a hint of disdain.

All around us, men showered off days, or even weeks, of grime. Less than five feet away, an elderly man leaned against a bench while a friend vigorously scoured his back with a brush. He arched his back, thoroughly enjoying the cleansing swaths of the brush's firm bristles. His pasty belly swayed back and forth as the other scrubbed.

"You wouldn't see that in the U.S. I guess homosexuality isn't very prevalent in Russia so the men don't get uncomfortable being naked together."

"It's definitely different," Matt replied as he hung his towel on a peg in the wall.

After rinsing, Eugene moved toward a heavy wooden door. He pulled it back and motioned for us to pass through quickly. Scalding air washed over our bodies as we entered. It singed our nostrils. Huge, bleacher-style benches led upward from the ground all the way to the ceiling, several stories high. They looked like stairsteps for a giant. Men lounged at every level, appearing as if they were floating in the mist. Eugene hiked toward the top, weaving through the maze of naked bodies that lined the benches. With each level that we rose, the heat intensified. Hot sweat spattered on us as the men we passed thrashed themselves and their comrades with birch branches. By the time we neared the top, our breath came only in small gasps. Our bodies were futilely trying to cool the air before it scalded our lungs.

Eugene indicated for Mike to lie down. When Mike had prostrated himself on the damp wood, he began lashing him with the birch branches. "It will open your pours and clean you very well," he explained.

"Must . . . get . . . more . . . oxygen," Mike sputtered, only half joking.

Matt and Jedd glanced at each other, trying not to laugh. Mike's face was tight with pain. Not only did the branches sting, but each swinging motion brought with it a blast of air so hot it was nearly unbearable. The effect was a surreal massaging sensation.

We rotated through the "thrash" and "be thrashed" roles for twenty minutes. By then, we were thoroughly cooked.

"We'll be out in the changing room, Eugene," said Jedd. He turned to the others. "I don't know how much longer I can take."

° ° °

Only a few days into our stay in Serpukhov, Trey caught a train headed for Moscow. He wanted to spend some time alone with his family.

 Trey's Reflections—November 27

I don't know if I'm going to be able to do any good at home, but I at least want to be there.

I just don't understand how everything could be happening like this. My entire life, I've idolized Dad. I dreamed of following his footsteps to West Point and the Special Forces. His military record and decorations have always inspired me to be brave and bold, but now . . . I don't even want to think about what the future may bring . . . honestly I am terrified. I would do anything to bring our family back together . . .

Red Corner

Eugene had suggested that morning that we seek an opportunity to speak to inmates of Serpukhov's high-security prison. It was a two-mile hike across town.

"Is there a chance we could all get in, Eugene?" Matt asked.

Eugene shrugged. "Not likely. I'm hoping for one or two. The prison rules say specifically that only one non-Russian can go in at a time. I have prayed, though. It wouldn't be the first time God has opened prison doors."

"Does everyone have their passports with them?" asked Eugene.

We all felt for the rectangular shape under our layers of clothing. A moment later, Sasha and Eugene began talking in rapid-fire Russian.

"Something wrong?" questioned Matt.

Sasha looked at us with chagrin. "Guys, I'm sorry. I forgot my passport. I didn't think I would need it."

"Didn't you know we were going to the prison today?" asked Jedd, disappointed.

"Yes. But I don't have my passport here in Serpukhov. It's in Moscow."

Mike jumped in. "Don't Russians always have to carry their passports when they travel?"

"We *are* supposed to have them on us at all times. I just forgot to bring it."

"Well, there's nothing we can do about it now," finished Matt.

"Who's gonna go in if Sasha can't translate for us?"

"Jedd," Mike volunteered without hesitation. "He knows the most Russian."

"I still wouldn't be able to say anything worth saying. I'll go, but I don't know that there'd be much point in it."

All except Sasha slid our passports to the guard beneath a thick glass window. He disappeared and returned several minutes later. "Through there," he said, motioning us toward the outside door. The small waiting room was little warmer than outside. A uniformed man puffed on a cigarette and eyed us warily from the other side of a heavily barred door. Another guard appeared next to the smoker and grunted for him to move, then nodded at us as he pulled back the door. Before we knew what had happened, we were in—all of us, including Sasha. We did not know why they bent the rules for us, but this was not the time for questions.

As we passed through the first set of iron bars, the front desk guard shouted, "Close the door this time, Fyordor." Its clang echoed dully through the dark, narrow hallway ahead of us.

Grimy passages turned this way and that, winding deep into the heart of the prison. Ancient brick walls, corroded and speckled with mildew, seemed to draw tighter as we proceeded, choking out life and hope. Iron doors, their peek-holes locked, lined the sides. The acrid stench of mold, bleach, blood, and urine added to the sense of suffocation.

"Why are you scowling, Matt?" Mike asked.

"I didn't know I was."

"You are."

"Maybe the weight of this place is getting to me. Just the thought of being locked in here is more than I could bear."

The guard turned to a side door and ushered us into a cell known as "Red Corner." The room was decorated with four rows of chairs, a few books, and a table with a small podium on it. A moment later, the guard left.

Eugene explained how terrible it was for prisoners here—he had experienced it firsthand himself. No TVs in the cells or well-stocked weight-rooms; just icy-cold cells and an occasional walk across the snowy yard. The diet consisted of two meals of boiled cabbage a day. The rare times they did get bread or meat, they were so thankful they hardly noticed the mold that inevitably pocked its surface.

Jedd said, "So who's gonna speak?"

"I just don't feel like speaking today," Mike stated.

"What do you say in a place like this?" asked Matt.

"Share from the heart, I guess," said Jedd. "Remember what Eugene said about these guys probably imagining that all Americans live in a paradise."

"Compared to the way they live, we do."

Jedd nodded. "And they imagine that we wouldn't have any reason for God since we have it so good. It makes me think . . ."

The deadbolt clanked, and the door creaked open. Twelve young men, hands behind their backs and eyes glued to the floor, hobbled lifelessly to their seats.

Russian Gulag

"I'll be back in an hour," the guard grunted to Eugene. He locked the door behind him, leaving us alone with the prisoners.

Matt's mind raced as he glanced around. *What would happen if these guys decided to take us out?* he wondered. *I don't see any intercoms or alarms in here, and there aren't any guards.*

We were thankful that Eugene seemed entirely at ease. He began by introducing us, lanky limbs gesturing enthusiastically as he spoke.

"Today I have brought with me three young men from America. They come from Santa Barbara, California, and they are here to share with you about their lives. Please welcome Jedd, Mike, Matt, and their translator, Sasha."

A lethargic clapping came from about half of the men. We could tell the prisoners were more concerned about their image among their cell-mates than creating a good impression on us. Yet surprisingly, they seemed to be thankful for our presence.

Jedd talked first. While he shared, Mike and Matt observed the prisoners.

Mike's Reflections—November 25

I can hardly believe it. These prisoners are not men; they're just boys. I don't think any of them could be older than eighteen. The youngest looked not more than thirteen. You can tell how much they just need a mother or father to love and hold them. Although their outer shells are hard, the younger boys feel no awkwardness sitting in the lap of the older. All they have is each other.

Matt spoke next. "I know my life is very different from yours. I'm from Santa Barbara. The weather there is almost always nice, and just about all the people are beautiful. They have big houses and nice cars. A lot of them, though, aren't any happier than you are here. I know a lot of you think that when you get out of here, life will be a lot better. Let me tell you—it will be. But even if you were to get out and move to Santa Barbara, you would still be carrying around a lot of pain and emptiness. Jesus said, 'Come to me, all you who are weary and burdened, and I will give you rest.' My question to you today is: Have you found rest for your souls? I have no idea if you have; there is no way I can tell. But if you haven't, I can guarantee that the only way you will find it is by coming to know Jesus . . ."

After Matt finished, there was only silence while the seconds passed. Then one of the older kids blurted out, "I don't even believe Jesus lived. How do you know He was actually a real person?"

Sasha translated what he was saying. Before we could speak, Eugene took over. "Why don't we watch this movie about Jesus? Perhaps this will answer some of your questions," replied Eugene.

We put *Man Without Equal* in the VCR we had brought with us from Eugene's church. Most of the inmates watched it intently, but afterward the conversation went downhill. Some of the prisoners were determined to begin a debate about Christian apologetics, and whether or not Jesus really lived. Were it solely up to us, we would have chosen to steer the conversation in a different direction. Unfortunately, our translator had a different idea.

We sat helpless, watching an impassioned Sasha enter a verbal wrestling match with three of the older prisoners. We tried to interrupt him, but each time we did, he neglected to translate. While listening to a whir of Russian words and an occasional rumble of prisoner laughter, we could only stand by, frustrated.

The guard returned in the middle of the debate. As soon as the door opened, the prisoners stood. They placed their hands on their backs, fixed their eyes on the ground, and filed silently out the door.

We emerged from the prison like men crawling from beneath a tornado-flattened house. The feeling clung to our clothing and hid in our pockets for days. There were men in there; boys, too. They *lived* there. Day in and day out, squeezed between those walls, sucking in and spitting out the fetid air, forgetting what it felt like to be free.

o o o

Maybe the tensions of the prison affected us more deeply than we realized. That evening, after Sasha had gone to bed, the three of us had a very difficult reconciliation time.

It seemed to Mike that Jedd always had to express his preferences in every little decision we made: what order we would speak in, what we would eat for dinner, what sports we would play with kids at the orphanages.

We continued for several hours. The tone rolled from discussion to argument and then back again. There were moments of learning, but at least as many of frustration and irritation.

Mike and Matt tried to avoid coming on too strong. For his part, Jedd tried to listen and learn; still, defensiveness snarled from time to time.

It was after 2:00 A.M. when we decided that most of the issue had been thrashed out. Not everything had been entirely resolved, but it seemed there was little to gain from continuing, bleary-eyed as we were. We prayed together and then went to bed. Jedd journaled some thoughts before turning out the lights.

Jedd's Reflections—November 27

I'm hurting. Once again, I feel I have been forced to confront how painfully far I am from the others-centered, unselfish man I want to be.

In normal situations, when you're not so intensely together with people, things like this might never be noticed. But if I'm totally honest with myself, I know that almost always in the back of my mind is me. What would I like? How will it affect me? I filter everything through the lens of "what do I want?" Many times, I give up the thing I decide I want, but always as a conscious sacrifice, rather than as a more relaxed "passing up."

I am thankful that I'm being forced to see this, even though it leaves me feeling like my guts have been given a once-over with brass knuckles. How else would I be forced to wrestle with these issues? Things like this would only be a significant problem in deep, long-term interaction. Of course, I could avoid the issue by avoiding deep relationships. But that would not solve the problem; it would only entrench selfish, self-centered thoughts and actions.

The question is, How can I change? In my day-to-day choices, I can try to not push my preferences, but that is only dealing with symptoms, not the root problem. Merely acting unselfishly will be a charade until my heart is changed. That is not something I can do on my own. I remember what Salomón said in Guatemala. The best (and only) thing I can do is seek to grow closer to Jesus. As I become more firmly rooted in Him, the fruit of unselfishness—and all other good things as well—will begin to flow out automatically.

nine

Village at the Edge of the World

Loly, Russia

two days later, we found ourselves forging north aboard another train whose tidy red cars appeared to have rolled right out of the golden age of railroad travel. At the end of the line waited Russia's deep north, the Gulag region. During the 1930s and 1940s, anyone who crossed Stalin was either immediately executed or shipped to the prison camps of the Gulag. For many such prisoners, a quicker death would almost have been preferred.

Steve's partner, Victor, volunteered to travel with us for the first week, Sasha remaining with us the entire time to translate. Christians in the city of Yemva, nearly a thousand miles north of Moscow, had planned work for us in their town and nearby villages. For most of the time, we planned to reside at an internot in central Yemva, heading out from there to speak in schools, prisons, orphanages, and wherever else we were welcome.

On the train, Victor and Sasha shared a compartment with two other Russians while the four of us filled a second. Two narrow bunks extended from either side of the small cabin, the lower pair doubling as seats. A small table protruded from the wall beneath the curtained window. Russian pop music crackled from the old radios in each berth. Though snow fell furiously outside, inside the train, it was warm, perhaps too much so. An unpleasant haze drifted in from the smokers in the cabin next door—it was too cold to open any windows.

Between rounds of cards in their compartments, the passengers thought of reasons to walk up and down the corridor and converse in the hallway. The train ride was a rest from the heavy labor that sustained most of them, and there was a friendly, almost holiday atmosphere among the diverse group. We met a woman from Tartar, another from Ukraine, and a swarthy Azerbaijani man who did not like Americans but still enjoyed joking with us. Sasha helped us converse with an old military officer who decried the "lack of commitment" in modern Russian youth. The car next to ours was full of conscripted soldiers, all in their teens, heading for two years of miserable duty at a military outpost on the Arctic Sea.

Trey climbed up to his bunk to capture the ride in his journal.

Trey's Reflections—December 3

Outside, everything is white. Even the wires that run parallel to the tracks look permanently frosted. Several hours out of Moscow, the birch trees gave way to dense forests of pine, perhaps as old as Russia itself. As we go, the landscape changes little, except that the snow keeps getting deeper and all of the rivers and lakes look as though they have been frozen for a very long time.

The time with my family this past week was bittersweet. Ironically, my relationships with Andy and my mom are better than ever—the difficult times have brought us together in an amazing way. Even with Dad, although part of me bristles with anger toward him, I still love him so much. Some of

Train to the North

the conversations we had gave me some hope that maybe my family's unity can be restored. I hope that it may be. Lord, I commit my family into Your hands. I feel like we have tried everything, Lord, and the one constant is Your presence. Please sustain us for the times to come . . . whatever they may hold.

A Belated Thank-You

When Trey climbed down from his bunk and stepped out into the hallway, he moved from window to window, looking out at the landscape, a sharp contrast of white and black.

"You are one of the Americans?" asked a gravelly voice with a heavy accent.

Trey turned, surprised. An elderly man with a sun-worn face stood peering at him with sharp, blue eyes. A rim of white hair encircled the man's balding head.

"I *am* American," said Trey, offering his hand. "My name's Trey."

The man nodded slowly and a smile took hold of his lips as he grasped Trey's hand. "My name is Vladim. Do you have time to talk to an old man?"

"Of course. Where did you learn English?"

"I'm a geologist. I studied English when I was on a research project in Nigeria."

"You're traveling to Yemva now?"

"Yemva's not the end of the line. The train goes even farther. Home for me is Archangel, up beyond the Arctic Circle. I've always lived there. That's one thing I wanted to tell you about."

"That's *way* up there."

Vladim nodded and smiled again. "I was born in Archangel not long before the Great Patriot War."

"World War II?"

"That's what we call it here. In the middle of the war, the Nazis cut off Archangel's supply lines. It didn't take long for the food to run out. Soon we were eating the dogs and the horses, and then they were gone, too." Vladim paused and lowered one of the pull-down seats built into the side of the passage. "Do you mind if I sit?"

Trey pulled down a seat.

Vladim continued, "Many people were dying. Some of the cold. Some got sick. My brother, he starved to death. I was very near to death, too, when the Americans broke through to us with their ships. They had supplies and food. I'll never forget my first taste of American chocolate."

Trey stared, entranced. Vladim spoke on, intent on telling his story. "During the Communist years, the government always said bad things about America. They said America was evil and her people were greedy and eager to destroy us. But I would never tolerate that. I would never let people speak bad about Americans. When I would hear them say bad things, I would say, 'That is not true. Americans are good people.'

"When I worked in Nigeria more than twenty years ago, I set myself to learn English. I wanted to learn English so that I could thank an American for what you did for me and my town. You are the first American I have seen since then, so I want to thank you . . .'"

The Real North

We closed the door to our compartment around midnight. Before turning the lights out, we read a chapter of the Bible and had our time of confession and reconciliation. The soldiers in the next car had begun drinking several hours before and now they were shouting and singing. Some of the folks in the neighboring compartment had a good supply of vodka as well and were passing the bottles around liberally. We drifted off to sleep to their songs and the rocking of the train.

When we awoke, the train was still rocking. Outside, the dark of pine needles, tree trunks, or an electric line infrequently poked through the blanket of pure wool. Like a black-and-white film, the vast forest continued to roll by. Occasionally, the woods were broken by an expansive, frozen river or by the small, mostly wooden towns that seemed to have been dropped from heaven; their only connection to the rest of Russia was the tracks on which we rode.

o o o

Twenty-seven hours after we departed Moscow, the conductor announced that we were approaching the town of Yemva. As the train slowed, we piled our bags, boxes, and backpacks near the door. When it halted, we hopped out into the deep powder. Many of the friends we made during the trip appeared in the doorway and began handing our luggage down to us. Vladim jumped down with us and worked furiously to get everything out before the train moved again. Our possessions unloaded, he climbed back into the car as the train started off.

"Good-bye, my American friends!" he cried out.

Others stood behind him, waving as they disappeared into the night.

Snowflakes flurried in the darkness. Whereas the jungles and hills of Guatemala had teemed with movement and noise, chatter and kaleidoscopic color, these ancient forests smothered all sound beneath their snows. But this realm did not feel less alive. It felt more so, like diving into a lake on a frost-covered morning. There was none of the mental dizziness caused by tropical haze and drowsy warmth. We felt as awake and sharp as the edge of a razor.

"It is only 4:00 P.M.," said Matt with some surprise. "But it's as dark as the middle of the night."

It hurt slightly to breathe in the icy air, but the tinge of pain brought adrenaline with it. "This is it," proclaimed Trey, "the *real* north."

From the station, a bundled shape of a man approached us, his mustache and glasses poking out from beneath a fur hat. It was our local contact, Igor, who welcomed us with a gloved handshake before leading us to a car parked nearby. A large man with a tangled black beard sat in the driver's seat.

"This brother will drive your luggage over to the rehab center. It is less than a mile. We can walk," explained Igor.

"What's the rehab center?" asked Jedd.

Victor responded, "Steve has told me about it. Next to the church is a building where ex-cons stay. When guys who've begun to follow Jesus in prison get out, they can live in Christian community while they learn job skills and adjust into normal life. The local church also has their services here on Sunday mornings."

We were all shaking with the cold when Igor finally turned off the road and led us through the battered front door of an old, ramshackle building. Doors opened to the right and left off a long, dim hallway. A glimpse through one suggested a small, simply furnished dormitory room with two beds.

"Ohh, that feels good," expressed Trey as we emerged into a large, well-heated room. The space was open, save for several long tables built from unfinished planks.

"Feel free to sit. I'll get some of the men," promised Igor, disappearing back into the hall.

A moment later, several rough-looking men appeared. We stood as they approached. A fellow in a dark wool coat, black hat, and calf-high fur boots approached, his smile revealing a missing front tooth. Without a moment's hesitation, he grabbed Trey by the shoulders and planted a kiss on his unsuspecting lips. Trey blinked twice and nearly fell back over the bench he had been sitting on. We had not been told that the Christian men in Russia's north took the apostle Paul's charge to "greet one another with a holy kiss" literally. The others greeted us in like manner and several proceeded to the kitchen to prepare a snack for us. A number of local believers and several more ex-cons stopped by to meet us as we enjoyed a snack of tea, bread, and jam.

"Igor says you'll be staying at the internot across the street from us next week," said a burly ex-con to Matt through Sasha's translation.

Matt nodded, although he had not been aware of the plan.

The man indicated Matt's guitar. "Come over. We all want to hear you play." The other ex-cons at the table nodded vigorously.

"I'm not so good," downplayed Matt. "But it would be fun to jam. You all play?"

"Some of us. We all love music."

Jedd leaned over toward Mike. "These guys are great!"

"Uh-huh," said Mike without really hearing what Jedd had said. His eyes roved the room anxiously. He focused on Jedd for a moment. "You see a bathroom yet? I've been holding it for the last three hours on the train so I could use a real one."

Victor glanced over. "Do you need something, Mike?"

"A bathroom."

Victor asked an ex-con, who explained that it was just behind the center. Mike left, but returned a minute later. "I need my flashlight. There's no light in the outhouse."

Approaching the small, homemade shack for the second time, Mike clicked on his flashlight and pulled back the plywood door. To his surprise, there was no seat. A pie-sized circle had been cut into the wooden floor. Pieces of two-by-four had been nailed to the right and left of the hole to serve as footpads. A sheet of yellowish ice, half an inch thick, coated most of the floor, including the footpads.

"I'm going to have to try to balance on that with my pants at my ankles?" wondered Mike. He glanced around for toilet paper. Strips of newspaper were all he could find.

107

Mike shown his flashlight into the hole. What appeared to be a thin brown post rose out of the pit almost to the level of the floor. With surprise, Mike realized the "post" was not made from wood, but from the instantly-frozen deposits of those who had come before.

"Well," Mike said to himself, dropping his pants, "thirty degrees below or not, you've gotta do what you've gotta do."

When Mike reentered the dining room, the ex-cons were already gripping our hands and thumping our backs in farewell.

Matt laughed. "We just met these guys and they are treating us like long-lost family."

"That seems to be just how they see it," said Jedd.

"We're heading out already?" said Mike, grabbing several slices of bread and cheese.

"We'll be back later in the week," responded Trey. "I guess we'll be staying at an internot near the rehab center. The next few days we'll be out in a village fifty-some miles from here."

○ ○ ○

The lights of Yemva faded behind us. We had divided up between the little car that carried our luggage and an old Russian army Jeep belonging to the pastor of Yemva's church. The vehicles slalomed along the frozen road. We had never traveled sixty-five miles an hour on ice before. Matt peered out the Jeep's windshield to see what was ahead, but could only make out the dimly illuminated blur of ice-blown firs.

After twenty minutes of driving, Trey's teeth were chattering like a telegraph.

"Are you really that cold, Trey?" Matt asked.

"Th-th-this little heater in the floor isn't pu-putting out much air."

"I'm feeling it, too," said Mike. "My feet feel like they're gonna fall off."

A few miles later, the Jeep's headlights illuminated a battered sign marked with the word *Loly* in Cyrillic. The road beneath us was nothing but white.

"This is it," said Igor. Soft light glowed through the windows of cottages that lay bundled in the snow. "You'll be staying in the gym at the school."

The gym was out behind Loly's school. The old physical education instructor, Alexander, answered our knock on its homemade door and grunted a greeting at us from beneath a bristly mustache. His face was grooved and weather-beaten like the side of an old barn, but his bare arms were strong and sinuous. We learned later that every day he cross-country skied five kilometers to school, played sports all day with the kids, and then skied home in the evening. He was also a hunter, often plying the northern wilderness for big game. Alexander challenged us to a game of "horse" before he left. He won, and then headed out into the frigid night for his five-kilometer ski home.

∘ ∘ ∘

Glimpses were all we had caught of the village when we arrived the night before—glowing windows and smoking chimneys. But now, our first morning in Loly, the eastern sky was ablaze with dawn. It felt as if we had awakened in fairy-tale land.

Loly lay in a small valley, surrounded on all sides by the dense forest. Most of the cottages had been crafted by hand from logs felled nearby. Icicles hung down over frosted windows. Tendrils of smoke climbed skyward from every chimney, filling the air with the rich aroma of wood smoke. The deep blanket of snow at our feet, like the clouds on the horizon, had turned to cotton candy.

Split-rail fences circled fields of snow, their summer grazers now tucked into barns. A mare stood patiently as her master used a pitchfork to unload a pile of hay from the sleigh to which she was harnessed. A woman dragged a sled to a well and filled her bucket. An old man chopping wood stopped to beat his gloved hands on his thighs to regain sensation in his fingers. Aside from a few power lines, there was no hint of the twentieth century.

After a few minutes of exploring, we walked to the front of the school and went in. It was warm and bright inside. A colorful mural of a boy in a cosmonaut suit covered the back wall of the entrance room. On it were emblazoned the words, *"Nam Noozhen Mir"*—We Need Peace. A teacher from the school, Tatiana, had volunteered to cook for us. She smiled shyly when we entered and indicated a table where she had laid out bread, cheese slices, and bowls of cottage cheese. Tatiana's Russian beauty had not left her, but she looked worn and very tired, dark bags beneath her eyes.

We learned that her husband had left her years before. With the little money she earned from teaching and odd jobs, she managed to support a daughter attending a university and a teenage son at home. Yet when we offered her a donation for our food, she staunchly refused. Only when we asked if we could give her a little money to help her daughter at school did she consent to any recompense for all her cooking.

On the Court

With Victor, we made a fivesome, so he had arranged a game for us with the Loly High School basketball team. Villagers packed the gym to see the contest. The crowd whooped for baskets made at either end of the court. Alexander had trained Loly's team skillfully; they were the regional champs. We played well, though, and Jedd became somewhat of a celebrity. After each of his baskets, the kids on the sidelines called out, "Jedd! Jedd!" and gave him thumbs-ups. The game was our first victory of the trip: Team USA 44, Loly High 43. After we handed out copies of *More Than a Carpenter* and signed countless autographs, Mike and Jedd spoke to those gathered about following Christ. The crowd listened intently as Sasha translated.

Loly's `Main Street`

Jedd's Reflections—December 5

The basketball game today was a great picture of how effective sports can be in building bridges for relationship and sharing our faith.

Many Russian Christians have traditionally seen athletics as "vanity." As we learned in church the other day, some still do. Victor says, though, that others are realizing that sports can be a great way to connect with people from outside the church, especially with men and boys.

Because Christianity was portrayed as only for the weak during the Communist years, males often will not approach anything that even appears like religion. Sports is one of the few things that can draw them in and help build the connection necessary for sharing the gospel.

Saturday evening we accepted the invitation to join the village youth at their weekly "disco"; the night before many of Loly's adults had gathered in the same small community center to hear what we had to say about Jesus. It was amusing to see the room's solemn, pre-*perestroika* decor, swimming in the dizzying array of colored lights that sprayed from the shimmering disco ball.

Jedd's Reflections—December 6

We had to put some thought into whether or not to go to the dance tonight. Many of Russia's more legalistic Christians see dancing as wrong, especially at a disco. We want to be respectful of these convictions, even if we disagree with them. And yet, it is also vital that we attempt to connect with nonbelievers. It is hard to know how to do both.

In Jesus' day, many frowned on His hanging out with prostitutes, making wine, and attending dubious parties. Jesus never sinned, yet He desired to be close to sinners and was willing to meet them in their environment. Many within the Russian church (and the American church as well) are unwilling to do this. As a result, they have been largely unable to make any real connection with the vast majority of nonbelievers.

I know that we must never compromise with sin. There is never a need to do something we know is wrong just to "make friends." And yet, as Jesus did, we must always be looking for opportunities to go to nonbelievers, to meet them on "their turf," and not just demand that they come to ours.

Mike's Reflections—December 6

Tonight at the disco I met some interesting characters. They were dressed much nicer than everyone else—designer pants and leather jackets in contrast to the old furs and army surplus worn by the locals. When they asked me to come outside to talk with them, Sasha whispered the disconcerting words, "I do not think they want to beat you up."

That made me a little nervous. It turns out they are members of the Russian Mafia on their way to a nearby town to "encourage" payment of a delinquent loan. They had heard some Americans were in town and wanted to meet us. We had seen mafiosi in Moscow, but it was a little *different to be talking to them. They asked if we would go drinking with them, but we declined. Doing so would not be the best witness to the kids around here, and, with the way they like to drink, I doubt it would have led to much meaningful interaction anyway.*

It was kind of funny. When we told them we hadn't been drinking, they asked how we seemed to be having so much fun. I replied, "Because we know Jesus, and He fills us with joy." It sounded like a line out of some cheesy gospel presentation, but it was as true as anything I've ever said.

Over the next several days, we had several opportunities to speak to classes at Loly's school. The day we left, the teachers had prepared a special dinner. Tatiana and the other teachers beamed proudly as they watched us gawk at the feast they had prepared. Before us lay deviled eggs, an entire sturgeon, sweet breads and jam, a small jar of caviar, tea and sparkling wine—all precious items that had been stored up for the long winter.

The meal began with a toast, each person telling a bit of their own history before raising a glass. Victor asked the teachers and all of us to share a little of our thoughts on God. The history teacher calmly but bluntly declared, "I am an atheist and Communist and will never become a Christian, but even so, I'm curious to hear what you believe."

We were especially excited about this opportunity, as, according to Alexander, the town of Loly did not have a single Christian and some of the teachers would be hearing the gospel for the first time tonight. We each shared our heart and Victor most of all. He gave his testimony with great passion. We could only understand snatches of what he was saying, but it seemed evident that God was speaking through him. Two of the ladies got up and left, apparently disinterested. A few minutes later, though, Matt noticed that tears were forming in the atheist history teacher's eyes. Tatiana sat next to her, leaning forward, intent on every word Victor shared.

"It is so much, *so, so* much to think of a God who loves us like this," the history teacher expressed. "Why have we not been told these things before?"

The meal finished, several more teachers said good-bye, thanking us for spending the evening with them. Tatiana and the history teacher, however, remained. We prayed with them and explained some of the first steps to following Christ. Victor also promised to talk to Pastor Willy from nearby Yemva about visiting them regularly in the future to encourage and teach them.

Later that night, Trey recalled in his journal, *"I was amazed at what powerful Good News we are blessed to know. I walked outside under the quiet stars in the deep snow to collect my thoughts. Yes, Jesus Christ is living and powerful and is here in Loly tonight!"*

Impact of a Backpack

It would be several hours before our ride to Yemva arrived. In the gym, Trey, Matt, and Mike began to shoot baskets and play on the gymnastic equipment while Jedd and Victor talked with Alexander in the little coach's office.

"After seeing you play basketball," Alexander said to Jedd, "I believe you could play for the regional team. You are a very good athlete."

Jedd thanked Alexander for the compliment but was hoping to confront the old coach with something else. "I have had some success in sports," he began, "but there is something I want to tell you, Alexander."

Alexander nodded and Jedd continued, "Even if I was to have all the success in the world, it would not be enough. At some point, I would have to face the reality that even success cannot fill my heart."

Alexander seemed a bit unsure how to respond. He waited for Jedd to go on.

"In high school, I was a very good athlete. I did very well. I expected to be a star in college, too. But when I got there, everyone was a great athlete. I spent most of my first year sitting on the bench. It was a very difficult time." He paused for a moment. Alexander seemed to be listening. "But through that experience, I began to realize that sports just are not a good enough place to build your life on."

Alexander waited as Victor translated, but then fired back, "That is because you weren't good enough. If you had been a better player, you would have succeeded. You would have played in the NBA."

"Maybe, but there are many, many men in the NBA who have won everything, been the best in the world, but you know what? At some point they say, 'That was great, but it is still not enough. I have everything the world offers, but I still feel empty.'"

"That is hard to believe," replied Alexander.

"It is true, and not only in sports. It is true of success in all areas: money, honor, fame, and power. They may be enjoyable for a time, but after a while, we realize that our heart has not been filled. I know businessmen and politicians and famous people who are extremely successful, but they are still some of the most miserable people in the world. They lack one thing. That one thing is Jesus."

It became clear to Alexander what Jedd was driving at. "I do not need God. God is for old women and children. I am an athlete. I am strong."

"Someday you will lose your strength, Alexander."

"Maybe, but God is for the weak. I do not need Him now."

"It is not weakness to admit that you have needs. We were created to fill our body's hunger with food, to quench our thirst with water. We also were created to be in relationship with God. Without that relationship, we will never be complete."

"I don't think so," stated Alexander with finality.

Alexander had been raised under Communism, steeped in atheism from birth, told time and time again that religion was nothing more than an opiate for the masses. Faith in God was for the weak, and no man, particularly one who prides himself on his strength, can easily admit weakness.

The conversation was over. Jedd moved out into the gym where the other guys were. Victor brought up another topic with Alexander, but kept looking for opportunities to challenge him further.

The four of us were discussing Jedd's conversation when Victor joined us. He smiled in exasperation. "Alexander does not want to admit that he might need anything. He thinks he is going to be strong forever."

Coach Alexander

"Hmm," mused Matt. "Is this the first time he has been challenged like this?"

"Like this, yes, I think so. But I think some Christians visited Loly once before. Tonight Alexander said to me, 'The last time you came, you people left me a *JESUS* film. Why didn't they leave a basketball instead, so I'd have something I could use?'"

There seemed to be little more that we could do. It would not be long before our ride arrived, so we began putting the last of our things in our backpacks. Alexander came out of his office and began shooting baskets.

114

"Nice backpack," he said to Trey. "It would make a good hunter's backpack." Trey smiled and Alexander continued, "Now, you guys want to play some 'horse' before you go?"

Everyone joined in the games of horse. Alexander and Jedd each won one. Trey appeared to be deep in thought. When eliminated from the third game, he went over to his backpack and began pulling things out. He did not stop until everything he had brought with him lay piled on the gym floor.

"Alexander, I want to give you something," Trey announced. Sasha translated. Alexander's face held a quizzical look as Trey continued, "I want to give you my backpack as a gift."

Alexander seemed to think Sasha had not translated correctly. He asked Sasha to repeat what he had said.

Trey continued, "I hope you enjoy this gift. I want it to be a reminder to you of the great gift that God gave all of us: His Son, Jesus."

A broad smile creased Alexander's weathered face and his eyes sparkled merrily. He stammered to Victor in childlike Russian that revealed his excitement. "I am hunter. This is my hunter backpack."

Trey helped him try it on and adjust the straps. The grizzled coach hopped all over the gym with it. He could hardly keep still. He disappeared into his office, and reappeared a moment later, his hands full of knick-knacks, gadgets, and other little items. He handed Mike a small Communist youth banner. He passed Trey a little red drum. "This drum is very old. It is used to call the pioneer youth to order," he explained, beaming. We protested that he did not need to give us anything, but he would not be dissuaded. Once he had emptied his load, he went back for more.

"You like to hunt?" he asked Jedd.

"Well, I've just done a little . . ."

Alexander pushed an old pair of hunting gloves into Jedd's hands. He turned to Matt. "You like this hockey banner?"

"It is very nice."

"It is yours," announced Alexander with gusto.

Alexander was still trying to pour gifts upon us when Igor arrived to pick us up. Heartfelt good-byes and thank-yous were exchanged as we moved out toward the two cars. We crammed our things inside, offered one last round of handshakes, and then squeezed in. Alexander was still smiling as we disappeared down the snow-covered road.

"What you did was awesome, Trey," said Jedd.

Trey was glowing, but also serious. "I pray that each time he puts on the pack, he will think of Christ."

"It just shows how a single sacrificial act can have more impact than all the words in the world."

The Jeep purred on, sliding this way and that on the white road. We settled into a contented thoughtfulness. Loly would never be far from our minds.

ten

Heart of the Gulag Region

Yemva, Russia

What life have we if we have not life together?

—T. S. ELIOT

An hour's Jeep ride returned us to Yemva, the town where we had met the ex-cons in the rehab center a week before. The forest was thinner here, and open fields filled the spaces between homes, apartments, and factories. A lonely stand of birch trees shivered slightly in the moon glow, which lit the road as our Jeep came to a halt in front of a stark, two-story house on the outskirts of town.

"You'll be living here the next two weeks," explained Igor. "The internot where you were going to stay got some new kids this week, so there weren't any beds for you. Our pastor said you could stay with his family. His name is Willy."

Trey slipped on the frozen walkway, barely catching his balance. Igor opened the door. "Hurry in," he said, disappearing through the blanket hung inside the door to keep the warm air inside. Passing through the blanket, we entered a central room bathed in heat from an oven that covered the entire wall. We shed several layers of clothing.

A motherly woman with graying hair smiled warmly at us as we entered. "You are welcome in our home. I am Luda."

Pastor Willy gazed over us with piercing black eyes. He shook our hands and introduced us to a twenty-one-year-old replica of himself—"My son, Mitya."

The single-room living area was simple but complete. In one corner, the counter, cupboards, and long table made the kitchen. The extremely cold temperatures made running water impossible, but a sinklike container could be filled with water drawn from a nearby well. At the other end of the room, separated by a wardrobe protruding from the wall, was a sleeping area. The stairs to the second floor remained blocked off all winter, since the single wood stove could not produce enough heat to make it livable.

With several local families who had come to welcome us, we sat down at a long, wooden table. Luda set tea before us all, then a funnel cake and strawberry jam. Mitya brought out his guitar, and singing mixed with the conversation for several hours. It was not until much later, as the families began to say good night, that we took note of the home's three small beds and realized that sleeping arrangements would be quite snug. Trey, Mike, and Matt row-sham-bowed for whom had to sleep with long, wild-sleeping Jedd. Matt lost. Each pair shared one of the twins. Victor, Sasha, and Mitya squeezed into the queen.

"Ready for lights out?" called out Willy as he climbed in next to Luda on a makeshift bed they had constructed in the kitchen.

A sleepy *"da"* came from someone and the room went dark. In the silence, we could hear the faint tinkling of ice pieces being blown against the windows. Through the night, Victor periodically tapped Sasha to stop his snoring. Matt fought Jedd for the covers for hours before digging out his sleeping bag. Mike and Trey slept peacefully throughout the night.

Cozy Quarters at Willy and Luda's House

Songs in the Night

For our first day in Yemva, Igor had arranged for us to speak in an orphanage for older kids, just behind the rehab center. A dozen children, eyes glowing, gathered round us. Their clothes had been worn in America once, back in the 1980s, the group of them together looking like a moving thrift-shop clothing rack. With their eyes gleaming up at us, they seemed much less hardened than children at some of the internots we had visited. We could not help but think this was due to their regular interaction with Willy's church.

Mike's Reflections—December 8

After sharing and singing with a large group of kids at the internot, we had a volleyball game scheduled at the internot's gym with a local women's team. It didn't go as bad as we expected. I think we're improving a little. More important, it afforded an opportunity to share the gospel with the women on the other team after the match.

A girl we met our first night at the rehab center—Lena—played on our team. There is something special about her. It is not just beauty, although she is pretty. She just seems to have a special spirit about her, childlike and gentle, yet glowing. I think Jedd likes her most of all. He tries not to show it, but I can tell by the way he smiles when she looks at him.

When we returned to Willy and Luda's for a late supper, several families from the church also sat around the room. The gatherings—except those at the church—never seemed to be planned; people just showed up at one house or another. Luda laid steaming bowls of garlic-thick borscht before each of us. It tasted like something for which the biblical Esau would have traded his birthright.

"Hey, Sash," Jedd said. "Tell Luda this is the best soup I've had in my life."

Luda beamed at the compliment, pressing her lips together and nodding her head with a humble sort of pride.

Victor glanced up from his soup with a grave look on his face. "I just remembered something, guys. There is something serious I need to tell you." The smiles faded from our faces. "A call came for me today from Loly." He paused as if he did not want to continue. "It was Tatiana. She says they are very angry at you all."

We looked at him with surprise. What could we have done? Victor could see our concern. A hint of laughter appeared in his eyes.

"Yes, they are very mad. Tatiana said that when you left, you took their hearts with you, and they want them back."

Victor's ear-to-ear grin mirrored our own. It brought us joy to think that we had brought such happiness to Loly. The feeling was definitely mutual.

Matt glanced around at the men and women and children who filled the room.

Only a few days into our stay in Yemva, we had already begun to see what an incredible Christian community they had here, from the weekly meetings at church to the informal evenings at homes. The marvelous thing was that they seemed to view us as every bit as much a part of it as those who lived there. Their community did not depend on one's location or familiarity, but simply on a shared love for Jesus Christ. It was clear these believers cared deeply for one another. They cared for us as well.

After several hours of conversation, Mitya and Matt brought out their guitars. Many of the great hymns have been translated into Russian, and we lost track of time singing back and forth: "Amazing Grace," "How Great Thou Art," "A Mighty Fortress." Like warm waves, a deep happiness began to wash over us: coziness and comfort in the midst of an ice-locked land . . . Slavic voices, rich and beautiful . . . a deep history of suffering and joy . . . a sense of community that filled the air like the smell of a baking pie . . . the serenity of home and the adventure of faraway all at once . . . laughter from the children . . . a contentment older than the earth . . . It was nearly two in the morning before people began to think of bringing the evening to a close. Our hearts yearned for more, but our eyelids were sinking lower and lower. It

The Yemva Church Sharing a Meal Together

was strange to us that children were still awake at this hour. It seems, however, that since the sun is only up for a handful of hours a day, the northerners are quite flexible with their sleeping patterns. Luda and another lady moved the dishes to the sink while Mitya drove two families home. We sat smiling, awash in warm joy.

Jedd shook his head. "That was so wonderful—the singing and the family-ness of everyone. I don't think I've ever felt as close to heaven as I did tonight."

Trey nodded. "The Russian music opens to me a world of beauty I've never known before. It reminds me how wonderful heaven will be—to be there *together*, worshiping in these ways."

The last of the friends said good-bye after 2:30 A.M. Though an icy wind piled snow against the house, inside all was cozy. Happy and content, we moved to our beds.

Matt's Reflections—December 7

There is something inexplicably moving about worshiping and fellow-shipping with Russian believers. I don't know what it is. Maybe it's that their perseverance through pain and hardship pours out through their melodies. I can only describe it as the sound of a melancholy joyfulness, a ringing of peace in the midst of pain, or the sight of beauty in the dead of winter.

121

Considering Sin

The following day, Mitya drove us to the Yemva train station to see Victor off to Moscow.

"My wife won't feed me anymore if I don't get home soon," he joked.

His big eyes and gloved hand poked out from the train as it moved away. "Keep up the good work!" he called out before pulling back into the car.

In the Jeep, Mitya huddled in his green down jacket. He kept his eyes fixed on the bleached road. He knew a moment's lapse of concentration when it was 30 below could prove disastrous. Even with the Jeep's heater blasting, our toes ached in our brittle sorrel boots. Jedd and Matt sat against the back wall of the Jeep, periodically scraping the buildup of ice from the windows.

"It was the strangest thing," Jedd said as he scooted forward and put his elbows on his knees. "I woke up really early this morning. The moment I popped awake, this thought occurred to me, like God just pushed it into my head. Do you know the verse that says, 'Love covers a multitude of sins'?"

"Yeah, I know the one you're talking about, but I'm not sure where it is," replied Matt.

"Anyway, I was wondering how love could cover sin, since the Bible teaches that there is always a penalty for sin. I mean, we don't believe that sin just evaporates or gets brushed under the rug when we're nice."

"Like Romans says, 'The wages of sin is death.' The price always has to be paid."

Jedd nodded. "Exactly. So I was thinking that to understand this verse, we really need to understand exactly what sin is. We often talk about sin as 'missing the mark.' That's true in a sense, of course, but maybe it's not the fullest understanding of what sin really is. It struck me that at its essence, sin is simply anything that breaks relationship—first with God, and second with others.

"For example, if a chemist were to tell you that the definition of cyanide was chemicals A, B, and C, he would be right. But the main thing we need to understand is just that cyanide will kill you if you swallow it. Sin *is* 'missing the mark,' but what we really need to understand is that sin causes death of relationship. *That* is why God hates sin so deeply—because He is so passionate about our love relationship with Him and with others.

"And that also explains how love can 'cover' sin: because love mends or heals the relationship between the sinner and the person being sinned against. For instance, if I stole Mike's Swiss Army watch and he found out, our relationship would be harmed. But if Mike loved me enough, even though he was mad at me for taking his watch, he would forgive me. Even though our relationship had been broken, it could be healed because of his love for me. The sin would be covered."

"So then how are the wages of sin 'death'?" said Trey, joining in.

"Because sin brings death to relationship. The fact that our bodies will someday die is part of it, but physical death is *nothing* compared to relational death. Adam and Eve eventually died because they ate the apple, but far more terrible was the fact that their pure communion with God was lost. Soon after, we saw the brokenness that resulted in human relationships when Cain killed Abel. You could go on and on describing the ways we see sin's impact today, from Rwanda and the Middle East to school shootings and broken marriages in the U.S."

Matt pulled on his beard, pondering. "That makes me think of 1 John. It says, 'Whoever hates his brother is a murderer.' I always wondered about this verse. How am I a murderer if I just hate someone? But in hatred, I really do destroy 'life' if we view things in the relational sense. John also wrote, 'If we love, we know that we have passed from death to life.'"

"This is really amazing!" Trey exclaimed, pausing for a second as he assigned words to his thoughts. "The idea that sin is anything that breaks relationship changes how you see everything. Wow, do you guys understand how this makes it all so much clearer? It shows how all the commandments and guidelines in the Bible are not just a random list of rules that God picked to rob us of our fun; they are a map for living in true relationship with God and others."

Matt nodded enthusiastically. "Exactly! And only love can heal these broken relationships. This isn't hard to see in our situation. If we are even going to make it through this trip, our love for one another must 'cover' all the mistakes we constantly make. The gap between us and God, however, was so big that all of the human effort in the world could not cover it. To heal *that* broken relationship, it took the sacrifice of Love Himself. As we accept His love and try to emulate it, we enter into the realm of restored relationships that God intended for us in the first place."

"The sages speak," said Mike, gently teasing.

"This is good stuff," defended Matt.

"Just joking. I think it is, too."

123

Matt's Reflections—December 9

Sin is any thought or action that breaks relationships, either between humans or between humans and God. Stealing, murder, adultery, envy, jealousy, malice, etc., are all sins for this very reason—because these things damage, or even completely destroy, relationships. But if you have love, even if you sin, these relationships may be restored—for love covers a multitude of sins.

This is why the Bible paints pride as among the worst and most dangerous of all sins. Pride isolates; it makes one think he or she is better than others, placing oneself on a pedestal, separate from, and therefore not in relation with, God or all of humanity.

The good news is not merely that we can go to heaven; it is that our relationships may once again be made right. Our relationship with God and with humans is restored through Christ's love. His sacrifice of Himself made it possible for us to reenter relationship with God. As He *lives in us, and as we seek to live out all He taught, we will also experience the types of relationships with one another that God designed us for. What an amazing gift!*

We made it back to the orphanage just in time to get recruited for another basketball game. Surprisingly, Willy, Luda, Mitya, and some others from the church had turned out for the game. Victor had told us that Willy, like many Russian Baptists, frowned upon athletic activity. The family did not cheer or make any noise during the contest, but they did follow with rapt interest. Perhaps it was the first basketball game they had ever seen.

When the contest was over, Willy, Luda, and Mitya seemed even more fascinated as they observed that an audience stayed to hear us speak about Jesus.

While the rest of us headed from the gym to the rehab center for a mid-week church service, Mike opted to return to Willy and Luda's house. He had pulled some muscles in his lower back during the game, and although he assured us he would be fine, we could tell he was in a good deal of pain. It was quite late when we finally left the center. For nearly two hours after the study, we had sung songs back and forth—English and Russian—with a group of the young people.

On the way home, Trey surprised Jedd with a blunt question.

"You've really got something for that Lena girl, don't you?"

Something flickered in Jedd's eyes, but he merely shrugged. "What makes you say that?"

"Even if I hadn't been your roommate for four years, I'd still have a pretty good guess. The little comments over the past week—'Doesn't she seem so sweet'; 'Isn't she a great volleyball player.' I know you were trying not to stare during the service," said Trey with a mischievous grin, "but I caught you looking while we were praying."

"So you had your eyes open, too, huh?"

"Just checkin' on my old roomie. If that wasn't enough, the whole time we were singing tonight after the service you were talking with her."

Jedd grinned. "There is something special about her."

"I wasn't disagreeing with that."

"Hey, I know it's silly of me, but I have to admit that I am kind of enchanted by her. I don't want her to notice. It would only lead to hurt feelings. Still, as much as my logical side is telling me to repress it, my heart is not going along."

Trey offered a sympathetic smile. *"Astarozsh"* (careful), he said in Russian. "I think she's pretty special, too, but don't do anything you'd regret."

Of Life and Death

As often as we were asked, we spoke. Mitya called the next day saying something about "church family." So off we went, having little idea where. The Jeep's engine growled to a start, heated air began to flow from the vents, Mitya yanked on the gearshift, and we lurched down the dark road.

We piled out in front of an apartment building and passed from the semilit street into the dark stairway. Most of the numbers had worn off the doors, so we had to take a guess at which was 304. We knocked and, to our relief, the door opened to reveal a bright coatroom full of people we had met at church.

"Dobre vecher!" (good evening) boomed Jedd as he strode in.

The reply was less than enthusiastic. *"Dobre vecher,"* whispered a few.

Hmm, thought Jedd. *They sure are not very friendly tonight.*

A man pointed with open palm to an adjacent room. Jedd and Trey looked in. Six or seven people were sitting on the couches that lined both sides. Alone, in the center of the room, lay a man in a wooden box.

Jedd bit his lip and turned back to the people in the coatroom. His face tried to convey an "I'm sorry, I did not know someone died" look. The people nodded at him solemnly. A few smiled faintly. Perhaps they understood. The daughter of the deceased, a middle-aged woman with a black handkerchief on her head, entered from the kitchen. Her eyes were puffy and red. Through Sasha, she requested that we sit on one of the couches near the coffin. The others in the room sat silently, alternatively gazing at the dead man and the carpet. A rough-hewn man with the look of a laborer sat like Rodin's *The Thinker*, breathing heavily. Occasionally, loud sighs broke the silence.

The dead man appeared to be in his sixties, his raven hair neatly combed, bushy eyebrows sticking out like small plants from his brow. Incense was burning, and pine branches lay piled around the coffin, but the smell of death could not be completely masked. The combination of odors and incense smoke made us feel lightheaded.

The minutes trickled by. From time to time, we looked at one another, asking, *What are we supposed to do?* with our eyes, but no one got up to leave. More than an hour later, Sasha, who had never entered the room in the first place, came in and motioned to us. We tried to hide our relief.

"Why did you guys stay in there so long?" whispered Sasha.

"We thought we were supposed to," replied Trey with a hint of frustration. "Why didn't you get us out earlier?"

We entered the small kitchen. Mitya, Lena, and several other young people from the church were sitting on the floor, quietly conversing. They welcomed us, and we joined the circle. With Sasha's help, Lena explained that Russians try to fill the bereaved's home after their loved one has died. "The more people that come, the better. It means a lot to her that you are here."

126

Jedd's Reflections—December 11

Being here in this place of death, I can't help thinking with some fear about Mom's cancer. I do not know what I'll do if she doesn't recover. Oh God, please make her well.

This world holds so much pain. A loving community makes it more bearable to go through loss, but the ache is still there. There is just no brushing it away. Many people—especially Christians it seems—try to make the world's pain seem not so bad. We throw out overused lines like, "All things work together for good." And, "They're in a better place now." Those things may be true, but they aren't a magic cure-all. It seems to me that it is far better simply to weep with those who weep. That is what Jesus did. The shortest verse in the Bible says a lot about what our response to human suffering should be: "Jesus wept."

The next morning, a funeral service was held in the deceased's apartment. People were packed, shoulder to shoulder, in the coatroom and in the room where the body lay. A lid had been placed on the coffin, and fresh pine boughs brought in, but the room smelled worse than the day before. The body had not been embalmed.

They sat us with the women and a few elderly men on the couches. Everyone else stood. People shuffled closer together as new arrivals continued to pour in. The service finally started with a prayer and a half-hour of singing. Pastor Willy delivered a short message and prayed once more. When the service was finished, we filed out the door and down the stairs in silence.

We all stood in the street, waiting. Everyone moved about to keep warm, but seemed to be trying not to look too energetic on such a sad day. Ice began to cake in our beards from our breath. Six men, mostly ex-cons from the center, carried the casket out and laid it on the back of a flatbed truck.

Moving forward slowly, we walked behind the truck, our heads down, crunching in the snow. At some unseen cue, the truck sped up and drove off and the procession stopped. We waited, our toes losing the last inklings of sensation. Those who had cars went back to retrieve them. Ice built in our beards with every breath; Matt's took on the appearance of a white tumbleweed. As the cars pulled up, people climbed into the one nearest them. Two ex-cons joined us in the back of Mitya's Jeep. Once inside, the monklike silence dissolved. The cons watched Mike with amusement as he beat his hands together to create some warmth.

A hefty one with close-cropped yellow hair laughed out loud. "Have you ever felt it this cold?"

Mike shivered. "Not even close."

"Are you starting to hate Russia yet?"

"Nope. I still love it."

The cars stopped near an arched gate on the edge of town where the pine forest led off into the distance. A black iron fence set off the cemetery. The graves were set between the snow-laden firs. Most plots were surrounded by waist-high fences, and many had permanent benches and even tables at which family members could sit, eat, and recollect. We were surprised to see that the great majority of the gravestones—even those erected during the Communist years—bore Orthodox crosses. It appeared that although the atheistic Communist state controlled almost every aspect of these people's lives, it could not hold them at the end. Some graves, however, boldly displayed the crimson star of the Communist Party, a final fist shaken in the face of eternity.

A number of men produced shovels and began plying the frozen soil at the appointed spot. Others lowered the pine box to the ground from the bed of the truck. It is customary to take one last look at the deceased before burial, and the men solemnly pried the lid from the casket. The man had been dead for three days, his face beginning to bloat, and turn purple and green. Blood trickled from beneath bulging eyelids and filled the creases in his cheeks. They took a final picture of father and daughter and then replaced the lid. The daughter began to weep softly as they nailed it down.

The grave dug, the bearers carried the casket into the cemetery and laid it next to the open hole. All was silent for a moment, save for the sound of shiver-wracked breathing. Heatless rays of sunlight filtered through the trees and touched our clouds of breath with gold. Willy looked at each face before offering a final prayer.

Then four men stepped forward and ran two long clotheslines beneath the coffin, lifting the box over the hole and lowering it. The daughter let out a forlorn wail as the coffin sank into the ground. One by one, the people stepped forward, grasped a handful of the freshly dug soil, and tossed it into the grave. When everyone had done so, we stood back and watched as the men who had dug the grave began to refill it. The shovels of dirt thumped against the pine, and the daughter began to sob uncontrollably. A girl from the church who had been standing nearby wrapped her arms around her and steaming tears fell upon the girl's neck.

When the shovelers had finished their work, women laid a cloth on the fresh mound and placed candies and meat-filled rolls they had made on top. The food was eaten slowly, thoughtfully. But as we ate, people began to talk quietly. The time of solemnity had passed. We could stop holding our breath.

People left in small groups. Willy was intent on remaining to the end, so the four of us climbed into the Jeep, which Mitya had running. We squeezed in as close to the vents as we could, wondering if there were still feet in our boots. We returned to the apartment for a traditional meal. A long table had replaced the casket and was covered in sumptuous dishes prepared by ladies in the church. The men ate first. When we had finished, we cleared our places and the table was reset for the women.

o o o

We gathered the following afternoon at Yemva's outdoor market. Mitya had asked us to join him and one of the ex-cons in staffing the small table of Christian literature the church always put out on market days. Matt stomped around in a circle. As much as the pounding hurt, sensation seemed to disappear from his feet every time he stopped moving.

"It's our coldest day yet," remarked Mike. "Negative forty-six."

Trey shook his head. "That's seventy-eight below freezing. You think Americans would do much shopping if our markets were this cold?"

"I'm going to go in that building for a few minutes," said Matt. "I can't feel my feet anymore."

"I'll join you," followed Mike. "My back's not doing too well. I wouldn't mind sitting for a minute."

"Mike must be hurting pretty bad," commented Trey. "I've almost never heard him complain about anything." Jedd did not seem to be listening. Trey studied him for a moment before asking, "What you thinking about?"

"What's that?"

"I said . . . Are you daydreaming about Lena?" Jedd smiled sheepishly but said nothing. "Wow. Lovely Lena again, huh? I've never seen you like this."

"I've never seen myself like this," said Jedd. "I feel like I'm in junior high. Only in junior high I usually didn't get like this, so I guess I'm going through junior high now."

"Could you ever see yourself marrying her?"

"No . . . I don't know . . . I don't think so. That's the stupid thing. There are a hundred reasons in my mind why I could not marry her, why even liking her is so foolish. We've got different backgrounds, different lives, different expectations. We don't speak the same language. For gosh sakes, I never thought I—"

"That's what's great about it. You're always so logical about things. And here you are tipsy over something that is totally irrational. I might expect this out of a lot of people, but never you. It's kind of funny."

"Yeah, I guess," said Jedd.

"Maybe you'll see her again tonight. I think we'll be going over to one of the believers' houses for dinner with some of the ex-cons."

Jedd did not hear him. He was off in his own thoughts once again.

∘ ∘ ∘

The pain in Mike's back was getting worse. He spent several days bedridden at Willy and Luda's until we decided it would be best if he went back to Moscow to recuperate. He limped onto the train and struggled down the empty corridor, dragging his pack behind him. It would be nicer to recuperate in the comforts of Moscow than in Yemva's Spartan accommodations. Even so, it hurt to leave like this, to miss out on the rest of the experiences, to leave the fellowship of the guys and the Yemva church.

"Compartment 16, huh? I guess this is it." He jerked open the sliding door. Inside, three Russians lay fast asleep, leaving only a top bunk available. Trying not to awaken the sleeping strangers, Mike heaved his bulky backpack onto the ledge of the open bunk. A sharp pain shot through his lower back. He leaned against the bedrail in a state of despair. Half wanting to cry, he laughed quietly at the ridiculousness of the situation. Here he was at 7:00 A.M., twenty-seven hours north of Moscow, alone on a train without anyone to whom he could talk. Worst of all, the excruciating pain in his back made him wonder if he would ever make it up into his bunk.

Gathering his strength, he placed one hand on the bunk's ledge and one on his neighbor's. Slowly, he began to hoist himself like a gymnast on a set of parallel bars. Once at the level of the bunk, he hurled his body's weight toward the bed. Grasping the bunk's far edge, he grunted as he pulled his legs up behind him. He lay there motionless, panting.

Slowly his thoughts turned from his pain to his departure earlier in the day.

Mike's Reflections—December 16

Although my train arrived at dawn, many of my new friends from the church made it to the station to say good-bye. As frustrated as I felt, it lifted my spirits to see them there.

My body aches. I haven't felt this bad in as long as I can remember. Even so, part of me wishes I could have stayed in Yemva . . . even stay there for the rest of my life. The rest of me wishes I was at home. It's been way too long since I've talked to the love of my life. I miss her so much. She's waiting for me at home.

Following dinner at Willy and Luda's, another group had gathered. An ex-con and Matt played their guitars in a corner. Trey sat on the floor, drawing on paper for a small crowd of children.

Mitya leaned over to Jedd. "What kind of work do you want to do in your life?"

"I want to be a university teacher, a professor, but I do not know what subject. I like many things."

"You believe that is what God wants you to do?"

"Yes. But if not, I want to do whatever He wants me to do."

"That is good. I also want to do whatever God wants me to do."

Willy, overhearing the conversation, joined in. "Have you considered being a missionary?"

"I don't think God has called me to that for now, but if He ever does, I am willing."

Sasha abandoned his bantering with one of the girls to help the communication. He translated as Willy continued, "More than half of the serious Christians in Russia have left since the end of Communism. They all went to the United States."

"I did not know that."

"There are many towns in Russia without churches, maybe without a single believer at all." Willy, normally emotionless on the surface, spoke with passion. "You know the verse about the harvest being ripe and the laborers being few? It could not be more true than in Russia today. So many people need God, but there are so few to tell them about Him."

Jedd responded, "It may be that God will call me back here someday. It would be difficult to leave my family in America, but if this is where God wants me, this is where I want to be."

"Think seriously about it, Jedd. I think you work well with the people here."

"And he is learning the language very quickly," added Mitya with a grin. Jedd smiled.

"There is need here, Jedd. When you are back in America, tell your friends. Tell them that we need people."

"I will," Jedd promised.

 Trey's Reflections—December 14

Another wonderful evening with the Christian family here. I love how deeply intertwined the lives of the Yemva believers are. It is more than Sunday mornings, Wednesday nights, and occasional dinner parties. It is more than committees and church outings. Like people everywhere, the church members have their distinct jobs and homes. Yet they have chosen to allow their lives to be woven together in countless ways, big and small: a mechanic drives over to the center to help Mitya fix his Jeep. Mitya walks across town to fix a door hinge for a widow. Willy and Luda invite the lady who lost her father to stay at their house as long as she wants. When the lady returns home, a girl from the church stops by daily to clean and cook. A few believers give Igor what money they can spare since he is out of work. Groups end up gathering nearly every night at one house or

131

another for no reason at all, talking, eating, laughing, and singing . . .
often until past midnight!

Of course, their life together is not without problems and bickerings,
but it's the closest thing to true community we have ever seen. For me, it
is a vision of what the church should be, what the church can be.

I think the main thing preventing Americans from experiencing the
community they do here is our frantic activity. Without any margin of
time or resources, all we can offer our brothers and sisters is a scheduled chunk of time on Sunday and Wednesday and a budgeted bit of
tithe. I do not wish to live that way . . .

"Da Svidanya"

We would leave Yemva in the morning. As we entered the church for
one last service, sadness washed over us. Part of us wanted to sink our fingers into the town and never leave. We each spoke briefly. We wanted to
encourage our brothers and sisters one last time to keep their focus on
Jesus alone, building everything else upon the foundation of a relationship
with Him. More than anything, though, we just wanted to tell them how
very much we loved them. Our words most certainly fell short. We hoped
they could see it in our faces.

As always, when the meeting ended, no one left. Circles of conversation formed here and there. We joined a group of young people around
the keyboard in front to continue singing. Back and forth we sang: "Father,
I Adore You," first in English, then in Russian; "On Christ the Solid Rock"
and then *Loobloo Muy Spasityel*" (I Love You My Savior). Children ran
hither and thither, yelling and laughing.

The knowledge of our departure made every little detail of that last
evening exceedingly precious: crushing embraces—and sometimes
kisses—from the ex-cons; Willy behind the pulpit speaking bold words of
exhortation; the passion on faces as the Russian believers sang out their
hymns; Luda's motherly gaze, looking upon us with love and sadness; a
burly ex-con spinning around with a little girl on his shoulders, holding on
for dear life; a babushka bent in prayer with a young woman, their hands
clasped in a knot.

Jedd sat down in back to watch it all. Two little children jumped up on him. Each straddled one of his legs, facing him. He bounced them up and down, and the children squealed with delight. Lena sat down next to them.

"You are happy?" she asked in Russian.

"Yes, very happy. And very sad also. I do not want to leave."

"I am happy and sad also," she said, tickling the children who refused to get off their horses.

"Only one more," Jedd told the children. He delivered the promised ride, and they grudgingly dismounted. Turning to Lena, he said, "I do not think there are many places like this in the world. I pray I can come again."

"Me, too," she said.

"Hey, Jedd, come here," shouted Trey from across the room. "Zshula wants to take a picture with us." Zshula had accepted Jesus at a music academy where we had spoken. We were excited to see her there at the church.

One of Zshula's friends snapped a photo of her with the three of us. We pulled out our own cameras and asked if we could take one with Zshula. A group crowded in for the shot. The flashes did not stop for several minutes.

Trey laughed. "I'm going blind. Let's sing some more."

Jedd returned to where Lena still sat. She had been crying. Sasha joined them. "What is wrong, Lena?" Jedd asked.

She responded, but Jedd did not fully understand her reply. Sasha explained, "Do you remember that boy from the school who became a Christian? He was here for the meeting."

"Yes, I saw him."

"Lena says his father just came in here a minute ago. He grabbed the boy by the arm and took him out. Lena followed them into the hall and asked the dad if something was wrong. He said to her, 'This is the first time and the last time this boy will ever come to church.'"

Jedd looked down. Tears dripped from Lena's cheeks to the floor. There was nothing they could do. The three prayed together for the boy before Trey again called Jedd up for more pictures.

It was nearly an hour after the service ended that things started to thin out. People moved into the hallway and pulled on their outerwear. A father buttoned his daughter's red coat and tied a scarf around her neck. Warm hugs were exchanged all around. "We are very glad you came," rumbled a big ex-con. *"Da svidanya"* (See you again), squeaked the little girl as she wrapped her arms around Trey's neck.

Lena and her mother requested that we come over for chai one last time. We bundled up for the long walk to their apartment, accompanied by Luda.

The cold did not prevent us from enjoying the walk over. In fact, we hardly noticed it. We talked and joked merrily. Jedd and Lena tossed snowballs at each other over the rest of the group. A misfire caught Trey's cap. He launched one into the back of Jedd's jacket. Light shimmered through the icy windows of the homes along the road. Jedd moved a bit in front of the group. He was carefully rounding a snowball in his mittens when he heard the crunching of footsteps running up behind him. Danger was approaching. Without looking back, he let the well-packed sphere fly over his shoulder. Slowly he turned. Lena stood a few feet behind him. Her arms hung at her sides, snow dropping from her face. Jedd brushed the snow away and tried to apologize. She feigned anger for moment, but could not keep from smiling. They walked side by side, talking, the rest of the way home.

Once inside the apartment, we settled in the living room. Lena helped her mother prepare chai and thin Russian pancakes. Lena's mother called us into the kitchen, and we squeezed around the small table. Coming over for tea had turned into a full meal. We gave thanks and began to eat. Lena's father had been working late and returned during our meal.

"So, you boys are leaving tomorrow?" he boomed. Sasha translated.

We nodded. "*Da, da.*"

"I wanted to give you some things before you left." He disappeared into the other room.

He returned and handed Jedd a long military knife in a leather sheath. "You like it?" he asked.

"Very much," replied Jedd. "It is very nice."

He pulled a switchblade from his pocket and handed it to Trey. "Be careful," he warned. Trey pressed the release and the blade flashed out with such force that the knife flew from Trey's hand onto the table. We laughed. Lena's father laughed the loudest of all.

"Jedd," Lena's father continued, "some of the men you played basketball against the other night are in my unit. They were very impressed with your playing. They were wondering if you played in the NBA." Jedd smiled and laughed as Sasha translated. "They asked me if you were related to me."

Jedd turned to Matt and Trey. With a grin he whispered, "Not yet."

Sasha gave Jedd a serious glance. "Luda translated what you just said."

"She what?"

"She understood what you said and repeated it to Lena and her mom."

Color flooded into Jedd's face. The room seemed very hot. Lena turned her head and looked at the floor for a minute. She stood and moved quickly to the stove, busying herself with some task that did not need to be done. Trey glanced at Matt with an "uh-oh" look. Silence boomed.

Lena left the room. It was a frozen minute before life and sound crept back into the room.

"Did they know I was kidding, Sasha?" Jedd asked softly.

"I don't know what they think," he replied.

Jedd was relieved when Luda suggested we ought to return home to pack. Luda said that Willy would probably be expecting us home soon. Lena's father told us that his military assistant could take us home. We moved into the entrance area and began donning our coats.

"I'll go out and make sure the driver is ready," said Lena's father.

Lena's mother gave each of us a long hug. Her eyes were moist as she said, "I hope very much it is not long before you come back to our home." She looked around her and called out, "Lena, the boys are leaving. Come out and say good-bye."

Lena emerged from her bedroom. Her eyes were red and puffy. A few spots of moisture that she had not managed to wipe away glistened on her cheek. *"Da svidanya,"* she said, almost inaudibly. She gave us each a soft hug, but said nothing more. Trey moved out the door with Sasha while the others continued putting on their jackets.

The others began moving down the walk. "We will be at the train station to say good-bye tomorrow morning," Lena's mother called out from the doorway.

Lena's father dropped his cigarette and crushed it. He gave directions to the driver and we all piled in. "This man will pick you up in the morning and take you to the station as well. Just tell him what time you want him to be there."

"Thank you for all the help," said Jedd.

"Da svidanya," he said with a smile as he shut the door.

∘ ∘ ∘

Back at Willy and Luda's we began packing our things. Although we could tell she was tired, Luda insisted on making one last pot of borscht for us. Jedd, wanting some time to think, went outside to chop wood. The night was relatively warm, probably not far below zero degrees Fahrenheit, the stars gleaming crisp and clear, like a pile of gems laid on black velvet. Trey came out a few minutes later to join Jedd.

"All right if I cut some wood, too?" Trey asked as Jedd brought the blade down on a round.

"Sure."

Trey watched Jedd swing the ax a few times before saying more. "Are you thinking about what happened tonight?"

"I'm thinking I was stupid. I can't believe I said that. I've been trying so hard not to send her any of the wrong messages. I know I may have a little bit, but I was really trying, and then with one stupid comment I blew everything."

Trey was quiet for a moment. "I don't know if it is all that bad. You probably shouldn't have said that, but you had no idea they would catch it."

Jedd sank the ax in the stump and turned to Trey. "I know. How *did* Luda translate that? I don't think she's said a word in English the whole time we've been here."

"Maybe it was a lucky guess."

"Yeah. Real lucky. You want to chop some?"

"Sure."

Trey placed a new round on the block and brought the axe down on it. Jedd continued, "From the beginning I've felt so foolish about this whole thing. It's totally irrational. I did not have good enough reasons for it. I just liked her. But I did not want to drag her down by it. I do have feelings for her, but . . . I mean, we're leaving here tomorrow. The whole world is our backyard. She'll probably be here the rest of her life. I just pray she forgets all this. I'd like to see her marry Mitya some day. I don't want her thinking about some American guy if Mitya ever does want to marry her. Shoot, I just . . . I just can't believe I said that."

The door of the house opened and Matt called out, "Time for borscht." Trey set the ax against the shed and they moved inside. "There's not much you can do about it now, Jedd. Don't let it kill you."

∘ ∘ ∘

The morning came too early. We said little as we dressed and stuffed the last of our belongings into our bags. A group of our friends were already at the train station when we arrived: Lena and her mother, several young people from the church, two girls from the internot, Zshula and a friend of hers, Igor and others.

Trey's Reflections—December 18

It is hard to sort through how things can be so sad and so deeply happy all at once. Pain and joy are often thought of as being on opposite ends of the spectrum. The truth is, though, they sometimes seem to wrap around and touch each other. Sometimes the most poignant and exquisite moments include both pain and joy intertwined.

I long for the day when we will live forever in the presence of our Lord and with these newly met brothers and sisters.

137

The train had not yet come and the sun was not yet up. The low clouds hung heavy, keeping the predawn light to a hazy gray. We brought everyone together for some final pictures and said a last good-bye to each person.

"Luda, you have been a wonderful mother to us during our time here," said Trey before embracing her. "We will miss you very much," said Matt to Zshula and her friend. The girls from the internot clung to Jedd's side, each squeezing one of his gloved hands tightly. He tried not to look at Lena. She stood by her mother in her long, black coat, tears trickling down her face. The falling snow landed on her beaver-pelt cap and did not melt.

The train pulled in for a two-minute stop. Jedd finally stepped toward Lena, biting his lip. She looked up at him.

"I will not forget you," he stuttered in broken Russian.

"I will not forget you, either," she replied. An impatient conductress was yelling at us to get on immediately. Jedd gave Lena a brief hug before moving toward the train with Matt and Trey.

We pulled ourselves on board and turned to say one last good-bye. The train began to creep forward. We waved and they waved back, calling out, "Good-bye, good-bye. Come back to us soon."

Jedd heard none of that. He had finally let his gaze find Lena. Their eyes fixed upon each other. For the first time, he allowed himself to look deeply into her eyes; he felt he was swimming in them. He did not stop looking at her until she was a small black smudge, hazy in the falling snow. Icy wind whipped across his cheek. He shut the door and moved down the hall to our berth, falling onto the seat. The train continued to pick up speed until the snow outside was slashing by the windows like falling meteors.

"You okay there, buddy?" Trey said with a smile.

"No."

Jedd sat next to the window for more than an hour, deep in thought, wondering if he would ever recover.

Waltzing through the West
From Moscow to the Mediterranean Sea

g o on in," said the large-eyed Austrian girl, smiling. "Mother and Father are expecting you."

Matt pushed open the oak door of the farmhouse and stepped out of the damp night into a bright entry hall. Set neatly by the door were two pairs of boots, the mud on them still wet from the morning pig feeding. The walls were decked with dozens of mounted antlers.

"Does your father like to hunt, Martina?" asked Mike.

"All the Austrian farmers like to hunt. Those horns you see are from ibexes my grandfather and my father and my brother have gotten in the Alps not far from here."

An hour before, Martina and Lily—two Austrian girls of about our age whom Trey met some years before—had picked us up at the train station not far from Salzburg, Austria. We had traveled west from Moscow and planned to stay at the home of Martina's parents until New Year's Day.

Taking off our shoes, we moved into the home's great room. Handcrafted wood covered the walls. The room smelled of the pine burning in the wood stove.

A rosy-cheeked man entered the room and strode toward us. *"Gruss Gott! Gruss Gott!"* he boomed in German, crushing each of our hands in turn.

Trey translated as Martina's father rolled on. "Welcome to our home! It is not since World War II that we have had Americans staying with us. The last group was a band of army officers who loved the chance to have a bath and sleep in a warm bed. They were very polite, those American soldiers."

Matt glanced around. "This must be an old farmhouse."

"Not so old. Only about two hundred years."

We smiled at one another. Europeans have a much different standard for what is considered "old."

"Would you like to come see the basement?" asked Martina's father.

"Perhaps tomorrow, if you don't mind," said Trey. "I'm feeling like I need some rest." Mike shot a sidelong glance at Trey. We were all a little tired, but it was not like him to pass up an opportunity to explore anything, even a basement. Trey had not seemed entirely himself since we left Moscow.

Martina began leading up the stairs. "Give them a chance to rest, Papa. We can talk later. They've traveled a lot in the last few days."

We had indeed been on the move—our goal: to work our way from Russia to South Africa on trains and planes in roughly two weeks. The night train from Moscow brought us to St. Petersburg the morning after Christmas Day. Trey's dad's company kept several rooms on permanent

Mike, Matt, Jedd, and Trey in Budapest

retainer at the city's five-star Grand Hotel Europa, and since no one was using them the two days after Christmas, we were able to stay for free.

The plush St. Petersburg hotel contrasted sharply with our accommodations in Russia's northland. Instead of feeble wooden structures, we saw towering marbled walls set with statues and gleaming chandeliers. No more drawing water from snow-covered wells or running to an ice-floored outhouse where pages of old magazines were used for toilet paper. Now, clad in thick robes, we could lounge in a bathroom complete with heated floors and an enormous tub where water flowed from polished brass faucets.

St. Petersburg, dubbed the Venice of the north, had plenty to impress out-of-towners. The Hermitage, a palace-turned-museum, contains enough masterpieces to keep an art aficionado enthralled for months. Elegant buildings run along St. Petersburg's system of canals, leading to well-tended parks, grand monuments, and imposing churches. Some say the beauty of her greatest cathedral, St. Isaac's, is second only to St. Peter's Cathedral in Rome.

From St. Petersburg we flew to Budapest, Hungary. Our lodging there was simpler, but the city proved to be magnificent and equally rich. From there, a train took us the rest of the way to Austria with a pleasant ride through rolling, mist-wrapped hills where shoots of grass poked up from dark soil and occasional snow patches lingered from a recent storm.

The days of rapid travel and sightseeing had been fun, and we had a few more to go. Tonight, though, we could not have been happier to climb under our heavy down comforters in the old Austrian farmhouse.

Trey's Reflections—December 28

As we were boarding the night train from Moscow to St. Petersburg, one of my worst nightmares came true. Dad helped carry my bags into our compartment, and before the other guys came aboard, he told me that he and Mom were planning on getting a divorce. Mom came in just as he was finishing and the ensuing conversation between them wasn't pretty . . . She was angry—even livid—that Dad had dropped this bombshell just minutes before I departed for four more months of travel.

I feel flat, unable to comprehend the enormity of this disaster . . . not just for me, but for Andy, too—he has to live at home through this. I've expressed some of this to the guys, but I feel like I can hardly talk.

about it without crying. How do people just move on with their lives when their family gets torn apart?

New Year's Waltz

Our time with Martina and Lily had allowed for enjoyable relaxation, including a foray into the Austrian Alps. Trey tried to keep a smile on his face, but he often slipped into an uncharacteristic quietness, thinking about his parents.

The end of our third day in Austria brought us to New Year's Eve. Trimming our beards, we cleaned ourselves up as best we could. Following the traditional wienerwurst and goulash dinner, we headed with the girls and their families to the New Year's Eve service at the nearby church.

"I'm surprised a little town like this has a church this big," stated Mike.

Lily smiled with a hint of pride. "Yes. It is beautiful, isn't it?" Our heads bent back as far as they could to gaze at the top of the building before us. Thick walls of stone shot up from the cobblestones at our feet, rising almost out of sight into the darkness above us.

"Some American churches are pretty fancy, but our best don't compare even to the country churches in Europe," concluded Mike.

Just a few electric lights aided the candles that burned in every corner and down the center aisle. It smelled of burning wax. Large paintings depicting the life of Christ and stories from the Old Testament hung between the intricately worked stained-glass windows. The long sanctuary was packed. The seats were all taken when we arrived, so we stood with a large number of others in the back. The place was abuzz with hushed conversation.

Mike leaned over to Lily. "There are a lot of people here. Do most people go to church?"

"Yes. Austrians are quite religious, especially compared to other Europeans. Most everyone attends church on Christmas, New Year's, and Easter."

"I didn't know that. To what extent would you say it impacts their lives?"

"Um, quite a bit at certain times of the year. Religion has always been a deep part of our tradition."

"The religion—would you say there is a real belief in God?"

"Some, I think. I know that *I* believe."

"What sort of things?"

"Well, you know, that it is good for people to be religious. It helps them live better lives. Martina and I even teach Sunday school."

"Really?"

"It is lots of fun."

"You teach kids how to follow Jesus?"

"We teach them to be good and polite and things. We play games and sing. To be honest, the only bit of the Bible I've read is one of the Gospels for a literature class once."

Mike's Reflections—December 31

It makes me sad to see that even in what are considered the most "religious" pockets of Europe, it seems that much of the general populace seems to view religion as little more than a good tradition, like an Easter egg hunt.

As best I can tell from history, the European churches—especially the Catholic, but more recently the Protestants as well—have frequently strayed into being more committed to ritual, tradition, and religious activities than to intimate relationship with God.

At least from the way I view things, this could very well be the reason why the vast majority of people in Europe have rejected the religion referred to by many here as "Christianity." If I thought that the rituals and traditions and trying to do a good deed now and then were all there was to Christian faith, I probably wouldn't stick with it, either.

As the priests entered, the buzz died away, and the congregation worked its way through a series of hymns and recitations. Then the lights in the sanctuary dimmed, only candles remaining, their flickering light insufficient to fully penetrate the darkness above us. The organ played mournfully as the priest read the names of the parishioners who had died in the previous year.

"Januar. Herr Dieter Heimler. Herr Friedrich Weiss. Fraulein Liesel Braumeister . . ." A deep bell tolled once for each name. "Frau Helga Bremen. Herr Peter Mueller . . ." It was sobering.

As the lights came up, we sang another hymn. After Communion was served and a few more words said, the congregation was released, people pouring out of the sanctuary, talking merrily, ready to get on with their New Year's revelry. Pockets of friends lingered here and there, their conversation punctuated by jovial laughter that sent thick clouds of steam into the crisp night air.

∘ ∘ ∘

We were driven to a nearby farmhouse, its dining room walls covered with more ibex antlers and a warm fire crackling in the stove. Joining a dozen of Martina and Lily's friends around a long wooden table, we ate a second dinner of lox salad followed by plates of raw meats, which we held over the open flames of little *stein kuchens* until they were cooked. As the hours slipped by, the cuckoo clock on the wall chirped ten times, then eleven.

Finally, the hostess—by now a bit tipsy from the punch—cried out, "It is almost time for the New Year. Outside everyone. Outside!"

As the small crowd filed out onto the driveway, someone set up a stereo near the door. A silky voice poured from the speakers in German.

"*Ein minut!*" shouted one of the girls.

From out beyond the misty fields we heard the fireworks and gunshots beginning. A firecracker exploded just behind the hostess, and she jumped forward, eyes wide. The young man who had lit it boomed with laughter and brought another string from a bag. When she recovered, the hostess began chasing him toward the barn.

Dinner with Martina's Family in Austria

The radio announcer broke into our consciousness again. "*Funf, vier, drei, zwei, eins . . . Gutes Neues Jahr!*"

Everyone—frozen for a moment—began moving, hopping around. The men shook our hands. With the girls we exchanged two kisses, one on each cheek. "*Gutes Neues Jahr,*" each said, "*Gutes Neues Jahr.*"

Then another sound came from the radio: music, a waltz by Strauss.

"This is it!" exclaimed Lily. "The New Year's Waltz."

She grabbed Trey and Martina took Matt. The rest of the group was doing the same. Round and round, smaller circles within a larger circular rotation. It was a bit dizzying. Two of the young men continued to light firecrackers and hurl them in the air. Another ran inside and returned with a box of champagne bottles, which he began to pour into glasses. Jedd and Mike exchanged partners with Trey and Matt, and the dance continued.

Martina laughed. "All over Austria they are doing this. Every New Year's Eve everyone listens to this national radio and we all dance Strauss's waltz."

"Whhhooooohoooo!" yelled Jedd. "I love it!"

It was after three when we finally climbed beneath our down comforters once again.

"That was great," whispered Jedd, as loudly as he dared.

"Yep," said Matt.

"It was magical," added Trey.

"What about you, Mike?"

A faint snore was all that came from Mike's bed.

145

∘ ∘ ∘

The next night we boarded a train in Austria to beat the sunrise to Rome. When we arrived, we left our backpacks in the station's "checked luggage" since we would be boarding another night train for Sicily that evening. Now we waited in a hotel lobby for a friend of ours who was vacationing in Rome with his parents. The four of us sat in pairs facing each other on plush red chairs in the lobby. The room would have seemed extravagant, almost gaudy in America. In Italy, it seemed to fit: intricate tapestries, marble statues, gold-rimmed mirrors, and lots of crimson velvet.

We had all been particularly happy when Trey had checked our bank account balance from an ATM earlier in the day. A number of people had sent money to help with our expenses, and to our relief, the account now contained enough to get us through the rest of the trip.

A young man—nearly as tall as Jedd—with a wide, slightly tilted smile hopped down the stairs toward us.

"Horse!" exclaimed Trey, a bit too loud for the setting.

"Hey, guys!" replied the young man.

We greeted our old college friend, nicknamed "Horse," with hugs.

"How you doing, buddy?" asked Mike.

"Mighty fine. Mighty fine." Horse rubbed Mike's bald head. "Nice do."

"You like it? Matt and I shaved our heads just before we left Russia."

"I bet you're driving girls crazy with that thick-beard-and-bald-head look."

"Oh yeah. They would deny it, but you know they love it."

"You guys took the night train down?"

"Yeah," said Trey. "It worked out pretty nice. If you take a night train, you don't have to pay for a hotel. Good deal, huh?"

"If you can find a place to sleep on the train," complained Jedd. "All the compartments were full, so I was on the floor of the intertrain compartment next to the bathroom all night. I was freezing."

Matt laughed. "Mike and I weren't freezing."

"Nope," replied Mike. "Matt and I were in a compartment with three classic Italian guys. The seats folded down to make this bed about as big as a queen-size. We were snoozing all night long."

"I'm jealous."

"Yeah, I bet."

Popes, Pizzas, and Piazzas

Our path through the streets of Rome took us first to St. Peter's Cathedral, said to be the grandest church in all the earth, one of the Seven Wonders of the World. In front of the massive structure stretched a vast cobblestone piazza the size of several football fields. Stone pillars, several stories high, encircled the area, the tops of the pillars connected by a stone railing that supported larger-than-life statues of saints from ages past. The cathedral had similar columns and statues set in its immense facade. A statue of St. Peter, guarding the entrance, held the keys to the kingdom in his outstretched hand.

"Amazing," breathed Trey.

The inside was even more breathtaking. A sea of colored marble lay before us. Rising from it, massive pillars rose to support the expanse of roof and dome hundreds of feet above. Statues of the popes guarded the tombs where their bones lay. Each artwork was a masterpiece: sculptures of saints and angels; paintings, some the size of small houses; even the stonework and carved writing revealed the touch of a master. Gold gleamed everywhere. It was too much to take in.

"We use the word *awesome* all the time," remarked Jedd. "But this place really is. You feel totally awed . . . It's overwhelming."

"You remember from history class how they paid for this place?" posed Mike.

"Indulgences, right?"

"Yeah. They got partway done building it and then ran out of money. So they sent out salesmen to sell indulgences for sin—just put enough money in the church's coffer, and you could be forgiven for just about anything."

Jedd smiled. "That would get pretty expensive for me—having to pay cash for every sin."

"Seriously, though. How can you get more opposite from the message of Jesus? God paid the penalty for our sins that we could never pay anyway and offers it to us as a gift. Then someone turns around and tries to sell it."

It was later in the day that we passed what is known as the Mameritime Prison. Narrow steps led beneath the street to a small stone cell in which both Peter and Paul, according to tradition, had been imprisoned.

Matt peered down the stone stairwell. "Kind of a contrast with St. Peter's," he remarked.

Mike nodded. "Yeah. You see the true roots of the church here: poor, rough, and simple. To be honest, I'd feel more comfortable worshiping down there than in the cathedral."

"I know what you mean. I would say that I feel worshipful in St. Peter's, but part of me wonders what causes the feeling. The awe I feel is almost more toward the church than toward God."

Mike's Reflections—January 2

When the Church is functioning as it should, it advances—as Jesus did—through bold sacrifices and selfless love. This was demonstrated so beautifully in the early church. Despite horrific persecution, their love and sacrifice shone brilliantly, even to those who sought to destroy them.

I remember a remarkable quote from the Roman emperor Julian, who led vicious attacks against the Church in the fourth century. Seeing the love of the Christians, he admitted in a letter, "[Christian faith] has been specially advanced through the loving service rendered to strangers, and through their care for the burial of the dead. It is a scandal that there is not a single [Christian] who is a beggar, and that the godless Galileans care not only for their own poor but for ours as well; while those who belong to us look in vain for the help that we should render them."

Compare the impact of this selfless service to the image presented by supposed representatives of Jesus in other times, when people who claimed to be followers of Jesus apparently attempted to accomplish their goals through power (as in the Crusades), coercion (the Inquisition), the awing effect of wealth and grandeur, or other of the world's tools.

This was never Jesus' way. He was ultimately victorious, but only through humbling Himself to the very point of death. He resisted the pressure to transform the world by becoming a political "King of the Jews." Instead, He changed the world by loving and apprenticing a few people. When the Church follows His example, transforming people through love, nothing could be more beautiful. When it does not, it often becomes absolutely despicable.

For lunch, we stopped by a small café, the proprietor taking delight in expounding the virtues of each type of pizza that lay on large, square pans behind his counter. We made our selections and took the slices outside. To stroll through Rome is like no other experience in the world. Unless a newcomer feels a desperate need to hit every "important" site, they are better off just to wander. Around every corner, a visitor will stumble upon ancient ruins, quiet piazzas, statue-covered bridges, marble fountains, or some little-known church that would be a major tourist site if located in any other city of the world.

"Eating pizza in Italy!" reveled Trey, a piece of tomato sauce glistening in his beard. "I'd say this is as good as it gets."

"The pizza is okay," replied Mike. "It's kind of ironic that pizza in Italy doesn't taste as good as American pizza."

"It's still pretty good."

Matt, a few paces ahead, stopped as he rounded the next corner. "Wow, guys, look at this." A circular structure hundreds of feet across loomed before us: the Coliseum.

The inside was like a football stadium. A stone wall surrounded the arena. Behind the wall rose hundreds of rows of stadium seats, enough to accommodate thousands of onlookers. During the height of the Roman Empire, Roman citizens could attend the daily events at the Coliseum for free. Often, the entertainment included gladiators—men trained to fight and kill for sport. Other times, animals were pitted against each other: bears against lions, elephants versus hippos. The arena could even be filled with water and mock naval battles waged.

Today, the floor of the arena is gone, and one can look directly down into the stalls where lions and other beasts were held before the events. Reportedly, the animals were kept near starvation so as to guarantee a blood-feast in the arena. We knew that many Christians faced martyrs' deaths in this place. During the worst years of persecution by the Roman emperors, even women and small children were turned out into the arena with the lions and other ravenous beasts. We took it in silently for a time before Trey spoke up.

"It must have been crazy down there under the arena, waiting to be brought up to the lions."

Matt nodded soberly. "I've read historical accounts of it. Christians would be down there in their cell, praying together, hearing the lions growling. Soldiers came and marched them up and out into the sand of the arena where the crowds made fun of them until the lions were set loose to devour them."

"And they knew that if they just denied Jesus, they would be spared," said Trey.

"You wonder how many Christians today could go through with it," commented Mike.

Jedd followed, "My faith gets a lot of strength from the stories of the early martyrs, especially the disciples. They knew Jesus. They were the ones claiming they'd seen Him risen from the dead. There is just no way they would have gone to such horrible deaths for something they just made up."

In college we had read the accounts of the disciples' deaths in *Foxe's Book of Martyrs*. All but one of them, history reports, were executed for their faith. Matthew was slain by the sword. Bartholomew was reportedly beaten to death with clubs. Peter, when led out to be crucified, asked that they crucify him upside down because he did not consider himself worthy to die in the same manner as his Lord. Andrew died over a period of three days, hung from an x-shaped cross. All except John faced similar deaths.

In every instance, the disciple endured the excruciating, life-ending pain without wavering from the claim that Jesus Christ was the Son of God, and that they had personally seen Him risen from the dead.

Jedd's Reflections—January 2

The lives of Jesus' disciples are an incredible evidence to me for the truth of Christian faith. Here was a group of rough and ragged young men. By their own accounts, they were immature, slow to learn, and often self-focused.

Then, wham! Something rocked their lives in such a way that they were transformed into passionate, selfless world-changers. They professed that they had been changed by a man who had risen from the dead, proving to them that He was Lord of all. They were even willing to die for this claim.

I know many people have died for their convictions, even for mistaken convictions. But these men weren't just "convinced" of things second-hand. They personally experienced the things they were claiming. Would they have accepted torture and death for something they knew was a lie? I find that hard to believe.

150

That night we boarded the train for Sicily. As we slept, it passed all the way to the tip of Italy's boot, then beyond, via ferry, to the island. For two days we explored the winding streets, hillsides, and coffee shops of Taormina, a small town set into a mountainside above the Mediterranean. Sapphire waters glimmered directly below us, while the fresh sort of sunlight one usually finds only in springtime poured down from above. In the distance, the volcano of Mount Etna puffed white clouds into the deep blue sky.

Three days after we left, the volcano blew, wreaking havoc on the Sicilian countryside and consuming some homes that had been built foolishly close to the cone. By that time, though, another train had carried us back to Rome where we had boarded Egypt Air flight 107, bound for Cairo.

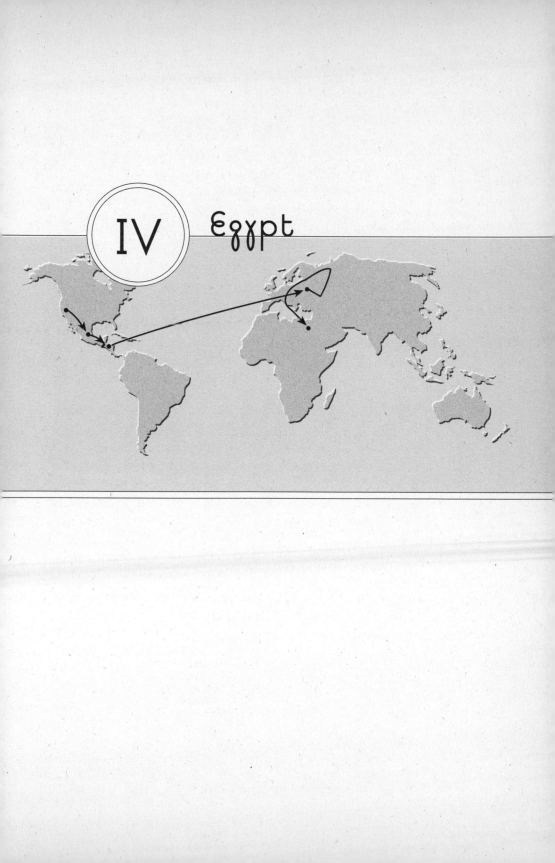

IV Egypt

With Professor Queloma in Cairo

twelve

Land of the Pharaohs

Cairo, Egypt

the world's airports are not incredibly different; some have more glass and carpet, others less. The people who fill them, however, vary greatly. In Cairo International, men in long robes with tangled beards shuffled by, their women never far from their side, often covered completely but for almond eyes peering out from a slit in their dark veils. Olive-skinned boys in loose white tunics had more freedom to explore; although, if they roamed too far, they were summoned back with a shout.

We took our place in one of several lengthy lines that led to passport control. By the speed we were moving, we knew it would be more than an hour before we were out of the airport.

"This is going to take a while," remarked Mike.

"We are pretty much the only non-Egyptians in here," Jedd noticed.

Trey replied, "It must be the shooting."

Just a few weeks before, a fundamentalist Muslim group had struck, gunning down two busloads of tourists in Egypt. Their goal was to force Egypt to become a fundamentalist state by cutting at the country's primary source of revenue: tourism. The murders seemed to have done the job, as there was hardly a handful of non-Arabs in the airport. With Egypt's economy so dependent upon tourism, we knew this would hurt everyone, from the richest businessman to the poorest beggar.

When our families read about the killings, they had hoped we would decide to cut Egypt from our itinerary. We were not sure it was the wisest thing to continue, either, but . . . well, we just wanted to go. "Besides," we decided, "the security will be so much tighter now; we will actually be *safer* than we would have been if no attack had ever happened." The makeup of the crowd around us suggested that few non-Egyptians shared our optimism.

"You sirs, you are American?" A young Arab in a dark suit stood before us. Matt looked at him suspiciously. "Yes. Why?"

"I am Habib. I work for the office of tourism. I am here to get you through this line."

"No thanks," replied Matt, shaking his head.

"No. I am not here for money. I am paid by office of tourism. I am just here to help you. It will be easy. Follow me."

We looked at one another as he headed off. "Have your passports ready," he said over his shoulder.

Mike shouldered his pack and set off after the young man. The other three exchanged looks. Trey shrugged his shoulders. "Why not?"

"Because maybe . . ." Matt trailed off as Jedd and Trey headed after Mike.

Habib led to an unused passport check on the far side of the room. A chain blocked the entrance to the metal detector, hung with a sign that read "Closed."

"Show this man your passports," Habib directed, indicating a security guard who stood nearby.

The man glanced at each document briefly, then nodded for us to proceed. He seemed to have no interest in x-raying our bags. Matt glanced back at the line in which we had been standing; it had hardly moved in the last ten minutes.

He was still not entirely convinced. "Are you sure . . ."

"Come now. You need a taxi?" asked Habib.

"That's all?" asked Trey, a puzzled expression on his face.

"That is all. You are in Egypt now. See? I told you it would be easy. We want to make things as simple as possible for tourist to enjoy Egypt." He waved to a barrel-chested man who had been squatting on his haunches on the sidewalk. "Elias? These young men need a taxi."

Along the Nile

An eerie wailing woke Trey from his slumber. The strange sound, something between a mournful prayer and a dying moan, echoed throughout the room. It seemed to be coming from everywhere. Trey rubbed his eyes and tried to remember where he was. It was still early, sometime before dawn. On the wall across from his bed hung a simple painting of an archer riding in a chariot. The wailing continued to reverberate.

Egypt. Everything fell into place. The wailing was the Muslim call to prayer, broadcast five times a day by loudspeaker throughout the towns and cities of Islamic nations all over the world.

We were staying at the apartment of a professor we had known at Westmont, Dr. Andrew Queloma, who now worked in Cairo. Trey got up and padded over to the window. A faint predawn glow hung over the quiet streets below. The air was already beginning to warm. It would be a hot one.

"Jedd. Wake up." Trey shook him again. "Jedd."

"Yeah, what?"

"Its about time to get up. Our ride out to the pyramids will be here to pick us up in forty-five minutes."

"Why are you waking me up now? I can sleep for another half-hour."

Trey moved out of the room. Jedd, unable to go back to sleep, pushed himself up with a faint scowl on his face. "What's he waking me up so early for?"

o o o

Small puffs of moistureless dust rose from each step as we hiked toward the pyramid's base. The sunlight was direct, sharp-edged. Russia's winter seemed a million miles away.

Trey, as usual, had his guidebook in hand. "Let's see here, guys. This Cheops pyramid was built around 2600 B.C. by some Pharaoh Khufu to serve as his burial chamber. It was originally covered by limestone, but over the years people took it off to use it for other things, so now what you see is this rough understone. Since they didn't have pulleys or cranes in ancient Egypt, archaeologists still are wondering exactly how they made it so high. This one is about 480 feet tall and as wide as two and a half football fields on every side."

Every step closer to the base gave us a greater appreciation for the pyramid's girth.

"Each one of those stone blocks is the size of a car," commented Jedd. "There's got to be thousands of them."

"Actually, over two million," corrected Trey.

Trey's Reflections—January 7

I feel a genuine sense of awe at the work of the ancient Egyptians. Their gigantic statues, the vastness of the pyramids, the intricate beauty of their artwork and jewelry, the craftsmanship of the Sphinx. I find it awe-inspiring. And to think that this very site has been viewed by Alexander the Great, Rommel the Desert Fox, General Patton, and countless greats . . .

It's all a tribute to man's genius and abilities. And yet, it is also a tribute to futility. These sites may be impressive, but the fact is that even if they last ten thousand years, man's greatest accomplishments will ultimately fade into dust.

Clash over Cash

Matt and Mike were paying little attention to Trey and Jedd. They were locked in a discussion of their own.

"I just don't feel right about spending the money that way," stated Matt flatly, shaking his head.

Mike kicked a dirt clod that lay in his path. It disappeared into a small cloud of fine dust. "I don't understand what the problem is. We are here in Egypt, we've been very careful with our money, and we're under budget . . ."

"I don't think we're under budget."

"Jedd just said we didn't spend all the money we had allotted for the last couple weeks."

"Well, whatever our budget is, it doesn't justify spending that much on one meal."

We had been offered tickets for a dinner cruise on the Nile that night at what was supposedly half the normal price. Mike was in favor of going. Matt viewed the expenditure as excessive. Jedd and Trey, usually quite vocal in a debate, had contributed little to the discussion thus far.

Jedd finally shared his mind. "Look, Mike, I'd really like to go on the cruise, too, and we are under budget, but it does seem it would be kind of extravagant. It is kind of hard to spend that much money when . . ."

"It is *not* that much money, especially for a dinner and an evening on the Nile! You guys don't make any sense. You know I'm not extravagant. Most of the time when we eat out, I spend less than anyone. I mean, man, Jedd, you eat more than me at every meal, but then when I want to do something special, you say it's extravagant."

Mike tossed the piece of foil he had been twisting on the ground and walked a few paces ahead.

"What do you think, Trey?" asked Matt.

"You know I'm usually a big spender," Trey replied with a hint of a smile, "but I kind of agree with you two on this one. I don't know if it would be the best use of money people donated to us."

Mike turned around. "All right. You guys don't think we should pay for this out of our general money? Fine. I'll pay for our dinner out of my own personal funds."

"Mike, you don't have to do—," protested Matt.

"No. I want to do this, and I think it would be stupid not to when we've got an opportunity like this. If we can't agree on paying for it together, then I'll pay."

Jedd suggested, "What if our group money pays for as much as a normal dinner would cost, and you could pick up the rest?"

Mike shrugged. "Whatever you feel comfortable with, but this is something I want to do."

Mike's Reflections—January 7

Sometimes it's pretty frustrating to hold our money in common. Deciding what to spend on and how much can be such a point of contention. Matt's so cheap, and Jedd thinks about it all way too much.

When I sit back and think about it, though, I guess I'm glad we're going through this together. For one thing, it is probably good preparation for marriage. Maybe even more important, Jesus spoke about the topic of money as much as about any other thing. I think He was referring to the importance of having a right perspective on money when He said, "If your eyes are good, your whole body will be full of light."

Holding the right view of money is so central to living the type of abundant life Jesus calls us to. I think that means living free from the entrapment of materialism, and generally avoiding extravagance so we can be generous with friends and share with the needy. At the same time, I believe God would want us to take occasion to freely enjoy His blessings at times. I think going on this Nile cruise would be doing just that.

Into the Mosque

Dr. Queloma led the way through a high, almond-shaped doorway into the mosque. The interior was cool and dark, a refreshing change from the late morning sunlight. At the entrance, we exchanged our shoes for slippers. The thick walls of clay suddenly quieted the constant blaring of horns—almost deafening on the streets. As we moved forward, the scuffing of our slippers on the stone floor echoed faintly in the silence.

In contrast to the churches in Europe, the mosque seemed stark. Smooth walls rose around us to a height of one hundred feet, but no paintings, statues, or stained-glass windows graced them. A pattern of geometric shapes in black and scarlet wrapped around the room at a height of about ten feet, the metal of the doors being worked with similar patterns. The only other adornment came from the immense woven rug set in the room's center. It could have covered a good-sized front lawn.

"Muslims take the second commandment very seriously," explained Dr. Queloma. "No likeness or any graven images allowed. Throughout the centuries, Islamic visual artists have channeled their creativity into this type of geometric pattern work and into remarkable forms of calligraphy."

"So no Muslim artists ever paint or do sculpture?" asked Matt.

"Well, some have found creative ways to get around it, but that is the general rule."

Dr. Queloma pointed to a small raised platform and podium. "Muslims hold their services on Fridays in mosques like this. That podium is where the imam speaks; it is always on the Mecca side of a room."

"Do they go to mosques whenever one of the calls to prayer comes over the loudspeakers?" asked Matt.

"You've noticed the call to prayer, huh?" said Dr. Queloma with a smile.

"It's hard to miss."

"They usually pray wherever they are at the time. Muslims don't have to be in a mosque to pray. The important thing is the direction their body is pointed: toward Mecca."

"That is one of the things Muslims do to earn salvation?"

"In a sense. There are actually five main requirements to pleasing Allah, called the five pillars of Islam. Prayer is one. Fasting is another. There is also almsgiving and the repetition of the basic creed, 'There is one God and Muhammad is his prophet.' The final pillar is pilgrimage: Every Muslim must travel to Mecca at least once during their lifetime."

"That's quite a list of requirements."

Dr. Queloma nodded. "It's a hefty load. And there is a lot more besides that if you really intend to be faithful. Muslims have a lot on their shoulders. Some do have a sense that no matter how good they are, they still need Allah's grace to be allowed to enter paradise. Even so, the underlying drive is that if you don't get pretty much everything right, you are going to be punished severely. There is definitely a lot of fear."

We passed out of the sanctuary into an open area surrounded by walls of dark clay several stories high. On the far side of the plaza, Dr. Queloma

159

Dr. Queloma's
Neighborhood
Grocer

mounted stairs that climbed to the top of the wall. A walkway six feet wide led along the top. Cairo spread out around us. Countless minarets and moon-topped domes poked up into the dingy, smoke-choked skyline. Honking and shouting drifted up from below, muted by the distance.

"Do you like living here, Dr. Queloma?" asked Matt.

"The first time I came here, I thought it was the last place I'd ever want to live. I still feel that way every once in a while. But other places seem kind of boring after Cairo. I love the amazing history of this place, and I really have come to appreciate the Egyptian people also."

"You have many Muslim friends?"

"Oh yes, quite a few."

"How do you feel about all that, I mean, what effect would you say that has on your faith?"

"I wouldn't say that I struggle with doubts at this point, if that is what you mean. A lot of the American students I teach here often do, though. Many of them have never lived outside of their culture. The whole environment is a shock for their system at first, and the more thoughtful ones wrestle with a lot of questions, especially in regards to their faith."

"What do you think causes that?" joined Mike.

"Growing up, they never fully understood that there are millions of people out there who see the world and God differently than they do, apparently just because they happened to be born in a different place. It is a shock for the students to realize that these people are just as devout and certain as they are."

"What do you say to these kids?"

"I usually try to give them as much freedom to work it out on their own as possible. If they want to talk about it, I'll share some of my thoughts."

"So what are your thoughts?" Trey probed.

Dr. Queloma laughed. "That's not the easiest question."

"I mean, after studying both Islam and Christianity as in depth as you have . . . what do you think?"

"Well, to be honest, as a historian, Islam really presents you with a lot of contradictions and problems. Christianity definitely leaves you with some questions as well, but an honest look tells you it has a very solid case on an intellectual level."

"What about differences in beliefs and stuff?"

"One thing I'd say that might bother some people is that Christianity and Islam have a lot more similarities than most people realize. Even so, though, there are some differences that deeply affect the core of belief."

"Like how we see Jesus?" questioned Jedd.

"That is the main thing. For the Christian, Jesus is everything. If it were proved that Jesus were not the Son of God, not who He claimed to be, then Christian faith would be empty and meaningless. For the Muslim, Jesus is only a great prophet, second to Muhammad."

"But Muslims do respect Jesus?"

"Oh yes, very much. At least, they do if they know their holy book. The Koran gives an amazing amount of honor to Jesus. It attributes a great number of miracles to Him, even while Muhammad never performed any, aside from receiving the Koran. The Koran even refers to Jesus as 'the one who sits near to God.'"

"Hmm." Matt nodded. "I never knew they viewed Him so highly."

Dr. Queloma continued, "The real foundational difference between the two faiths, though, is how God is viewed, the contrasting 'portraits of God.' For Christians, He is great and awe-inspiring, but also tender and loving. Love is His central attribute. He is seen as a gentle shepherd and even as a Father. This view of God is largely unknown to Muslims, who see Him as glorious and fearsome, but certainly not as a tender Father who desires to be intimate with His children."

Jedd's Reflections—January 8

Sometimes I simply take for granted the qualities that the God of the Bible uses to describe Himself. Growing up as an American Christian, the fact that "God is love" sometimes seems no more remarkable than the fact that the sky is blue.

But when you think about it, it really should shock us to think that this same God who could take burning stars in the palm of His hand and hurl them into the heavens also tenderly bends down to tell us that He loves us, and that He knows us and desires that we would seek to know Him. The pictures that God gives us of Himself—like that of a Father running out to hug His wayward child, or passages depicting Him doing things like "rejoicing over us with singing"—are almost scandalous.

Perhaps most astonishing of all is the fact that He would become a rag-clad baby, screaming in a manger.

After spending a good portion of the day in the Egyptian National Museum, we wandered the streets with little agenda, pulled into shops here and there by aggressive shopkeepers. The sun was fast becoming a bright orange blob as it dipped low in the smoggy sky. Trey kicked an empty can along the road before booting it toward the large mound of trash heaped against the building. It seemed that every street corner—with the exception of the nicest areas of Cairo—had at least a small pile of garbage. Dogs devoured what food scraps and small bones could be found in the refuse, but the less edible items, we guessed, were picked up periodically by garbage men of one sort or another.

"I'm enjoying the chances we have to talk with Dr. Queloma," remarked Mike.

"Definitely," affirmed Matt. "I thought it was fascinating what he and his friend at the office said yesterday about Muslims coming to faith in Jesus."

"I didn't catch that; I was in the other room."

"Basically, they told us about several different men and women who grew up Muslim and really wanted to seek God. A lot of these people had dreams or visions or something of Jesus coming to them, telling them that He actually was the Son of God, and these people put their faith in Him."

"That's interesting. I wish I wasn't such a skeptic, but deep down I always wonder about stories like that."

"I know what you mean, but it did sound like at least a few of these people were believable. There were even a couple of Muslim professors who had these visions. Dr. Queloma and his friends know some of these people personally. If nothing else, they at least experienced *something* that changed their lives."

 ## Mike's Reflections—January 8

Miraculous happenings and weird dreams and those sorts of things have always sent up red flags in my mind. Most of the times I have seen someone talking about them—like some of those so-called evangelist nuts on TV—they have seemed so transparently fake to me.

I know I can take my skepticism too far, though. The work of a few charlatans should not cause me to rule out the possibility of God choosing to work outside of what is considered "normal."

It is certainly not impossible that He would choose to reveal Himself to those who seek Him, whoever and wherever they are. Perhaps dreams *are one way of doing this. Even on a purely logi-cal level, I see little reason why the Muslims Dr. Queloma told Matt about would make up a story about a dream and then become Christians—they had little to gain and much to lose by making such a choice.*

A horse-drawn cart, laden with cucumbers and tomatoes, pulled out of the alleyway in front of us. An old man in a long white robe walked alongside the horse, occasionally snapping a cord to keep the lethargic animal moving. Along the sidewalk, as always, men and boys stood talking and sat at games we did not recognize.

Two overweight merchants lounged in front of a shop, smoking a water pipe. The men puffed on the thin hoses that led from the pipe, which sat on the ground between them, roughly the same size and shape as the base of a table lamp.

"You like to join us for a smoke?" invited one of the merchants.

"Ah yes, please join us," followed the other, gesturing wide with his arms.

Matt, having spotted Mike's "let's give it a try" grin, laughed and rolled his eyes. "Go for it if you want, Mike."

Mike stopped for a moment, admiring the pipe's craftsmanship.

Trey looked back at Matt and Mike. "Are you guys coming?"

The merchant took a small puff. "This pipe gives very good smoke. Please, sit down."

"I'd like to, but my friends don't want to wait," replied Mike.

The men nodded good-naturedly, and Matt and Mike jogged to catch up with Jedd and Trey.

"You don't see a lot of women on the streets around here," commented Jedd.

Trey agreed. "And Egypt is a lot freer than most Islamic countries. From what I've heard of many Muslim places, women are pretty much treated like cattle a lot of the time."

Jedd's Reflections—January 8

One serious strike against Muslim countries is their treatment of women. Females are often seen as little more than a piece of property, to be made use of for practical purposes and pleasure.

Even knowing that women have been mistreated in virtually all times and places throughout the world's history, some of the stories about the abuse of women that come from places like Iran or Taliban, Afghanistan, are still shocking: harems of women kept as sex slaves, the execution of women who enter public without covering their faces, legalized wife beating . . .

What a far cry from the words of the apostle Paul, "Husbands, love your wives, just as Christ loved the church and gave himself up for her . . ." [Eph. 5:25].

Being in a place like this, one sees how ignorant it is to view Paul as a "sexist" when he explains that God gave men the responsibility of leading in the home and the church. If anything, Paul was a radical. He affirmed a male role of leadership, but also championed women as possessing the same value as men. He commanded men to love and honor their wives and even to put their wives' needs above their own.

Some say Paul's words about the respective roles of men and women were only a reflection of the culture of his time. Nothing could be farther from the truth. Paul laid out a vision for male-female relationships that stood in sharp contrast to what had generally been the status quo of most cultures since the beginning of time. Paul was able to supersede culture because he was not looking to society and its norms for his source of truth, but to God's design in creation and to the value God places on each individual.

Especially considering the culture of his time—which bore many similarities to the culture in many Islamic countries today—Paul's message was nothing short of revolutionary.

A Coptic Witness

Halfway through our flight to South Africa, Jedd moved to the back of the plane to have a row of seats to himself. Matt and Mike dozed. Trey pored over a map of flight routes in the airline magazine.

Few Americans have a sense of the vast size of Africa. The distance from Egypt to South Africa is twice the distance between San Francisco and Washington, D.C.

"Would you like a beverage, sir?" a young, dark-haired steward asked softly.

Jedd glanced up from his journal. "Cranberry juice, please."

The man set an empty cup in front of Jedd and poured from a can. "How did you like Egypt?"

"I liked it a lot. You are Egyptian?"

"Yes. And you and the other young American men—you are traveling together?"

"Pretty obvious we're Americans, huh?" Jedd smiled. It usually was.

"What are you traveling for? Business?"

"Not really. We are visiting a number of countries in different parts of the world. We live and work with local Christians in each place we go."

"Then you are Christians?"

"Yes."

The young man glanced up and down the aisle. "I will come back. I need to serve drinks now, but after that, I would like to talk."

"Sure. Whenever you are free."

Thirty minutes later, the young man returned. "Is it all right if I sit here?"

"Sure, please do."

"I wanted to talk with you because I am a Christian, too."

"It's good to meet you. My name is Jedd."

"I am Orel Al Messiah. I am a Coptic Christian."

Dr. Queloma had told us a bit about the Coptic Church. Long before the start of Islam and prior even to the introduction of Christianity to much of Europe, Christian faith thrived in Egypt. Muslim armies conquered Egypt in A.D. 642 and have ruled ever since. The Coptic Church, however, has maintained its presence in Egypt even to the present day. Dr. Queloma informed us that like the Russian branch of the Eastern Orthodox Church, the Coptic Church was often more focused on tradition and ritual than on relationship with Christ. He also shared that even while they endured persecution from Muslims, some Coptic leaders worked against the growing number of evangelical churches in Egypt, seeing them as competition. Even so, many Coptic Christians, Dr. Queloma believed, were devoted to Jesus and His kingdom.

Jedd smiled at his new friend. "I'd really like to hear more about what it's like to be a Christian in Egypt, Orel."

For the next hour, Orel shared the challenges of seeking to follow Christ in Egypt. The picture he painted was quite different from that suggested by some of the Egyptians we had spoken with on the streets.

"A person is born either a Christian or a Muslim," he explained. "It is marked on your birth certificate and on all your identification papers. A born Christian will face persecution all his life—in education, in jobs, in finding a house . . ."

"Can a person change their religion?"

"A Christian can change to Muslim. There are rewards for doing so. But a Muslim who wants to become a Christian will fight battles. His papers will probably never be processed, and the government will make his life very hard for him in the meantime."

"What do you mean, 'hard for him'?"

"The government usually doesn't officially do violence to Christians, but the police or other government employees might do bad things to you. Just two weeks ago, the police were checking everyone's papers as they came out of my church. There was a man whose papers identified him as a Muslim. They made up a fake charge and put him in jail for a week."

"Is there any recourse in a case like that?"

"Not really. A few judges might try to make a fair ruling, but usually not. We feel helpless."

"And angry?"

"Sometimes I have a lot of anger toward the people who oppress and insult us over and over again."

"I can see why. Do you feel like you're able to love your enemies in the way Christ said to?"

"If we try to act loving to them, they think we are fools and just stomp on our backs even harder."

Jedd was silent for a moment. "I'm sorry, Orel. I honestly have never experienced anything that tough."

"Sometimes I think I would give anything to live in America. I have—"

A stewardess tapped Orel on the shoulder. He jumped slightly. "Orel? We need to prepare for dinner now."

"I'll be right there."

The young lady continued on toward the rear of the plane.

Orel offered his hand. "It has been good to talk with you, my brother."

"It has. I promise you, Orel, my friends and I will be praying for you, especially that the Lord will give you grace to love your enemies."

"We will meet again, although it may be in heaven."

"I look forward to that."

Jesus' command to "love your enemies" is pretty easy to follow when the closest thing to an "enemy" in your life is no more than a person who might make things a little difficult now and then. What if they could literally steal your chance for an education or ruin your career? Would I be able to keep that from gnawing at me all the time?

When push comes to shove, Christ's teachings in the Sermon on the Mount are the exact opposite of the American sense that "If someone messes with my rights, I'll make them sorry." Someone who is truly trying to follow Christ will never seek revenge or retaliation, or even harbor feelings of hatred, no matter how justified it might be. I know this must be incredibly hard in situations like Orel's.

Even so, I can see that those who live out the forgiveness, mercy, and grace that Jesus taught are the type of people I want to be. They are free, unburdened, and gracious in a way that the vengeful never can be. I pray that I might be that way, even if I face real persecution someday.

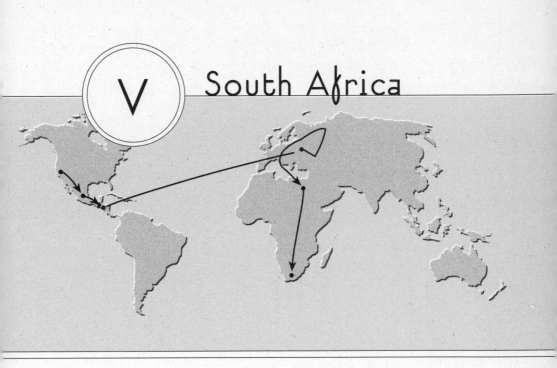

V South Africa

thirteen

Beauty and Strife

Abundance does not spread, famine does.
—Zulu saying

Pretoria, the capital of South Africa, sported gleaming office complexes, bright shopping malls, and landscaped acres surrounding corporate offices. The city, from the air, appeared surprisingly similar to an American metropolis.

As we deplaned into the airport, we waded into a sea of signs welcoming business travelers: "Coca-Cola—Mr. Hamm." "Kodak for Eric Smythe." One sign caught our eyes: "Four American Guys." The sign's bearer was Mr. Thys de Beer, a sober but kind South African with a mustache that wrapped down around his lips. A friend of Jedd's had met Thys during a business trip to South Africa. She had asked Thys to serve as host for a few days to four young men he had never met.

Within hours of our first meeting, Thys and his family had offered to wash our clothes, fix a hearty meal, and provide a room in their small home. They even gave us use of their new minivan so we could drive over to the Lesotho embassy to acquire Lesotho visas. Since Lesotho's airport had few direct international flights, we had flown into Pretoria instead and would catch a short connecting flight a few days later.

Jedd sat at the wheel of the minivan as we ventured into downtown Pretoria.

"Why don't you take a right here?" suggested Trey. "I think the Lesotho embassy is up either this street or the next."

"Jedd! The curb!!!" blurted Mike.

Jedd jerked the wheel and steadied the van in the middle of our lane. "Sorry," he offered, a bit irritated.

It was the second time he had nearly clipped the sidewalk. He was still getting used to driving on the "wrong" side of the road. As in all former British colonies, drivers in South Africa operate on the left side of the road with steering wheels on the right.

"Slow down," directed Trey. "I need to get a look at this street sign up here."

172

The green of a large park stretched off to our right. Tall buildings rose on our left, allowing only narrow slats of sunlight across the boulevard in front of us.

"What are those ladies up there so excited about?" asked Matt.

A group of six or seven middle-aged black African women were jumping up and down, waving and shouting on the sidewalk just ahead.

"Careful, Jedd," warned Trey. Two of the women—apparently not noticing our approach—had moved out into the street, still hopping and shouting. The group seemed to be cheering on an invisible marathon runner off to our left.

Traffic brought us to a near halt as we drew even with the women. Mike rolled down his window, but we could not make out anything they were shouting.

Suddenly, Trey caught something out of the corner of his eye.

"Oh my gosh. What the . . . ," he exclaimed.

He stared down the crossroad to our left. Question—perhaps fear—showed on his face. What looked like a river of ebony flooded toward us between the high-rises. It took a moment for our minds to put it into focus. Several hundred Africans were charging down the street in our direction, chanting, shouting, and smashing windows along the way. Many wielded traditional African weapons, mostly spears and short clublike instruments. A car alarm sounded as clubs crashed against a Range Rover that was parked along the avenue. It appeared that the street behind the rioters was littered with the glass of car and shop windows.

"Aye ya, aye ya, aye ya!" A rhythmic chanting boomed between the buildings and washed over us. The mob's nucleus seemed to bounce up and down in unison, matching the rhythm of the chant.

Traffic began to move forward, slowly. The cars whose drivers could see what was approaching were honking madly.

"We've got to get out of here," breathed Trey.

Two policemen seemed to come out of nowhere. They charged toward our vehicle, each bearing an unslung short-barreled shotgun.

"Go! Go!" one shouted. "Get moving!"

The officer nearest us yelled as he waved his free arm, swinging it in a full circle, desperately signaling us to move

"Hit it!" cried Trey.

Jedd did not need prodding. The minivan lurched forward into the open right lane, narrowly missing one of the ladies who was still cheering on the mob. *Whappp!* She slapped the van as we drove past. Trey glanced back to see the policemen running into the park, shouting and motioning to a pair of afternoon joggers. Two blocks up the road, Jedd took a fast right turn, wheels chirping. Trey caught a glimpse of the mob's front runners reaching the place we had been. Past the next stoplight, Jedd slowed and began to pull up along the curve.

"Let's keep going. I don't think we're far enough away to stop," said Matt.

"What the heck was that?" exclaimed Mike.

"Some kind of riot," said Trey.

Jedd shook his head. "I hardly had a clue what was happening at first. I thought those policemen were going to commandeer our car or something."

Trey's Reflections—January 10

That riot seemed so strange, so out of place. The city appeared every bit as "normal" and modern as the financial district of San Francisco or Chicago. We looked down a street, expecting nothing but businesspeople in suits, but instead encountered a sea of rioters raising spears and smashing windows. What a bizarre thing to witness!

"We call those kind of riots 'toi tois,'" explained Thys de Beer later that night as we sat around his living room with cups of African "bush" tea. "You were very fortunate to escape as you did. At the very least they would have destroyed the car."

"You boys are getting a pretty good dose of South Africa on your first day here," remarked Dierdre, Thys's wife.

"Do these toi tois happen often?" asked Mike.

"Pretty frequently," replied Thys. "Any time the blacks are unhappy with something—you know: wages, rent, some perceived unfairness in government—they go on a toi tois; smashing windows, burning cars, sending people to the hospital . . ."

"Aren't things better now that apartheid is over?"

"No," said Thys flatly.

"It depends on who you talk to," explained Dierdre. "For South African whites, definitely not. There is crime everywhere, the schools are terrible, businesses are closing, and our money is hardly worth half of what it used to . . ."

"But for the blacks?"

"Things are better in some ways. They are much freer and can vote and such. The terrible things done to them by the government under apartheid have been abolished. But they expected everything to suddenly become perfect when apartheid ended. Of course, it's not. In fact, even for blacks, some things have become worse. Frustrated expectation creates the anger . . ."

Thys cut in, apparently feeling a bit of anger himself. "I'm not saying apartheid was good. We never liked it and it needed to end, but basically, our country is going to hell now."

Matt spoke up. "I've heard a lot of whites are leaving the country."

Thys nodded. The flash of anger passed from his face as quickly as it had appeared. He seemed to settle back into the resignation of one who has given up hope that what he has lost will ever be recovered.

"That's true, just about anyone who can afford it is leaving, mostly to Australia and America. This isn't because they want to go. Our ancestors have lived here for four hundred years. But it's getting too scary to stay. Just look at the print." He lifted a newspaper from the coffee table and held it up for emphasis. "Every day you read about a half-dozen carjackings happening right down the street. They just jump out when you are at a stop sign, put a gun in your face, and take your car, sometimes in broad daylight. It happened to me once. I was lucky, though. Half the time they'll just kill you."

Matt's Reflections—January 10

It is hard to know what to think about the whites of South Africa. I know that many people condemn them for the apartheid system they lived with for so long. When I see the miserable situation they now face, my first thought is that they deserve it after allowing all the evils of apartheid.

I still cannot help but feel sorry for them, though. Their ancestors have lived in this land much longer than mine have lived in America, and now they see the social and economic stability of their country falling apart. Going through that would be hard for anyone.

175

A deeper investigation of South Africa would have to wait. Before the trip began, we had purchased a flight from Pretoria to the Kingdom of the Lesotho, allowing for only a brief stay with the de Beers.

"Anytime you guys are in town, you're welcome to stay with us," Thys said warmly as he dropped us off at the airport. He meant it.

fourteen

The Mountain Kingdom
Maseru, Kingdom of the Lesotho

Set amid the African plains, the Maseru airport consisted of little more than a small terminal and a pair of runways. With the twenty or so passengers who had packed into our small aircraft, we made our way across the dusty concrete toward the terminal. The building was nearly empty save for two uniformed attendants, a green-clad man with a machine gun, and the few small circles of welcomers that had swallowed our fellow travelers.

"You're sure they knew when we were coming, Trey?" questioned Matt.

"I think so. I even called the guy who directs a couple different schools here when we were in Russia to firm everything up. But you can never quite be sure. I'll tell you—the semester I spent in Zimbabwe, I never knew exactly whether someone understood me just right. If no one comes in half an hour . . ."

A deep voice broke into Trey's reply—"Brothers?" Several people turned to look at the thickly built African who had just entered the room. He did not wait for a reply but strode directly toward us. The fact that we were the only whites in the building apparently made him certain we were indeed the appropriate "brothers."

"I am Samuel!" He beamed as he drew near, wrapping each of us in a hug that left us short of breath. The man appeared to be thirty or thirty-five, clad in a bright red shirt. His skin was so dark it seemed to swallow the light around him. Though a beret tilted across his wide forehead, the almost silly nature of the fellow's grin told us he was no soldier.

He held Matt at arm's length. "You were afraid I would not come? Yes, I see it in your face." His laughter boomed around the room. "We would not forget you. I've been thinking about you all day. Here, let me take that bag."

As far as we knew, he would be taking us to the nearby city of Maseru. From there, we would head deep into the mountains, where for the next several weeks we would teach various classes for the junior high students at an African-run mission station. We had not traveled far in the truck Samuel had brought when we noticed a series of steep plateaus—several hundred yards high—rising out of the plain.

"Where'd those come from?" questioned Matt. "Everything around the airport looked totally flat."

"Most of Lesotho is hills and mountains. That is why they call us 'the Mountain Kingdom,'" said Samuel. "You'll see."

The plateaus grew larger and closer together as the city neared. Groupings of homes began to appear between them, sometimes springing up between the cliffs. Most of the cement-block buildings were roofed with tin or corrugated metal. Unlike suburbs in the United States, the neighborhoods were not quiet and lonely in the middle of the day. Men and boys leaned against fences or sat in the shade of trees. Women went about daily chores, hanging laundry or shucking corn with small children playing at their feet. The dress was mostly Western, although no women wore pants—only loose cotton dresses. Our road continued on into the central part of Maseru. It had only a few main avenues—just two lanes each, lined with shops and markets. Despite a population said to be several hundred thousand, it did not feel very citylike. Rocky hills, draped in a tenuous green, rose as a backdrop on every side.

∘ ∘ ∘

"What is this place?" inquired Matt, shutting the door of the truck behind him. A collection of buildings—some wood, some cement—surrounded the grassy field where Samuel had parked.

"The Masuru Bible College," answered Samuel. "It's where Christian pastors are trained. The director is hoping you'll be able to do a lot of repairs on the buildings while you're here."

"So . . . we'll be working here for the next few weeks, Samuel?" asked Jedd.

Samuel nodded. "Your coming is perfect timing. It is vacation time, so the Bible college students are gone. You can stay in the dorm."

Jedd shot a questioning glance at Trey. "I thought . . ."

Trey shrugged. "So did I."

A short while later, we were situating ourselves in one of the dorms. "Not a bad setup here," said Mike, throwing himself down on a bare mattress.

The dorms were simple—three large rooms with cement floors, white walls, and metal bunks; perhaps more like military barracks than anything else. Matt was already busy putting up a mosquito net around the bed he had chosen.

We had just finished a brief meeting with the director, who asked if we would be willing to spend our time in Lesotho making repairs on some of the college's buildings. He mentioned the mountain mission station only as a place we might want to visit for a relaxing weekend.

Mike sat on the edge of his bunk. "It's kind of weird that the director had told you we'd be teaching classes to junior high kids up in the mountains."

"He probably just didn't think about what time of year it was," responded Trey. "There's no point in asking about it now. All the students in the country are on vacation. I'm glad we'll be of use around here at least."

Mike laced his fingers behind his head and leaned back. "If we're able to finish those projects he wants done, maybe we could do that little retreat idea."

"What do you mean?"

"Remember a while back Jedd had the idea of doing some kind of little retreat. We could do that up at the mission station. I was actually thinking it might be pretty neat if we spent a few days fasting."

Jedd's voice came from another room. "*I* didn't suggest fasting."

"We don't have to," replied Mike, "but I think it could be a really good experience."

Jedd entered the room, mosquito net in hand. "I hate this net I have. You guys have those great hanging nets. This little wire thingy is supposed to arc around my head, but it's too small. The net always ends up in my mouth after I fall asleep." He dropped the mesh onto an empty bed and sat down next to Mike. "So how long do you want to fast?"

"I was thinking three days."

"You've got a little more stored energy than I do, Mike," Jedd gibed, patting Mike's belly. "I'd pass out on day two."

"I'd be willing to give the fast a try," said Matt seriously.

"What about you, Trey?" asked Mike.

"Yeah, I'd be up for it."

"Well, I'll fast if you guys are going to," said Jedd, "but, to be honest, I don't feel like I'd know *why* I'm doing it. I know fasting's been important to a lot of Christians in history, but I also know a lot of people did it for the wrong reasons. I'd just like a clearer sense of why it's supposedly valuable."

"Maybe you won't know 'til you do it," said Mike. "Not that I claim to be an expert. I haven't done it very much myself. But the few times I have, it really has helped me to direct my thoughts to interacting with God, praying, and listening to Him."

"Well, let's see what happens with work here. I don't want to be a naysayer, but I never feel great when I miss even one meal, let alone three days' worth."

Mike laughed. "We'll see what happens . . ."

Cows, Women, and Song

"I need another nail, Mike," requested Matt.

Mike lifted his head and spoke through clinched teeth. "I can't let go of this board. Can you grab one out of my mouth?"

Matt reached down from his perch on the roof and picked out one of the nails Mike held between his lips. The two had been working with Samuel for several hours to replace rotting boards on the eaves of the dining hall. Samuel and Mike held the new two-by-eight in place while Matt set a nail and began to pound. It was still quite hot out, despite the fact that the sun had begun to sink into the trees at the far end of the seminary grounds. Mike's face and forearms glowed a sunburned red. Matt, always diligent in the application of sunblock, merely sweated. A large, salty bead dripped from the tip of his nose and fell directly into Mike's eye.

Samuel, Mike, and Trey Repair a Roof

"Dang, Matt! Watch it," he grunted.

"Sorry."

Samuel stood and arched his back. "You can sure get sore doing this." He pointed to a swath of pasture across the road.

"See those guys?"

"What guys? Those cows?" questioned Mike.

"I had to pay thirteen of them for my wife."

"Who'd you pay?"

"Her parents, of course."

"Does every guy have to pay cows for his wife?"

"Yes, it is the tradition."

"What if you don't have cows?"

"You can pay the amount they're worth in cash, but you always bargain with the parents in cows."

"So is thirteen cows pretty standard?" asked Matt.

"No. Not many women require *thirteen* cows. The average is around eight, I think." Samuel spoke extra matter-of-factly, trying to hide his pride.

"How do you know how many cows a wife is worth?"

"There are many factors: beauty, reputation, skin color . . . things like that. Education, too—if she is more educated, she is worth more cows."

"What if you can't afford the number of cows she costs—can you get your wife on credit?"

Samuel did not catch the hint of joking in Mike's voice. He answered, "Almost no young men have enough wealth to pay for their wife when they get married. Almost all have to use credit. Sometimes you owe your parents-in-law for the rest of your life. I know men who work in the mines in South Africa eight months at a time for years just so they can pay off their cow debt."

"So do you still owe cows?"

"I've paid off nine cows, but I still owe four."

Matt interjected, "So, Mike, how many cows do you think Brittney's parents are going to want for her?"

180

Mike smiled. "Probably a lot more than I have."

Around the corner, Trey and Jedd continued to scrape paint from the side of the dormitory. It peeled off in small white flakes, cascading into their hair and sliding down their shirts. They looked like they had just come out of a snowstorm.

"Do you know what we're planning to do the next few days?" asked Jedd.

"We'll be going to church tomorrow and then maybe sometime next week we'll have a chance to head up to the mission station."

"Are you still thinking of trying Mike's idea of a three-day fast up there?"

"I'd like to try. Have you decided whether or not you will?"

Jedd shrugged. "Like I said before, I will if you guys want to. I wouldn't say I'm excited about it, but I do have this feeling that it could be really good for us."

Trey teased, "So you aren't going to wait to fast until you figure out exactly how it works?"

"You know I overanalyze sometimes," Jedd replied with a smile. "And I would like to understand fasting perfectly before I did it, but, like Mike said the other day, it probably doesn't work that way. We can talk about fasting all we want, but I probably would never begin to understand its value until I actually do it."

○ ○ ○

Sunday morning the four of us and a local man ventured out to a residential area outside of Maseru. We made our way through the cement-block homes, ducking clotheslines, stepping around loose chickens and small children. The metal-roofed church was nearly empty when we arrived. For the first half-hour of the service, church members filed in, joining the singing as they made their way to an open bench. Now the church was packed.

Matt's eyes were closed. The sound washed over him and swirled around in his head. There were no musical instruments, just voices. Rich, deep sounds of men; altos and tenors from the women; even the unripe tones of children—all blending, weaving together in what seemed to be perfect harmony. He could almost *feel* it.

Trey whispered, "It's like we get to sit in the middle of the Brooklyn Tabernacle Choir."

"Better," Matt replied without opening his eyes.

The women were dressed in their finest—brightly colored dresses of rough cotton, matching scarves or ribbons adorning their hair. The men and boys wore plain Western attire—slacks and a shirt, sometimes a tie. Everyone sang, clapped, swayed; many even danced.

Mike noticed Jedd shaking his hips as he sang. "Nice moves," he gibed.

Jedd shrugged and smiled. "I got a little groove. Go for it, Mike."

Mike, a lopsided grin on his face, shimmied back and forth as he turned a full circle.

"Not bad for a beach bum, not bad at all." Jedd laughed.

The song ended. Clapping and praises in the African tongue filled in for a moment; slowly the room quieted, growing almost silent before a strong female voice rose up. "Ahhhhyyyahhhh . . ." One by one, the entire congregation joined in the song as if guided by a masterful director. The individual voices, each so different, melded together perfectly, layer upon layer.

It was nearly an hour and a half into the service when Jedd was asked to come to the front to deliver his sermon.

"Why is it that we were created?" he started.

The woman translating for him seemed to have a perfect grasp of both English and the local language; she began before Jedd had finished his sentence and matched his tone and emphasis exactly.

"We were created to walk in relationship with our Maker . . ."

An "uh-huh" sounded from the congregation, along with two "Amens." Jedd paused for a moment, a bit surprised. He continued, "When Jesus was asked what commandment was the greatest, His reply left no room for doubt. Our purpose on earth comes down to two simple responsibilities: love God with everything that is in us, and love our neighbors as ourselves . . ."

Several more "Amens" erupted from the crowd. Jedd grew a bit more animated.

". . . First Corinthians 13 tells us we could do every good deed in the world . . ."

"Uh-huh."

"We could give every cent we have to the poor . . ."

A Lesotho Village

"Amen."

"We could even give our body to be burned . . ."

"Yes, yes."

"But if we are not motivated by love for God, if we have no love for those we are serving, if it is just a religious exercise or a noble gesture . . ."

"Uh-huh!"

"Then it is all worth absolutely nothing!"

"Amen! Amen!"

Twenty minutes later, Jedd was glowing as he made his way back to his seat.

"Good job," whispered Trey. "Man, you were sure getting into it."

Jedd smiled. "I couldn't help it. When they're telling you to preach it, you've just got to preach it."

More singing began, followed by announcements; more singing, then another sermon. This one lasted a good forty-five minutes, then more singing.

183

Mike's Reflections—January 18

I could hardly believe how long the church service today was. Between all the speaking, praying, and singing, it went well over three hours. As strange as it sounds, the man we were with said that this service was a short one.

I did find it all interesting, and I absolutely loved the singing, but I have to admit that I was getting tired of it all by the end.

I guess they just have a very different view of church—and of time in general—than we do. We sometimes see church services as little more than something we "need to do." We arrive, say a few hellos, work through our songs, sermon, offering, and announcements, and then get out.

Church in places like this is seen as the highlight of the week . . . not only spiritually, but socially as well.

If I'm honest, I know the reason I see a three-hour service as unbearably long is nothing but my expectations and attitude. After all, I have no problem watching a three-hour movie.

I wouldn't say I admire everything about the church in Lesotho, but I wish the church at home (myself included) could come to see Sunday mornings together more as a happy, highlight-of-the-week type thing as they do.

Cultural Shocker

We were on our way back to Maseru when Matt pointed and asked, "What's going on over there?"

A dozen or so women hopped and spun in a tight circle, wearing only grass skirts; their chests, arms, legs, and faces were painted white. Neighbors gathered around, cheering on the participants.

"Looks like some kind of ceremony or something," responded Trey.

"Oh . . . it's a female circumcision ceremony," the driver of our truck explained.

Mike grimaced. "Is that common?"

"It is less common now than it used to be, but many still do it. Among some people here, a girl is still not considered marry-able until she's been circumcised."

The women forming the circle chanted loudly. Hands on knees, they faced the middle and bounced together in a circular motion.

"A lot of Western groups have worked in Africa to try to stop female circumcision, haven't they?" questioned Matt.

Our driver nodded. "They have, but old cultural traditions aren't easily changed. A girl will spend six weeks at a special camp in the mountains where they'll perform the actual circumcision. The tribal rites are celebrated upon the girl's return."

"It is interesting that Western groups are trying to change aspects of local culture like that," stated Mike.

Trey glanced over at him, surprised. "Why? You think female circumcision is okay?"

"Absolutely not. Female circumcision is despicable. It puts women through excruciating pain and robs them of pleasure God meant for them to have. What I'm saying is that some of those Western groups that generally embrace moral relativism are being somewhat hypocritical when they come over here and try to change the culture."

"I'm still not following you."

"See, because I believe there is an absolute right and wrong, I have no problem with trying to change another culture if it has practices I believe are inherently wrong. The Bible says a man is to love his wife and serve her, not dominate her and reduce her to a tool for pleasure. If a culture promotes things contrary to this, it is morally right to change it. The ironic thing is that a lot of the people in these international organizations from the West claim there is no absolute truth, no ultimate standard of right or wrong—only the standards of each culture."

"That is true," responded Trey. "I sure saw that during the semester I spent studying in Zimbabwe. A lot of the vocal international-activist types totally write off Christian morality and basically argue no one should push their morality on anyone else."

"Exactly," said Mike. "Then they turn around and condemn practices in other countries like child labor and female circumcision."

Mike's Reflections—January 18

Many people today—especially in Hollywood and on college campuses—are constantly working to destroy the idea of an absolute right and wrong.

I find it so ironic when many of these same people end up in crusades for "human rights" or other causes around the world.

As a Christian, I believe I have a right—actually, a DUTY—to battle against injustices like female circumcision, slavery, or wife abuse anywhere in the world. This is because I am convinced that there are absolutes that are higher than any cultural norms or traditions.

But where do those who believe there are no absolutes find any "right" to try to change other cultures? They claim morality is just a matter of preference. If that is true, then an American has no right to interfere with the culture in another country, no matter how much his own "preferences" tell him otherwise. If there are no absolutes, no culture has any basis for judging any other culture.

Three Days without Food

A red-hued boulder shaded Matt from the late morning sun. The day was already a scorcher, and the cool surface of the rock felt good against his back. Today, we had begun our time of fasting, halfway up the side of one of Lesotho's larger mountains at the Mount Tabor mission station. With only one African man and his family currently residing at the station, the mission station itself would have provided sufficient solitude. Even so, we decided to seek the added seclusion higher up, near the top of the mountain. Water, sleeping bags, Bibles, and journals were all we needed for the three-day excursion.

Matt glanced out over the expanse that stretched out before him. From this vantage point, the massive plateaus and deep river gorges below seemed to be all at the same level. Nothing in the scene seemed to move except for a small cluster of clouds on the distant horizon that slowly dragged its sheet of rain across the plane. It seemed to Matt that he had not felt this at peace for months. He picked up his journal and began to write.

Matt's Reflections—January 22

Ordinary life, especially in America, is so full of noise. Almost every waking hour is flooded with frantic busyness. At work, we move from one task to the next to the next. Then we go home and work madly at our to-do list. Whenever we find a "free" hour, we gorge ourselves on entertainment and distraction: CDs, TV, movies, the Internet, phone calls, e-mails . . . There is rarely a silent moment.

If God wants to speak to us with a "still, small voice," it seems unlikely that we would be able to hear anything. Listening to what God has to say in the context of our normal lives is like trying to have a conversation with someone in the front row of a U2 concert. In order to really hear what our Creator has to say to us, our mind and body must be still and silent for more than just a few minutes at a time.

I hope that during this time up here we can really quiet ourselves. If we discipline ourselves to be truly quiet and to listen, most likely we will hear things God has been trying to communicate to us for quite some time.

A meadow opened on the mountainside just below Matt. Jedd and Trey sat together on the grass, drawing to the end a conversation they had begun earlier. There had been a good deal of friction between them for the past several weeks, and both wanted to set things right before seeking God in prayer.

"I'm glad we've been able to talk through all this," said Jedd. "The way things have been has frustrated me so much. It seemed like there was constant on-and-off friction beneath the surface."

Trey nodded. "It's weird how we work through smaller, day-to-day issues during reconciliation each night, but we never really talked about some of these bigger things that go back so far."

"Yeah. Like the birthday thing from junior year. I really appreciate that you brought it up this morning."

"Well, I never said anything before because I felt stupid for carrying around resentment about something like that. I mean, worrying about someone forgetting your birthday? That's a girl thing to do."

Jedd Talks with Basotho Shepherd Boys

"I'm glad you told me, Trey, and seriously, I don't think it was a small thing. You put together that incredible surprise party for my birthday that year, and then when your birthday came I forgot it . . ."

187

Trey's Reflections—January 22

The reconciliation time with Jedd this morning was really good. I know we both are committed to each other, but recently there's been a lot of silly little conflicts.

We talked through a few issues that should have been dealt with years ago. I also shared some things about my family situation that I hadn't told anyone about before. I don't want to use it as an excuse for being short-tempered, but I know that thinking about my parents getting a divorce puts me on edge. Jedd has been worrying about his mom's cancer, too. Her chemotherapy is going fine, but I know it's hard for him to be so far away from her at this time.

More than these challenges, though, I think the root of the friction we sometimes have is just that we are both strong-willed guys who still have a lot of selfishness. That is something that would still be there even if circumstances were perfect. The change of heart we need can't occur through our own strength; rather, God must make it happen over time as we stay connected to Jesus. God's work in me will enable me to always believe the best, hope the best, and to strive toward being the tender-hearted man I want to be.

For now, it is just so refreshing to come to God knowing that things are right between Jedd and I. I know I can never truly draw near to God if I'm harboring bitterness or irritation.

The stars took over the sky even before darkness set in. We had only one small flashlight, so as the last shades of red drained from the sky we began setting out our sleeping bags and preparing for bed. Soon we lay on our backs, four in a row, watching the stars grow more and more brilliant.

"I don't think I've ever seen 'em so bright," Matt remarked.

"Me neither," seconded Jedd. "The African sky is amazing. All day long I've been watching the colors and the clouds and the shadows they cast on the ground below. It's unlike anything I've seen before."

By now the darkness was nearly complete. No clouds obscured the sky above, but there seemed to be a storm moving across the horizon. Tiny jags of lightning—appearing no more than a few inches long—streaked between distant thunderheads and the nocturnal plane. We leaned on our elbows for several minutes, watching the show.

Mike's Reflections—January 22

I've been thinking today that deep down I have been overly critical of the culture here. I can't say there aren't some good reasons for that. There are the customs, like female circumcision, that seem so cruel to me. I also haven't noticed a very strong work ethic, and I think I'd go crazy trying to interact with the locals if I lived here permanently.

But I am beginning to see that there are some really beautiful things as well. Most of all, the great sense of community that most of the people here seem to have. There is also the genu-ine, expressive warmth and friendliness that seems to pour out of many of them. The men can even hold hands; friends wave to each other with abandon. They can laugh and talk so loudly. Their music is so beautiful, and I love the way they give themselves to it, moving and dancing.

And now I am falling more and more in love with the beauty of this land as well—the vast planes and substantial sky. Africa truly is a remarkable place.

"Did you hear that?" asked Trey, poking his head out of his sleeping bag.

Jedd was already drifting off. "What?"

"That sound. Kind of a rumbling, like thunder."

Matt rolled onto his belly and peered in the direction in which we had seen the lightning. "I think that storm might be getting a little closer. I hope it doesn't hit us."

"I don't think it will," said Mike. "I watched a storm moving across the planes all day. It never came near. The wind isn't moving in this direction."

Two hours later, though, we had to conclude that the storm was getting closer. The faint rumbling Trey had noticed was indeed thunder, and it was growing noticeably louder.

"The wind is sure starting to pick up," remarked Jedd.

"The time between each lightning flash and its thunder is getting a lot shorter," Matt observed. "A couple minutes ago I counted fourteen seconds and on the last one I counted twelve."

"You guys think we should try to head down to the mission station?" questioned Mike.

"As much as I'd like to stay, it probably wouldn't be smart to be up on a mountainside in a lightning storm," Trey admitted, disappointment in his voice.

"I think we'd better get moving right away," said Matt. "It is going to be hard enough getting down the mountain with only one flashlight."

We worked as quickly as we could in the darkness, rolling up our sleeping bags and returning our belongings to our packs.

"Man, that gust just about blew me off . . ." Trey was silenced as lightning washed the mountainside in phosphorescent light. Thunder boomed only a moment later.

Matt raised his voice to be heard above the wind. "Let's get moving. Lightning is gonna be hitting this mountain *soon!*"

We moved in line, trying to stick as close together as possible. As clouds obscured the stars, near total blackness enveloped us. Matt's Mini Maglite helped little, illuminating only a small patch of ground around his feet. It was almost easier to work from lightning flash to lightning flash. The wind had become a near gale when the first raindrops began to fall—fat, hard-hitting drops. The frequent flashes revealed a strange world of boulders, twisting trees, and bushes—everything a milky blue.

"Shoot!" cried Mike. He had slipped over a small ledge and tumbled several feet.

"You okay, Mike?" yelled Trey.

A flash provided a glimpse of Mike—on his knees, peering at his elbow. "Yeah, fine. Just scraped my elbow."

"Does anyone know if we are moving in the right direction?" questioned Matt.

We knew we would not see the mission station until we stumbled directly upon it. Its electric lights operated on a generator that shut off at 9:00 P.M.

"I think we've got to head a little more to the left," said Trey.

"I had thought more to the right," said Mike. "But I'd trust Trey more than myself in . . ."

Mike's words were erased as a blaze of white light arrived simultaneous with a bone-jarring crash.

"Man! That one rattled my head!" yelled Trey.

"It must have hit just a few hundred yards up," said Matt.

We moved to the left and a short while later found ourselves in a grove of leafy trees. The wind whipped us with the wet branches as we pushed through, but the covering provided shelter from the driving rain.

"If these are the trees I think they are, the station is just a little ways down that way," predicted Trey.

As we emerged from the grove, Matt's flashlight illuminated what appeared to be a trail. We had not been on it for more than a minute when another lightning strike on the mountain above lit up the scene before us. The mission station and surrounding buildings stood not more than a hundred yards away.

"I'm glad to see that place," declared Matt.

The ground flattened out, and we moved toward the station's front door quickly. We were almost to the front steps when an explosion of angry canine growling sounded just to our left. Jedd, who had been in front, jumped back into Mike.

Matt flashed his light in the direction of the sound. Two large German shepherds, teeth bared, snarled at us from the porch. With eyes reflecting green, they began to bark loudly.

We started to back away . . . slowly, carefully. One dog began to follow, but as he reached the steps his chain went tight.

"That scared the heck out of me," breathed Jedd.

"I don't think we'll be getting in through the front door," remarked Trey dryly.

We moved along the outside of the building, shielded partially from the rain by the eaves. The side door was locked and several minutes of knocking produced no result.

Mike stroked his chin, squeezing raindrops out of his beard. "It is going to be a long night if we have to spend it out here."

"You know," said Trey, "I think I may have left the window open in the room I slept in last night."

We followed Trey around another corner to a small window. He pushed on it, but it did not yield.

"Give me a hand here; I think it's loose."

With Matt and Trey lifting together, the window slid open. Trey was soon inside.

"I'll come around and open the side door."

In a moment we were sitting on beds in Matt and Mike's dark, dry room.

"Well, that was an adventure," stated Matt, peeling off his soaked shirt.

"And still two days of the fast to go," followed Trey with a grin.

o o o

Jedd's Reflections—January 24

The fast is just about over. It's the longest I've ever gone without eating, but I feel so full of joy and contentment. I feel like I still don't totally understand fasting, or all the reasons for it, but I do have a deep sense that it is valuable and important. The last three days have been an incredibly rich time of growth with the guys and nearness to the Lord. I put together a little list of some of the benefits I see:

—Fasting reminds us of our frailty. I often see myself as competent, strong, and self-sufficient. Yet one day without food and I already begin to lose my strength. In this, fasting is especially important for prideful young men. It gives an inescapable sense of how fleeting our strength is and how dependent we are upon God's provision.

—Fasting gives us greater compassion for the hungry and also helps us appreciate the blessing of food and eating.

—Fasting frees the time that would have been spent eating or preparing meals for prayer, and hunger throughout the day can serve as a reminder to pray.

—Fasting causes us to depend on God for energy and helps us to see how His strength is "made perfect in weakness."

—Fasting can be an act of sacrifice and devotion. If it is done with the right spirit, God will bless it. Also, any time you sacrifice for something, you become more committed to it.

—Fasting helps us gain discipline and control over human desire. We learn that as nice as it is to get our meals when we want them, we can go without them.

Even more than these things, though, I think fasting may be mainly about listening. It is a time to quiet ourselves and focus on God. It allows us to hear what He desires to say (and most likely has been wanting to say for quite some time).

I think maybe God has been providing some guidance about the future, too. I'm so excited about the thought of living with the guys next year. We're even toying with the idea of writing a book about the trip together. Doing something like that definitely seems beyond us, but that is part of the beauty of it: If it is going to happen, God is going to have to be the one to bring it about.

For my part, I'm just thrilled to get to be going along for such an incredible ride.

The Road to Durban

dozens of vans were parked at the Lesotho–South Africa border where a dusty lot served as the transportation station. A man in a hole-pocked T-shirt moved between the vehicles, shouting orders at drivers and directing riders to the appropriate vans.

"You're still sure you want to do this?" questioned Samuel.

"Yes, Samuel, we do," Trey assured, a bit more forcefully than the previous three times Samuel asked.

"If you want, we could go back to the airport and see if they have a flight to Johannesburg today," he said.

"Look, Samuel, you told us yourself you thought it was safe during the daytime. Have you heard stories of whites being robbed in the taxis or something?"

"No," replied Samuel with a half-grin, "I've never heard of whites riding the black taxis at all!"

The vehicles Samuel referred to as "black taxis" were not actually taxis, but the minivans that serve as the primary method of transportation for most black South Africans. The public transportation system had no set departure times. As riders arrived, they found a van headed in their direction, paid the driver, and then sat down to wait. When every seat was filled—be it in fifteen minutes or fifteen hours—the van departed. It was not exactly Swiss precision, but it was the cheapest way to get where you wanted to go.

The driver of our van waved toward us. "We full now, time to go," he announced.

"You are lucky," said Samuel. "Less than an hour."

Our backpacks were already buried with the other passengers' luggage in the miniature trailer that was hitched behind our van.

Jedd put his arm over Samuel's wide shoulders as we walked toward the van. "It's been great getting to spend this time with you, Samuel. Thanks so much for everything."

Samuel laughed his deep belly laugh. "No, brothers, thank you."

"We'll be praying for you," said Matt.

"Me, too, of course," Samuel promised.

"And Mike, we'll see you in a week in Durban," said Trey.

Mike nodded.

"You're positive you don't mind going it alone?" Matt asked Mike.

"Definitely. Not that I don't love you guys and all"—Mike gave a wry smile—"but I'm looking forward to some time to myself. A chance to hit the surf will be nice, too." Mike would catch a different van to the coastal city of Durban. The other three planned to spend a few days with a family in Johannesburg, then drive down to Durban to meet up with Mike before our flight to India.

"Let's go, Matt," urged Trey, who was already buckling himself into his seat. "I think they're waiting for us."

Only one "seat" remained for Matt, a space of ten inches between the side door and a large, fleshy woman whose hips seemed to be twice as wide her shoulders. She did not return Matt's smile, but wriggled a bit to the left to create more space as he climbed in. Samuel slid the door shut behind him.

The van moved forward, weaving between the vans and honking repeatedly at any person who was not quick to move out of the way. Matt glanced back. Mike and Samuel stood side by side, waving. Samuel waved with both hands, ivory teeth gleaming out of his dark face.

Home and Hearth

The van's motor was located beneath a raised section in the middle, rather than in front, where its growling and grinding dampened any prospects for conversation during the journey. Our fellow travelers slept or stared out the windows glumly, eyelids hanging low.

Initially, rolling prairie dominated the vast spaces that spread out on either side of the two-lane road. Farmhouses—each with its own windmill—appeared here and there, usually set back into the hills. As we drew closer to Johannesburg, the geography lost most of its charm, the expanse becoming flat and dry, spotted with a few scrubby plants. The only contours came from random mounds that bulged out of the plain, often several hundred feet into the air and surrounded by high cyclone fences topped with razor wire.

"Those are mines," explained Trey, "probably diamonds or gold. The mounds are the tailings they take up from underground."

Jedd peered at one mound a few hundred yards from the highway. On the near side of the mound, he saw a tower of rusty metal. Going around at the top was a massive wheel of iron, lowering a line of cable into a gaping space of blackness in the ground below. Not far from the tower, a long row of bunkhouse shacks leaned precariously, appearing ready to fall over at any moment.

"Not the nicest worker accommodations," Jedd whispered to Trey.

"Yeah, I've heard the miners aren't allowed out of the fenced-in area very often either," replied Trey. "It is a big deal going out because they have to strip-search them for diamonds."

Jedd subtly pointed toward a wiry man who slouched forward in the front seat, sleeping, his head bouncing against the dash. "I think that guy up front said something to the driver about being a miner."

"He is," affirmed Trey. "You can tell because he's wearing the big gumboots. They wear those in the mines."

"A lot of the guys at the station were wearing those."

"Remember how I told you Lesotho's number one export is labor? If a man from Lesotho wants to make any money, he doesn't have much choice but the mines in South Africa. On average, these guys spend fifteen months working in the mines for every month they live at home."

"What a miserable way to live."

Trey nodded. "Very sad. They accept this horrible life so they can make

195

money for their families, and then they often end up frittering a lot of it away trying to find a little pleasure on alcohol and prostitutes. When they do go home, a lot of them bring AIDS with them."

"I know; it's crazy. I read an article recently that said nine out of ten new AIDS cases are in sub-Saharan Africa. It said that in some countries in the region as much as 50 percent of the working-age population is infected with HIV."

Jedd's Reflections—January 29

It gives you a good sense of how poor and miserable the conditions are in much of Africa that people will travel hundreds of miles to work in these mines. I honestly cannot grasp what such an existence would be like. When I think about a career, I always think in terms of what would be most fulfilling and what I would enjoy most. So many throughout the world think only of finding a job, any job, that can bring in enough to feed themselves and those they are responsible for taking care of.

This luxury that I've been given—to actually choose my vocation—I had better not take it lightly. God didn't give it to me just so I could find the easiest or best-paying job or so I could seek some self-centered self-actualization. Like Queen Esther, I've been given an incredible position and resources so I can accomplish God's purposes; I must use them well.

For the entire ride, Matt had not been able to place more than half his rear end on the seat. He sat at an angle, one hip well in front of the other, knees jammed against the seat in front of him. He turned awkwardly to glance back at Trey.

"You guys doing all right?" he asked.

"Not bad for having seventeen people in a minivan," Trey replied. "You?"

"I've had better travel experiences," answered Matt dryly. "What's the plan once we get to Jo'burg?"

"We'll stay with the Claassens for two nights, then meet up with Jedd's friend."

Matt twisted his neck farther so he could see Jedd. "So what is the deal with your friend? I never even caught the reason she's in South Africa."

"Charlotte is my cousin's wife's cousin."

Matt gave a slightly puzzled look.

"We call each other cousin-in-law. Anyway, we've been friends since we met at my cousin and her cousin's wedding. She's the one who knew Thys de Beer and his family and set it up for us to stay with them. She just happens to have a business trip here this month."

"And we can ride with her all the way to Durban?"

"Right. She's a really generous gal. When I set this up a few months ago, she offered to drive us anywhere we needed to go. I guess a South African friend of hers is coming, too."

"So there will be five of us making the trip from Johannesburg to Durban?"

"Right, and um . . . I need to talk to you about this part. See, apparently the South African friend—her name's Jacqui—thought we were just on vacation when she got reservations for places to stay on the drive down. She got reservations at these nice lodges in wild-game parks. I'm not sure what I think about that."

"They're planning on staying in the same room with us?"

"No, not that. We'd have different rooms. It's just that we don't have all that much budgeted for the rest of our time in South Africa. Staying in game parks would probably put us a couple hundred dollars over budget."

"Hmm, I don't know," responded Matt. "I didn't mind taking a little vacation when we were passing through Europe, but I don't think that we should be spending a lot of money on a little safari tour through South Africa."

"Well, look," replied Jedd. "I don't want to blow money, either, but Charlotte has really gone out of her way to help us out here. She's even getting a car so she can take us to Durban."

"It'd still cost a lot."

"Well, let's just think about it," suggested Jedd. "We can decide later."

Matt's Reflections—January 29

I don't feel completely comfortable with this little side-trip idea. The people who helped support this trip knew we'd do some sightseeing, but they gave us the money to support service, not a world vacation.

Spending three times as much as we'd need to spend so we can stay in game park lodges really doesn't seem like the best use of money to me. I'm thinking we may need to tell Charlotte we just can't do it.

We arrived at the home of Neels and Marietjie Claassen in time for dinner. Trey and Matt watched as Neels leaned over the barbecue and carefully peeled back the edges of a foil-wrapped bundle. The smell of peppers, onions, and spices mixed with hickory smoke.

"Ahh, almost ready," he stated, glancing up at Matt. "Sausages prepared over the *braai* are my favorite thing."

Matt had to smile. Nothing about Neels suggested the coldness or calculation one might expect to find in someone of his position. The whole of Neels's wide face smiled with his easy grin, and though his eyes were sharp and intelligent, they seemed to offer more grace than judgment. Many whites had been removed from positions of authority during South Africa's rapid transition out of apartheid. Only Neels's lifelong reputation for being fair and genuinely committed to justice for black South Africans enabled him to retain his seat as a justice of the South African Supreme Court.

Matt glanced around at the thatch-roofed patio and well-manicured backyard. "We sure appreciate your letting us stay with you—even letting us use your car and everything," he said.

Neels used a pair of tongs to flip one of the foil packages. "It's really our pleasure. We enjoy having people stay with us."

"Do you have guests often?"

"We do. Marietjie and I see our primary ministry as one of hospitality. In fact, that is why we built this house. It was bigger than we needed, even when the kids were still at home, but it's been a great resource to use for showing people the love of Christ."

"What kind of people do you have stay with you?"

"Over the years, we've had hundreds—businessmen, groups of kids on missions trips, people who've lost their homes, travelers like you boys . . ."

"They usually stay for a couple days?"

"As long as they need to. It's been anywhere from an evening meal to" —he paused to think— "one couple I remember stayed the better part of a year."

Matt glanced at Trey. "This is very cool. It sounds like what we've talked about in theory: an active, intentional ministry of hospitality out of the home."

"Definitely," agreed Trey. "So, how do people find out about it, Neels?"

"We've never announced it or anything, if that's what you mean. When you make your resources available, word gets around fast. One month the church might call to ask if a visiting missionary family can stay for a few weeks, the next someone calls from Australia asking . . ."

A woman's voice floated out of the open back door of the house. It was Neels's wife, Marietjie. "We'll be ready in a few minutes, Neels."

"Would you mind watching the *braai* for a moment?" Neels requested, handing Trey the tongs. "I've got to take care of a bit inside before dinner."

Trey's Reflections—January 30

It is exciting to see people living out the very idea the guys and I have talked about—making an intentional ministry of hospitality.

Throughout this trip, we've experienced what an incredible gift it is to be taken in and taken care of. There's just nothing that conveys love and acceptance like an open home and hearth. I hope whoever I marry will also be excited about this kind of ministry. Especially since it is so rare in America, a married couple who have committed themselves to showing lavish hospitality could really impact many lives.

199

It was well after dark by the time we finished dinner, and we all helped carry our dishes to the kitchen, then returned to the backyard with cups of tea and slices of a berry pie Marietjie had made.

"Neels," began Trey after we had settled back down at the picnic table, "I've been wanting to ask you your thoughts on the future of South Africa and the postapartheid government. We haven't met anyone who seems to have much hope."

Neels nodded thoughtfully. His lips held a sad smile. "You've seen enough to know that South Africa is bleeding severely. Anyone who'd deny that wouldn't be telling the truth. But I am hopeful. There are a lot of good people out here, both white and black."

"There's a lot of frustration and disillusionment, isn't there?" asked Matt.

"There is," affirmed Neels, "for blacks as well as whites. Blacks thought all their problems would disappear when Mandela became president. They were bound to be disappointed. Whites knew tough times were coming, but I don't think many foresaw how bad it would get. A lot of them didn't really understand the apartheid situation from the beginning."

"Are you saying white South Africans didn't know what was going on during apartheid?" probed Matt.

"That is not exactly what I meant, but there is a sense in which that is true also."

Marietjie interjected, "Imagine the horror a lot of Germans felt when they found out about the Nazi concentration camps for the first time. In certain ways, this is how some whites feel about the grisly details of apartheid. You see, whites knew things were not right, and we all bear a collective guilt of inaction, but most had no idea how terrible the details of apartheid really were."

"How could that happen, though?" questioned Jedd. "It seems like the facts would be unavoidable."

"Part of it was a chosen blindness, I think," responded Neels. "But there was also another element. The goal of those within the government who designed apartheid was to keep the races apart—hence the word *apartheid*. They were quite successful in this effort. During the apartheid years, as you've probably heard, blacks were confined to *townships*; these were basically large walled ghettos on the outskirts of the cities. Blacks were not allowed to exit the townships into the so-called 'white areas' unless they had a government-issued passbook authorizing them to do so. At the same time, whites were also not allowed to venture into the townships without special government permission, so unless you were part of the police or were illegally inquisitive, you never really knew how the other half lived."

Marietjie added, "It has been a shaming and horrible time for many as our history is exposed."

Neels did not immediately follow his wife's words, but peered for a moment up into the night sky. We remained quiet, not sure how to respond.

Finally Neels spoke up again. "What you see today is a nation reaping what it has sown. I do have hope for the future, but I believe we have much whirlwind yet to harvest."

"Are you thinking of moving out of the country?" Matt asked quietly.

"Many are already gone," Neels answered, shaking his head slowly. "But we will not." He glanced over at his wife, who smiled back at him. "No, Marietjie and I believe we've been placed here for a reason. It is our home, for better or worse."

Trey's Reflections—January 30

In some ways, I find it hard to believe that any—let alone most—white South Africans didn't have a pretty good sense of what was going on during apartheid. And yet, Neels and Marietjie don't seem to be trying to avoid blame. In fact, they seem willing personally to accept more than they deserve, considering both of them worked to help bring justice to black South Africans long before apartheid ended.

If what they say is true—if many whites were able to avoid seeing the realities of apartheid—then this is a powerful example of how easily humans can choose to remain blind to the pain and suffering going on around us.

As I think about this more, I question my right to judge the South Africans. I cannot help but wonder if in condemning them, I might be condemning myself as well.

Is it not possible that the world system of countries and national borders is only a much grander apartheid system that carefully keeps the misery of so many out of sight and out of mind? Are we totally absolved of any guilt because we call the townships that we choose to ignore "Third World countries"? Does the greater distance mean we bear no responsibility?

Are those who know that abortions terminate human brain waves and stop beating hearts any better when we—just as ordinary, decent Germans during Nazi times—choose to ignore the grisly "medical procedures" carried out at local hospitals day after day?

We had better examine ourselves before throwing any stones.

A Challenge for Jacqui

On the morning of our third day at the Claassens', a Mercedes pulled into the driveway. It was Jedd's "cousin-in-law" Charlotte and a friend she brought along. Charlotte offered an eager wave through the windshield as she parked. Fair skin and strawberry hair suggested her Irish-American roots. The girl in the vehicle next to her seemed Charlotte's opposite. Jacqui was a South African of Indian descent with dark features and flashing eyes that hinted of her sharp-edged wit.

We still were not certain if it was the best use of our funds to join them for a mini-vacation road trip to Durban, but we couldn't really think of any good excuses that would not hurt their feelings, so we decided to make a go of it. The two of them would be our traveling companions for a week.

。 。 。

"Do you guys mind if I crack my window a bit?" asked Charlotte.

"Go for it," responded Trey. "I'm kind of warm, too."

"It's the American hot air," piqued Jacqui. We were quickly getting used to her sarcastic humor.

We were surprised to learn from Jacqui that a substantial number of the Indians—which make up 15 to 20 percent of the population in South Africa—are Christian. Jacqui herself had grown up in a nominally Christian home and had an aunt who continually encouraged her to take her faith more seriously. For Jacqui, though, Christianity had always been an Easter- and Christmas-only event. She seemed intrigued that we saw it as more than that.

"So," she asked, returning to a conversation begun earlier in the day, "do you guys go to church *every* week?"

"Most weeks," responded Matt. "But it's not because we have to . . . we want to."

"My aunt would like me to go to church more often. It's hard to get up on Sunday mornings, though."

Trey grinned. "That's why I go to a church in Santa Barbara that meets in the afternoon."

"That'd be nice . . . at least once in a while. I'd get tired of church if I went too often."

The car fell quiet for a moment, save for the faint hum of tires on black-top.

。 。 。

In several leisurely days, we reached the coast and found a nice game preserve set on the St. Lucia Estuary, just a few miles from the ocean. A stretch of grass had been carved out of the woods within a stone's throw of the water and set with a dozen round, thatch-roofed cabins known as *rondovals*—a somewhat sanitized version of the traditional tribal home. A sign posted on the community bathroom read, "Warning: Be on the look-out for hippo in the camp at night."

Late in the evening, we sat around one of the rondovals talking. Matt strummed his guitar from the top of his bunk bed.

"You got any more of that repellent, Matt?" asked Trey.

"In the side pocket of my pack there," Matt answered. "You going out?"

"Yeah. I'm thinking about walking down to the water's edge. Anyone want to come?"

Charlotte and Jedd indicated that they would join him. "I think I'll just play my guitar here for a while," said Matt. "I was down by the water earlier today."

"I'll stay here and protect Matt from the hippos," said Jacqui.

When the others had left, Jacqui returned to the table that still contained the remnants of a chicken and rice dinner.

"This is nice," she said. "I don't get all that many chances to take vacations."

"So you don't mind taking your vacation with three guys you'd never met before?" asked Matt with a smile.

Jacqui turned serious for a moment. "Not at all. I really am enjoying getting to know you fellows. I honestly haven't ever met guys like you."

"Is that good or bad?"

"Good," she continued. "And for once I'm being serious. I mean, I know you guys aren't perfect, but . . . I don't know. It just seems like you *have* something."

"Thanks. I guess if we have anything different, it's just our commitment to Jesus."

"Yeah, but I've known a lot of Christians . . . ," Jacqui said, her voice trailing off.

"There is so much more to following Jesus than calling yourself a Christian. Many people who call themselves Christian don't really try to follow Him and live as He taught. We're not necessarily the best examples of it, but we're trying."

"Yeah. I guess I've never taken faith stuff too seriously. I don't mean it hasn't been important to me—I do *want* to be good and go to church and stuff, but you know how it is." She paused for a moment, thinking over what she had just said. "Or maybe you don't."

"More than you'd think," responded Matt. "I grew up in a Christian home,

Jungle Jedd

but I hit a point where I got pretty tired of trying to keep up with all the requirements for what I thought I needed to be and do. I wasn't sure I wanted to stick with it. Honestly, I don't think I would have if I still thought that doing all the Christian stuff was all there was to my faith."

"What do you mean, 'Christian stuff'?"

"Just the things everyone associates with being a good Christian: go to church, study the Bible, say your prayers, don't do bad stuff, be nice to people."

"But you still do those things."

"Yes, but . . . it's totally different now. I had fallen into thinking of those things as a big list I had to keep up with if I wanted to be good."

Jacqui tilted her head slightly. "So God doesn't care if we're good?"

"Of course He does. But He's more concerned about us being good on the inside than the outside. We might look good to others by going to church or Bible studies or doing good things, but unless we allow God to change the core of who we are, we'll never be truly good."

"I guess I've heard that. And the bit about believing in Jesus. I don't see how just believing is going to change much."

"It's not, if by 'believing' you mean nothing more than agreeing with certain facts *about* Jesus. Even Satan knows all the right facts. It's *faith in* Jesus that brings us true life. Faith is not just assenting to some religious doctrine or idea; it's a total confidence in Jesus and all that He taught. That confidence is what can cause us to abandon ourselves totally to Him, to accept His death as the payment for our sins and to pattern our lives according to His teachings—*that's* what begins the transformation in our lives."

Jacqui thought for a moment. "I like the concept, but you can't just drum up this 'total confidence' out of nowhere."

"I agree, you can't. The Gospel of Mark tells about a man who asks Jesus to heal his son. When Jesus tells him that anything is possible for those with faith, the man falls on his knees and he begs, 'I do have some faith; please build my faith where it is weak.' I do that often myself."

"So I should just ask for faith and then wait?"

"That's a good place to start, but also . . . if you want to build confidence in someone—or at least see if they're worthy of your trust—how would you do it? Spend time with them, right? Get to know Jesus. Find out what He said about life and relationships. See how He lived."

"Is that where studying the Bible and prayer and other Christian stuff comes in?"

"Exactly!" replied Matt, excited. "Jesus is worthy of your confidence, Jacqui. You just need to get to know Him."

"I want to. I feel like I still really wonder, though, what—"

Jacqui was cut off as the door flew open and Trey burst into the room. Charlotte and Jedd followed on his heels. "Whoa! That had my heart pumping," he gushed.

"What?" questioned Matt, a bit annoyed with the sudden interruption.

A Questionable Trail

205

Trey did not notice. He continued, breathless, "We were down by the water, and we saw these two shiny green eyes with our flashlight. We lost them for a second, and then they appeared closer. We started moving up the bank, and when we shone our light back down, they were right by the bank—it was a crocodile. They run faster than a person, so we got out of their pretty quick."

"What am I going to tell your families if you get eaten by a crocodile?" Matt asked, beginning to smile.

"Tell 'em we were crossing a river in the middle of a jungle, trying to bring medicine to a dying missionary," replied Trey.

"Yeah, right here in the middle of a game park," gibed Jacqui.

"Then say we were trying to save a baby that fell into the water," suggested Jedd.

"I'm in the presence of superheroes," said Jacqui, suppressing a fake yawn. She looked at her watch. "I actually am getting pretty tired. You about ready to head back to our cabin, Char?"

o o o

By daylight, the water's edge was a different place. Like a silver gray apron, the estuary stretched out, its bankside edges tangled with rushes and water lilies. The early morning cool was fast giving way to a humid warmth, the moisture in the air giving the horizon a smudged appearance. Birds and monkeys chattered from the dense brush surrounding the clearing.

In an open grassy space along the bank, Matt lounged in the sun a few feet from the water, reading. A short distance away, Jacqui balanced comfortably in the limbs of a thick-trunked tree, a dozen feet in the air, her legs drawn up to her chest.

"What're you doing, Jacqui?" asked Jedd, who had just walked down from the cabins.

"Looking for hippos . . . I haven't seen any yet."

"Did you know your leg is bleeding?"

"Yeah. I scraped it climbing up here. It doesn't really hurt."

Jedd paused, looking out over the water for a moment. "Mind if I sit in the shade here and read?"

"Your Bible?"

"Yeah."

"Why don't you read out loud so I can hear, too."

Jedd sat down with his back against the tree's trunk. "Anything in particular you want me to read?"

She thought for a moment. "No. Just pick a couple of your favorite parts."

Jedd thumbed through his Bible, glancing at a few different passages before settling on one. "Here, this is Psalm 139. It's one of my favorites— it gives a picture of how intimately God knows us and of the type of relationship that . . . well, I'll just read it:

> O LORD, you have searched me and you know me. You know when
> I sit and when I rise; you perceive my thoughts from afar. You discern
> my going out and my lying down; you are familiar with all my ways.
> Before a word is on my tongue you know it completely, O LORD. You
> hem me in—behind and before; you have laid your hand upon me.
> Such knowledge is too wonderful for me, too lofty for me to attain.
> Where can I go from your Spirit? Where can I flee from your presence?
> If I go up to the heavens, you are there; if I make my bed in the
> depths, you are there. If I rise on the wings of the dawn, if I settle on
> the far side of the sea, even there your hand will guide me, your right
> hand will hold me fast . . .

When the passage was finished, Jacqui was quiet for some time. Jedd glanced up at her; she was gazing out over the estuary. He looked at Matt, who smiled back at him. The small waves lapped in slow rhythm against the shore.

"What're you thinking?" he asked finally.

"A lot, I guess. Can you read a little more?"

"Sure. As much as you want."

Jedd read several more passages before she said anything, and then only a soft "Thanks." She wanted to think for a while, he could tell. Matt joined him as he moved up toward the rondovals.

"Jacqui really seems to be soaking it all in," Matt remarked.

"Yeah, I think so," Jedd agreed. "Let's take a sec and pray for her."

Months later, Jacqui wrote to Jedd, "For the first time that morning, I began to see the breath and life in the words you were speaking. Something touched me in that moment. Perhaps on that morning my life and my future were placed right there on the cusp, and then something moved me. I think it was the true turning point in my life, where I made a conscious and yet unconscious move toward Christ."

Matt's Reflections—February 2

It's kind of funny how Trey, Jedd, and I had such big questions about the money it would cost to spend time touring with Charlotte and Jacqui. I was pretty convinced this side trip was not the best use of our funds.

Now it seems to me that the side trip is exactly what God wanted us to do—particularly to become friends with Jacqui and challenge and encourage her.

I feel doubly foolish for fretting about it, especially since Charlotte has been so generous in helping us pay for most of the side trip.

I need to keep in mind that my idea of how money should be used is often quite different from God's. Frugality may be a virtue, but it is definitely not the highest one—God often seems to be anything but frugal.

Meanwhile, in Durban

Mike spent the morning surfing. The waves were not ideal, but the sun was out and the water felt great. A shower in his room at the youth hostel washed the salt away and primed him for lunch.

As he walked out of the hostel's lobby, Mike glanced at the hand-printed message on a sign that hung above the doorway: "Do not go left after exiting, or you will put yourself in danger." Mike had to smile. "That's what's great about South Africa," he mused. "Every time you begin to think you're in paradise, something smacks you upside the head." Heeding the sign's advice, he turned right toward the boardwalk that ran along Durban's most popular beach.

A few hearty wave-riders were still out beyond the breakers, bobbing up and down in the gray water. Along the boardwalk ran Durban's famous water park—wading pool after wading pool, each with a unique combination of water-squirting works of art, sculptures, and slides. The pools had once teemed with the children of white vacationers. Some still came, but from what Mike could see, it was much different now. Thoughtful parents would never let children out of their sight while playing in the pools for fear their child might become another South African crime statistic.

The smell of roasting chicken pulled Mike's attention away from two small black girls who sat in a pool facing each other, playing patty-cake. In the window of a street-side shop window, a dozen golden-brown birds, dripping gravy, circulated on a rotisserie. He offered a "hello" to the security guard—a thick-armed black man—who stood near the entrance. Nearly every shop had one. The fellow offered a sleepy nod in reply. A Thanksgiving-like smell caught Mike as he entered the café. An attractive girl with soft blue eyes smiled at him from behind the counter.

"How are you today?" she asked pleasantly in a thick Afrikaans accent.

"Well, thanks. And yourself?"

"Pretty good, but I'll be much better when my shift's over. What would you like?"

Mike considered the menu for a moment. "The chicken dinner special looks good to me."

"Yeah, it's really not bad." She disappeared through swinging doors into a kitchen area. "I'll be back in just a moment."

She was still in the kitchen when three young black men entered. Their clothes were stylish, but shiny patches in the knees of their jeans and loose threads hanging from their collars suggested the outfits were worn daily. Mike offered a half-smile, but they seemed not to notice him.

"Excuse me, does anybody work here?" demanded one, a squat teen with large bags under his eyes.

"Hey, we wanna order," followed a second.

The counter remained empty.

A terse "Just a moment" sounded from the back.

"Hello? Excuse me!" The young men appeared to be getting agitated.

"HELLO!"

The young woman appeared through the door carrying a plate covered with mashed potatoes, green beans, and a half-chicken. The look on her face wavered between irritation and fear.

"Hello, honey, are you finally going to help us?"

"I'm not your honey."

"Oh, come on, baby."

"I'm not your baby!"

"Oh, come on, don't be like that, honey."

"Hey, why don't you show her some respect?" Mike blurted out awkwardly.

"Why should I? She didn't show us no respect."

Mike wasn't sure whether he felt silly or scared. "She didn't do anything to you."

"Oh no, nothing at all—didn't even ask us what we wanted when we came in the door."

Mike shook his head slightly. "She didn't know you were here. She was busy making my food."

"No, you were ignoring us; weren't you, honey?"

"That's it!" she exploded, her face growing red. "I'm calling security."

Mike glanced toward the door. The large, green-clad man was still out in front.

"Oh no, she's going to call security," the stocky fellow mocked.

The girl set Mike's plate on the counter and called toward the guard, "Security. Security!"

The young fellows laughed as the man entered.

"What's wrong, miss?"

"These guys are harassing me. I want them out of the store."

"We're not doing nothing, just trying to get some food. She won't serve us 'cause we're black. She was just ignoring us."

"She couldn't hear you," Mike interjected.

The third young man, who had said little up to this point, responded, "Yeah, right. You Afrikaaners always side with each other."

"I'm not Afrikaans—I'm American. I'm just saying what I saw."

"Well, you don't know what it's like for us here. They always treat us like this."

The security guard said something Mike did not catch. Shaking their heads, the young men moved toward the door. The squat one shot a disdainful glance back at the girl; she returned it with equal venom.

Mike's Reflections—February 2

What I saw today was just a minor incident, but I think it says a lot about the turmoil that South Africa is going through at this time. It seems like too much to hope that there will ever be more than isolated cases of racial reconciliation. It is a much more difficult situation than in America. The wounds of apartheid are still so raw, and they only seem to be getting more aggravated with every passing day.

The black people of South Africa have suffered innumerable injustices. It would be almost impossible to expect that there would not be a great deal of hatred toward whites. It is also easy to understand the fear and frustration of the Afrikaaners as they watch their country fall apart. I hope I am wrong, but I fear that South Africa will travel down the path of continual conflict, just like neighboring Zimbabwe.

We rejoined in Durban as planned. Our final days in Africa were restful: a last meal with Jacqui and Charlotte at the home of Jacqui's parents, and time with another special host family who confirmed both the hope and the anguish of South Afria.

Trey turned out the lights as we climbed into South African beds one last time. "Enjoy a good night's sleep, guys. It may be your last for a while."

"You think India's going to be rougher than the places we've already been?" questioned Matt.

Trey shrugged. "I don't know, but from the things I've heard, the crazy part of this trip is just beginning . . ."

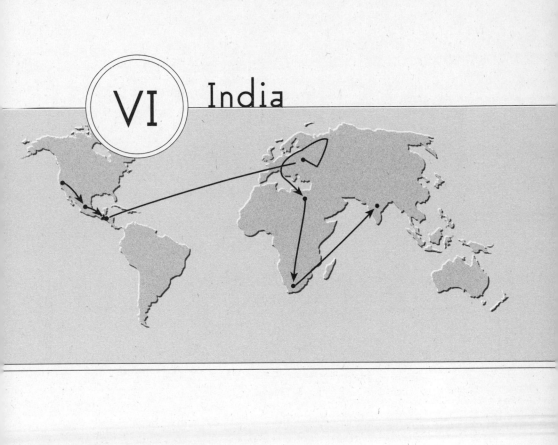

VI India

Indian Rickshaw Rider

sixteen

Rajas, Rice, and Rickshaws

no words, just bony fingers attached to bony arms, stretching out toward us, eyes pleading, sunken, and jaundiced. The closeness of the bodies, the smell of urine and sweat, the sheer desperation of the need was suffocating, maddening. Our hearts longed to help, yet something else inside just wanted to swat them away like a swarm of mosquitoes.

"Aye, aye! Get back!" a voice shouted harshly.

Most of the beggars retreated a few steps. One woman with matted hair and a leathery face clung to Trey, tugging on the sleeve of his shirt. We spotted the source of the voice—a man dressed in slacks and a long-sleeve shirt despite the night's wet heat. The accent on his English was almost too thick to understand. "Yhou neet rite to otel? Mhy taxi fit you ahh."

Trey slid several rupees into the hand of the woman who had been pulling on his shirt. She took the money and stepped back, her face still deadpan. Seeing her good fortune, three other beggars took her place. Trey shook his arm and stepped away from them.

"Aye, aye!" shouted the driver, shooting a fierce glance at the beggars. They drew back slowly, passionless. "Yhou neet rite?" he asked again.

"No thank you, sir," said Jedd. "A friend is meeting us here."

The man snorted and tramped off in search of other potential riders. A few beggars approached again. Trey spotted a fair-haired man walking in our direction. "I think that may be Mr. Alter," he guessed.

The fellow called out as he approached. "You're the four from Santa Barbara?"

Matt stepped forward. "That's right. I'm Matt."

A friend of Matt's in the U.S. had asked Tom Alter to meet us at the airport. From what we had heard, Tom was one of India's more popular television actors. He had grown up in India, the grandson of American missionaries. His white skin and fluent Hindi opened doors into the major studios. Apparently, his Robert Redford looks and theatrical prowess had helped him become a national television star.

Despite being nearly 1:00 A.M., traffic was still heavy. Strangely enough, most cars forged through the night without headlamps. It seemed they relied on the noise of their constantly blaring horns, rather than light, to alert others of their approach.

Trey was trying to pay attention to Tom, but he could not help staring out the window. In every country thus far, he felt as if he had stepped back in time. Now he could not shake the sensation that he had been cast forward—not to a future of brilliant chrome and glass, but to a post-Armageddon doomsday world. Moldering shacks of cardboard and wood scrap were hardly distinguishable from the heaps of refuse piled alongside the road. Shapes of people lay in the gutters and across the sidewalk, wrapped in tattered blankets. Rats skulked among them, foraging for anything edible.

"I feel like I'm in the Twilight Zone," commented Mike soberly.

Tom offered a sad smile. "It's hard to digest, huh? I'm so used to it all I hardly notice it most of the time, but every once in a while I still think, *This is crazy.*"

Perhaps most disconcerting was the heavy darkness. It seemed to hang over everything like a tangible substance. Even here in the middle of the city, only a handful of lights shone, usually from the larger buildings. These appeared orange and muted, as if they were dying, hardly able to penetrate the murky smog that filled the air.

"Yieez! We almost hit that cow!" Matt exclaimed. He reached for his seat belt, but there was none to be had, so he placed his arm forward against the seat in front of him.

Jedd shook his head. "There're cows everywhere, just grazing on the trash and wandering in the road. The way everyone's driving, I bet there are cow wrecks all the time."

"These cows being free to just roam around—it's the Hindu thing, isn't it?" questioned Trey.

"Right," Tom affirmed. "Don't mess with the bovines."

"Now what's this?" wondered Matt. Directly ahead, a series of new buildings rose incongruously out of the gloom. They shone, clean and bright, as if they had been transported from downtown L.A.

Tom explained, "Believe it or not, there is quite a bit of wealth in Bombay. It's just a lot less well distributed than in the States—there are hordes of dirt-poor people, a small group of the rich, and not too much in the middle."

"It's that way in most Third World countries," asserted Mike.

"Right. But here it's formalized by the caste system. There are five official levels, with subtiers in each level as well."

"Is the caste mentality still dominant?"

"Definitely. You see it get a little watered down in some of the more Westernized families, but the caste system is still very much the rule. People will rarely marry anyone out of their caste. The upper levels won't even associate with the lowers. The lowest tier are called the untouchables, and they're just that: less-than-human things that no one would even think of touching."

"How do the wealthy make their money?"

"A lot of manufacture, usually for export. Some have huge landholdings that they rent to peasant farmers at a premium. The main thing in Bombay, though, is the movies."

"Movies?" questioned Matt.

"Bombay is second only to Hollywood in movie production. I can't say they're all on par with American films, but for sheer quantity, Bombay's the place. Don't forget, you've got a nation of nearly a billion people here."

Tom directed the driver to a side street and then turned back to us. "Listen, here's your hotel. I've already negotiated a good rate with the owner, just tell them who you are. Give me a call tomorrow and you can come over for tea, late morning. I'll give you some tips before you catch the train for Hyderabad."

Train Tracks to Hyderabad

Our train would carry us to the town of Hyderabad, where we would stay for several days with a local pastor and his family. Beyond that, we had not yet decided what we would do with the rest of our time in India. We planned to volunteer with the Sisters of Charity in Calcutta during the week before leaving for Bangladesh, but that left a week open for visiting the Taj Mahal or other famous Indian sites.

The train compartment did not feel big enough for six people. Three tiers of narrow beds clung to the walls on either side of the doorless, six-by-eight-foot space. During nonsleeping hours, the middle bunk folded up and the bottom one served as a bench for three. No glass covered the windows, only bars. Open to the air, wind continually rushed through the compartments, in the open countryside providing relief from the heat, but in the populated areas, where shacks lined each side of the tracks, casting dust into our mouths, along with the taste of tin cans and rotting food. Matt turned to record the scene in his journal.

 Matt's Reflections—February 6

The squalor of the dwellings growing along the train tracks in the city areas is bitter. No permanent structures, just myriads of handmade hovels, built from creative combinations of garbage.

The people, though, aside from the poorest beggars, do not appear degraded, but generally content in their world. They are extremely diligent in their work and, despite the filth around them, keep their own clothing spotless and are attentive to personal hygiene. The men are often cheerful and quite affectionate with one another, and the women's flowing saris add a glimmer of brightness to every scene.

I am also impressed by the industriousness of the agricultural endeavors here. Nearly every square inch of farmable land appears to be cultivated. I guess that is a necessity in a nation of more than 900 million people.

Rising from the bench seat and moving into the aisle, Mike said, "I'm going to walk around. My back is bothering me a little."

"I'm sorry, Mike," offered Matt, seeing the grimace on Mike's face.

Mike was never one to complain, but we could all tell his back was still very uncomfortable much of the time.

Matt turned to Jedd, who sat across from him. "The train station back in Bombay was impressive, wasn't it?"

"Yeah. It looked more like a gothic cathedral than a train station. A lot of those buildings the British built during the colonial days don't seem to belong here. It's weird to see such incredible architecture surrounded by shacks made out of garbage."

"India's just wild and foreign all the way through. All the travelers I've known who've spent time in India say it's the craziest place they've ever been."

Jedd nodded. "It's a constant assault on all your senses—everything's so intense. The smell of curry and people and garbage. The color of the women's saris and the Hindu temples. Constant noise and motion. The humid air and the crush of the crowds. Even the food is unlike anything I've ever had before."

"It leaves me dizzy, but I like being on the train; aside from the vendors, it's almost peaceful."

Jedd turned to look out the window for a moment. He could just make out the shape of mountains on the horizon, hazy in the humid air. Rice paddies filled the space in between while a dirty ribbon of water wound through the fields, spotted in many places with colorful dots washing their clothes.

He turned back to Matt. "What Tom told us yesterday about some of the Christian churches here in India having trouble with struggles between the classes was sad. It sounds like elements of the caste system are very present in the Church."

"Yeah, I didn't like hearing that, either. I knew Indian society was extremely stratified—it's a central part of Hinduism. The different castes are hardly supposed to touch one another. But that's so the opposite of Christ's way . . ."

Jedd interjected, "From what Tom said, not all the churches allow society's hierarchy to affect the way they do things. Many have totally rejected caste norms—people fellowship together equally."

"I know, but it still makes me mad that anyone who claims to be a Christian would force one group to sit on the floor and take Communion last and things like that."

"I agree. To us, it seems so obviously counter to Jesus' ways. But I can see how it would be difficult for Indian Christians to avoid falling into things like that. When the whole world around you just seems to assume certain things, no matter how wrong they might be, it's hard to go in the opposite direction."

Jedd's Reflections—February 6

I know that in any culture, there are elements of the status quo a person has to resist if they want to follow Jesus.

It's hard to identify these elements, especially within your own culture. For me, it might be feeling like I have to achieve the "American dream" by climbing the ladder. Or maybe that I should "fight for my rights" whenever I've been taken advantage of. I often just assume those values are correct. But they are American values, not necessarily Christ's. Discerning between the two is not easy when you've been soaked in your culture from birth.

I guess that is how it is for some of the Indians with the cultural norm of social stratification. It is very hard for them to shake the view that the wealthy and wellborn aren't somehow inherently higher and better, or at least rightly entitled to certain privileges.

The reality is that anytime we fail to weigh our cultural assumptions against what Christ taught, we will be slaves to those assumptions— blindly obeying them. It is only when we allow Jesus and His words to reshape our view of the world that we can rise above the status quo.

Mike was exploring the train, passing from car to car. He noticed that between some of the cars, a ladder led up to the roof. *I doubt anyone would care if I went up there,* he thought.

Before he could begin climbing, a voice broke into his thoughts. "Excuse me. Are you and your friends Christians?" A man in his midthirties stood before him. He had a handsome face—relatively light-skinned for an Indian, jet-black hair, and ebony eyes.

"Yes. How did you know?"

"I saw your friend's guitar," the man replied, beginning to smile.

Mike smiled, too, though not quite understanding what the man meant about the guitar. "What is your name?"

"My name is Samuel. I am a Christian, too. You have some time?"

Mike nodded, "Sure."

The two spent the next several hours talking. Samuel was delighted to hear of our experiences with other believers throughout the world. Mike was equally interested in Samuel's story.

Although well educated, Samuel had been unable to find work enough to support his family anywhere near his native town of Chirala. When he was presented with the opportunity to earn nearly $3,000 a year working for an Indian businessman in Africa, Samuel saw it as the only way to keep his family from slipping into total poverty. Upon arrival in Africa, however, the reality of the job was nothing near what had been promised. The man running the business was a crook who worked Samuel mercilessly, knowing that Samuel had little recourse. After six months, Samuel still had not even been able to save enough money for a return trip to India. Fortunately, the believers in the church he attended in Africa saw his need and together purchased his ticket home to be reunited with his family.

"Come by our berth when you get a chance," said Mike as they parted. "I want the other guys to meet you."

o o o

The train slowed, the brakes shrieking—metal on metal—blending with the sounds of an approaching crowd. Another stop. We braced ourselves for the onslaught of hawkers and beggars. A vendor in a white robe moved sideways down the aisle, bearing what looked like an old-style milk can. Somehow he had boarded the train while it was still slowing. "Coffee! Coffee! Coffee!" He pushed three mugs in front of Matt's face. Matt held up his hands and shook his head.

A deep voice boomed from the other side, through the bars of the window. "Dinner? You want chicken and rice? Fifty rupees—chicken dinner." Sensing he was being ignored, the man stopped walking alongside the moving car and allowed it to move past until the next window was even with him. "Dinner? You want . . ."

A small hand slid in through the window, palm up, followed by the gaunt face of a little girl against the bars.

"No, sorry," Trey said shaking his head uncomfortably at the girl. Jedd looked down from the top bunk where he was reading, glad that for once he was not in the line of fire.

The smell of black tea and cinnamon reached Mike's nose. He stood and nodded at the *chai* salesman who peered in from the aisle. The fellow produced a ceramic cup from nowhere and wiped it with his shirt before filling it with a slosh of the sweet, milk-based tea.

"I bet that shirt-wipe is the only washing those cups get all day," mused Mike as he handed over several coins. "Oh well. When in Rome . . ."

Matt shook his head with a smile, "It's your stomach."

Mike grinned at him. "Hey, the tea is hot. It'll kill the germs."

The flow seemed endless. More beggars at the window . . . a girl with a basket of baked goods . . . a man carrying bamboo cages filled with chickens trying to squeeze through the aisle . . . a boy with a sack of papayas. The venders moved quickly, desperate to maximize commercial opportunities before the train's motion resumed.

With a metallic groan, the station began to slide across the window, warning the last straggling entrepreneurs to close their sales.

222

"What do I do with this?" wondered Mike, holding up his empty cup.

An arm shot into the compartment from the aisle and the cup disappeared. A moment later, Trey caught site of the chai seller leaping from the train back onto the vanishing platform.

° ° °

Mike reentered the compartment and sat down on the bench. It was rare to see him so excited. "Guys, listen. I was just talking with Samuel some more . . ."

"Who's Samuel?" asked Trey.

"You know, the Christian guy I introduced you to earlier, who worked in Africa."

"Oh yeah."

"Anyway, his whole family is Christian, and his father is a pastor of a church. He pretty much begged me to come and visit him in his town. What would you guys think about doing that?"

"I don't want to cut things short with our plans in Hyderabad, but if it works out I'd be up for it," Matt responded.

Jedd was not so enthusiastic. "Yeah, well, we can keep it in mind. We'll just have to see how things work out time-wise."

Trey added, "We just aren't going to have much time. India's a lot bigger than it seems, and if we're still planning to make it up north to the Taj Mahal, we're already pushing it if we are going to work in Calcutta at all."

Mike was not put off. "I know we don't have much time, but I think we should seriously consider going there. I don't exactly know why, but there's something about Samuel that I really like. I don't think he'd just ask us without good reason."

"It sounds great, Mike, but with all our plans and stuff I don't really see it working out," Jedd said flatly.

"Well, I've got his name and the name of a station where we can telegraph him. I think we should stay flexible if God wants to change our plans."

○ ○ ○

By nightfall, the novelty of the train ride had disappeared; we were ready for the noise and constant activity to stop, hoping it would when the lights went out. As we prepared for bed, a boy who shared our compartment suggested we lock our bags to the wire loop that hung from each bunk.

223

"Thieves will take right from under your nose," he warned.

Matt and Mike lowered the middle-tier bunks and lay down. Jedd and Trey were already laid out on the top tier.

"Ready for lights out?" asked Matt. Hearing no objection, he flipped the switch and the compartment went dark.

The rhythmic clacking continued, loud but steady enough to be almost sedative.

This just may be a decent sleep, thought Mike.

Several hours later, we knew otherwise.

Along with the always-boarding and unboarding passengers, the salesmen seemed to have no sense that a compartment with its lights out meant "We want to sleep." Every half-hour throughout the night, they returned, especially the chai sellers. "Chai, chai, chai! Coffee, coffee, coffee!" they'd cry in a shrill voice, flipping the lights of the compartment on and off. Finding no buyers, they would move to the next doorway, usually leaving the light on behind them.

Trey pulled the sweatshirt he had been using for a pillow over his eyes, groaning as he rolled closer to the wall. Jedd tensed in anger, muttering loudly, "What's wrong with these people? Why the heck doesn't anyone shut 'em up?" No one answered his question. We just stared silently at the bunk a few inches in front of our faces. Our train pulled into Hyderabad at 6:00 A.M. There was just enough light for us to recognize that our white T-shirts had turned a brown-gray. As we stepped off the train, Matt shook his head as he glanced at a sign hung above the platform. It read, "Cleanliness is next to godliness."

Matt's Reflections—February 7

Last night was about the worst night's sleep I've ever had. The train rumbled, passengers coughed, chai vendors shouted and turned the lights on every thirty minutes—not to mention the bites and stings from insects.

The apostle Paul said, "I have learned the secret of being content in any and every situation, whether well fed or hungry, whether living in plenty or in want . . ."

I wish I could say I've learned the secret as well. I feel like maybe through this trip, I'm becoming at least a little more flexible and content. Even so, I know I still have a long way to go.

My parents always taught me that I am the only one that can control my feelings. Even if someone does something horrible to me, I still have the choice to choose my reaction. While I know this in theory, it is often hard to live out. I want so much to grow in this, for I believe that joy is always accessible to those who have learned to be content in all circumstances.

Worlds Apart

Although not yet seven in the morning, the streets of Hyderabad were alive and buzzing. Moving things of all shapes and sizes teemed over every inch of blacktop. They flowed in and out, around—almost on top of—each other like a swarm of cockroaches. Pedestrians kept as close as they could to the three-storied shacks on the sides. Colorful rickshaws, ancient taxis, ox-drawn carts, motorcycles, the cab of a semitruck, entire families on single scooters, and old army Jeeps jockeyed for position in the flow. They buzzed and beeped and screeched, conversing continually with the shrill bleating of horns. From the sides, vendors threw their voices above the blare of traffic, proclaiming the benefits of their products. The pulse of the city was nearly deafening.

Meeting us at the train station was a local Indian pastor named Anil. He haggled with a crowd of minitaxi drivers for several minutes, drawing the fare lower like an auction in reverse. When only two men remained interested, we proceeded to squeeze into their three-wheeled, doorless carts. Trey and Matt were packed together in the rear of one, with Anil in front, balanced on the single front seat with the driver. Trey leaned forward as the vehicle lurched out into the traffic.

"We'd better make sure the other guys' minitaxi doesn't get left behind. They would probably be lost for days."

"Don't worry, I gave their driver clear directions," Anil assured.

Matt laughed, half serious. "We'd still better keep an eye on 'em. If there's any possibility of getting lost, Mike and Jedd will probably find it."

A stoplight brought the wheeled insects to a halt, not in an even line, but in a mashed-up blob. Despite the rushing cross-flow, the pack edged farther and farther into the intersection. The light turned green, and Trey leaned his head and part of his body out of the vehicle. His greasy locks waved in the wind like a not-so-well-groomed golden retriever.

"Check out the cows grazing in the trash!" he said, pointing. "Someone hung beads around their horns."

"Those cows don't look too holy to me," declared Matt.

"Maybe not," Anil agreed. "But you still better not plan on having any hamburgers while you're in India."

"Wow! What is that?" asked Trey.

What looked like a fairy castle—complete with spires, sparkling domes, and turreted towers—rose above the filthy street at least two hundred feet into the sky.

"I think it was built by the raj of this area for one of his favorite wives, but I'm not sure," responded Anil. "There are quite a few buildings like that in Hyderabad."

"What a contrast to the way most people here live." remarked Matt.

"That is the way India has always been."

225

Trey in a Crowded Street in Hyderabad

The minitaxi driver turned from the main thoroughfare down a narrow lane that wound between whitewashed cement homes. The noise instantly diminished. Although the walls and street were in various states of disrepair, the neighborhood appeared refreshingly tidy.

Trey questioned Anil, "Matt said that you run a training center for pastors here in Hyderabad."

"Yes. I am a pastor, too, but some time back I realized that many pastors here in India, including myself, needed more training and a deeper understanding of the Bible. It has been an evolving process, but now for six months out of the year we have pastors and teachers from Australia and America come to teach at the little training center we have here."

"Is there a dormitory for the students?"

"Not really. A few students stay with us, and some stay with local believers. Depending on how many come, we sometimes rent places as well . . . and here we are at home now."

We were still climbing out of the taxis when four boys poured out of the house. The smallest child wrapped his arms around one of his father's legs while the other three stood respectfully, smiling slightly, and glancing between their father and us.

Anil ruffled the little one's hair, then said, "David, stand with your brothers. Now, boys, I'd like to introduce you to four American brothers who have come to spend some time with us: Matt, Mike, Jedd, and Trey. This is Terry, Melchizadeck, Sunny, and David."

A woman appeared in the open doorway. Her eyes were dark and bright, like the boys. A brilliant orange sari hung over one shoulder and wrapped around her waist.

"And this is my wife, Annie," announced Anil, obviously quite proud.

Annie shook our hands warmly—something we had come not to expect from women in Third World countries. "Breakfast will be ready soon," she advised. "I've made toast and eggs—something, I think, you have not had in some time."

"We'll go wash up in back," promised Anil.

∘ ∘ ∘

That night for dinner, as for the prior two meals of the day, we sat in a circle on the floor in the living room. Annie passed us each an aluminum plate piled with steaming rice. A large bowl of a lentil curry waited in the center while Anil prayed. Then Annie ladled the sauce onto each of our plates in turn.

"Is that spicy?" questioned Matt.

"I made it less hot than usual," assured Annie. "Sometimes visitors have a hard time with the food we normally eat."

Anil could tell we were still unaccustomed to eating without utensils. He encouraged, "Eat well, boys. Annie is the best cook in Hyderabad."

Anil dug in with his right hand, swishing and smashing the curry around in the rice and then squeezing it into tiny balls that he plopped into his mouth. Mike tried to follow suit, but somehow the rice did not quite make it into a ball and only a few grains made it as far as his mouth.

Annie laughed. "Like this, Mike," she said, easily rolling another perfect ball on Anil's plate and feeding it to her husband.

It seemed strange to us, but women in India feed their husbands first and then eat their own dinner afterward with the children.

227

"Can I have some more water?" Matt asked, pursing his lips and taking in quick little breaths.

Anil smiled. "Water will not help," Anil explained. "After you are finished, you will eat some curds. It cools the fire in your mouth."

"Don't worry, we love this spiciness," said Trey. "Next time make it as spicy as you normally do."

Jedd, his mouth full, nodded eagerly.

"I'm not sure . . . ," said Mike, shooting a slightly fearful glance at Matt.

Trey, however, was already on to the next subject. "A guy we spent time with in Bombay was telling us a little about the election that is going on now. He said the Hindu Nationalist Party is really on the rise."

"It is," Anil affirmed. "There has been a substantial shift in political power in the last year."

"Is that good or bad for you?" asked Mike.

"Well, the BJP, the political party that is gaining strength, is largely a radical Hindu movement. They've been riling people up, especially the youth, and we Christians are very wary. India's never been pro-Christian, obviously, but our government has generally left us alone."

"Has the BJP caused any major problems yet?" Matt questioned.

"Not so much for Christians, but a number of Muslim mosques have been vandalized and even burned to the ground by BJP supporters. This is a warning to us as well."

"Is there a reason that the violence has been directed only at the Muslims?"

"About 15 percent of the population is Muslim, so they are a much more visible challenge to the Hindus than the 2 percent that are Christians. There is also a long history of violence between Muslims and Hindus. I don't know if you knew this, but when the British pulled out of India, they helped establish Pakistan as a Muslim country so both religious groups could have a part of former British India. This has helped to quell some of the religious civil wars, but the peace between India and Pakistan has been a tenuous one. When there are problems between the countries, it increases the tension between Hindus and the Muslims who live in India."

Mike's Reflections—February 7

Living a Christian life would be such a different experience in a place like India. We're so used to living in a culture that is permeated by elements of Christianity in every realm. Of course, there are times when it is very unpopular to be a Christian. But whether they like it or not, everybody in America has been shaped in some way by ideas that have roots in Christianity. I can't imagine how much harder it would be to live among a people with such radically different assumptions about life.

"May I interrupt for a moment?" said Annie, emerging from the kitchen. She carried a bowl of a white, creamy substance—the promised curds. The curds were a form of yogurt made from goat's milk. They tasted a bit sour, maybe even rotten, but helped to soak the spices from our tongues.

Annie sat down next to Anil, and he took her hand. "A very good meal, Annie," he said. "She is an excellent cook, is she not?"

We each added our wholehearted agreement.

A moment later, Mike launched back into our conversation. "Is it difficult to share Jesus with people in this environment?" he asked.

Anil nodded. "Sometimes it feels next to impossible. On the surface, Hindus are very tolerant when one initially speaks of Christ. In addition to the main gods like Brahma, Vishnu, and Shiva, their pantheon contains hundreds of other gods. Some of their holy men claim that in the universe there are actually millions of deities. In a system like that, it is not difficult to accept Jesus as another one of the gods."

Jedd spoke up. "When we were riding the train, I noticed a wall alongside the tracks painted with pictures of a bunch of different gods. There was the big elephant guy, and a lady with a bunch of arms holding skulls—"

"That was Kali," interjected Anil.

"—And a bunch of other guys also. The interesting thing was that they had Jesus up there, too."

"Exactly. They have no problem with people worshiping Jesus, or with people worshiping just about anything else, for that matter. The problem comes when you encourage people to accept Jesus for what He claimed to be: the only true way to relationship with our one Creator."

"Strange as it may sound," began Jedd, "it is a lot that way in America, too. People don't have much of a problem with anyone believing just about anything they want to believe."

"Right," affirmed Mike, "but as soon as you present the idea that God chose to reveal Himself through Jesus, and that all of our religions and other efforts are destined to fail, that is when people start attacking you and calling you closed-minded bigots."

Jedd's Reflections—February 7

I've often thought of attacks against Christians coming from only two groups: people who want to force atheism on everyone, like in Communist states, or from authorities who want to enforce a single religion, like in Muslim countries.

Historically, though, some of the worst attacks against Christianity have come from people who would be fine with Christians being Christians as long as they would not insist on following Christ as their only Lord.

The Romans, for instance, were generally very tolerant. Had the early church been willing to worship the emperor and some of the Roman gods in addition to Jesus, they may have faced no persecution at all.

But when Christians claimed Jesus was "the way, the truth, and the life" and refused to bow down to any other god, the authorities were so enraged that they threw Christians to lions, burned them at the stake, and did countless other terrible things.

I can see it becoming increasingly this way in America now. Christian faith is fine as long as a person is willing to acknowledge the validity of every other idea as well. But those who refuse to bow down to our culture's other deities—especially the god of politically correct tolerance—are despised. I have little doubt that the consequences of refusing to bow will likely only become more severe in the years to come.

Of course, the Bible tells us to be gentle and respectful toward those who disagree with us; we have no business forcing our views on others. But for the Christian, there can be only one Lord, and we must be willing to pay the consequences for obeying Him alone.

"Jesu Raja"

"Aye taxi, aye taxi!" called Anil, signaling to a minitaxi on the far side of the street.

The colorful transport zipped across the flow of traffic and pulled up before us.

Somehow, all five of us squeezed in, Anil next to the driver, Trey on Mike's lap, Matt on Jedd's. Three young Muslim women, dressed from head to toe in black, tried to hold back their giggling as they passed us.

Mike elbowed Matt and whispered, "I'll give you ten bucks if you pull off one of those girls' veils."

Anil wheeled around. "Don't even think about it. The men in that mosque would kill us if you did that."

"Sorry, I was just joking," Mike responded.

"It's not even something to joke about."

At the bus station, drivers of full-size taxis approached us, promising to undercut the bus fair to wherever we wanted to go. We ended up in the back of a long, white vehicle that looked like it belonged at a classic car rally.

"This car looks like a vintage 1940s roadster, but the interior is pretty new," remarked Matt.

"They still manufacture these in India," Anil explained.

"Just like this?"

"Yes. The British started making this model in India over fifty years ago. Until recently, they've been producing the very same model."

The buildings and traffic became less and less dense as we drove on. Finally, the urban sprawl gave way completely to open countryside.

"Where exactly are we going, Anil?" asked Jedd.

"The church in Hyderabad is my first responsibility, but I also pastor in the small village where we are going. Since the services in Hyderabad are Sunday mornings, I hold services at this village on Sunday nights."

"Every Sunday?"

"No, there is a third church that I pastor also, so sometimes I go there on Sundays and visit this one during the week."

"How far is it?"

"It will take us about three hours. This car will only bring us to where the paved roads end. Then we will have to hire a Jeep to take us to the village."

. . .

It was after dark by the time we got into the Jeep and started bumping along the rough dirt road that led through the jungle toward the village.

"This is tiger country," stated Anil, peering out at the dense foliage that lined our road.

"I've heard that tigers sometimes grab people right out of their villages at night. Is that true?" questioned Matt.

"They've been known to. You have more to fear from the cobras, though. There are lots of them."

Trey winced. "Most wild animals don't bother me, but I hate snakes."

As if to confirm Anil's words, a mongoose, mortal enemy to the cobra, darted through our headlights.

It was nearly half an hour later when the trees and bushes that had pressed on us for miles suddenly moved back. A full moon cast silver over two rows of simple dwellings, some built of mud, others of cement, a few topped with corrugated metal, the rest with thatch. Behind them, an extensive space of the jungle had been cleared out and cultivated with rice and other crops. A single electric line ran through the center of the village. Some of the houses appeared to be connected to it, but the moon-glow was much brighter than the timid light that spilled from their open windows. When the Jeep's motor stopped, silence rose around us. The quiet felt tangible after days of constant din in the city. People milled about here and there, doing chores by torchlight or conversing with their neighbors. Some men brought out a wicker-matted bedframe and covered it with a quilt for us to sit on.

"What time does the service start?" asked Matt.

Anil answered, "The people in villages like this do not have the same sense of time that we do. They don't use clocks but do things when they feel the time is right."

"So how do they know when church will be?"

"The believers know a service is planned for this evening. When the time is appropriate, they will begin to gather."

As Anil predicted, a short while later a small crowd began to form in the open area in the center of the village. A trio of men worked to connect a wire into the electric line, forming a hook at the end of a wire and tossing it up over the line. Several times the hook caught and sparks burst from the connection. On the fourth try, the light bulb flickered to life and the men carefully set it atop a long stick that they planted in the ground.

The men completed the preparations by laying out bamboo mats for the congregation and setting a row of wooden chairs for us, facing the mats. By the time the service began, a group of about forty was present. On the left sat the men, their white cotton shirts contrasting markedly with their dark faces. On the right were the women, their hair almost indiscernible from the night, but their saris glowing in brilliant shades, lending grace to even the most shriveled faces. Standing behind the seated Christians, curious Hindu neighbors looked on, intrigued by the four pale-faced visitors. A few yards away, a goat nibbled on a small pile of garbage. Slowly, a man began to strike a drum with his open palm, the instrument reverberating in the cool air. He played for several minutes before, as if on cue, the congregants began to sing, accompanied by a tambourine. The beat grew faster; strong, driving, the pulsating tones pulling us into the spirit of worship.

"I've never heard music like this," whispered Trey. "Their voices aren't great, but there's something powerful about it."

"I like this song where they keep saying, '*Jesu Raja,*'" said Mike.

Anil leaned over toward us. "*Jesu Raja*. It means, 'Jesus the King.' It is about time to speak. Are you ready?"

Trey and Jedd both nodded.

After the service, the believers gathered around us, smiling. Their teeth and eyes shone in the moonlight. Anil translated. "Thank you for coming to our village," said a kindly faced man, placing his hands together in front of his face and bowing slightly. A woman stepped forward. She said nothing, but took each of our right hands in turn and pressed them to her forehead.

"Would you please pray for my son?" asked a young father. He held a three-year-old boy, who lay quietly on his shoulder, eyes wide. "He has not been able to walk since an accident a year ago."

"We would be glad to pray for him," replied Mike.

We prayed for the child, and his father thanked us humbly. As he moved back into the crowd, an elderly man hobbled forward, leaning heavily on a staff. Two men supported him as he moved.

"He has been unable to walk right for a long time," explained one of the men. "Would you please pray that God will heal him?"

We laid hands on the man and Jedd began. "Lord, we come before You in the name of Jesus and ask that You heal this man. We stand here humbly, Father, but we ask that if it be Your will that You restore his legs . . ."

The others followed, requesting healing for the crippled man. Something stirred our assurance. Our faith was as strong as it had ever been. Never in our lives had we prayed so specifically, directly for a person to be healed, but somehow we believed it was what we were supposed to do. We each felt a near certainty that the Lord was going to restore the man's legs.

Trey said, "Amen," and we opened our eyes. The man opened his eyes as well. They were full of expectation, so were those of the crowd. The man pushed against his staff, lifting himself upright and moving his weight onto his legs. He stood there, supporting himself, eyes wide. The villagers seemed to take in a collective breath. Before they could exhale, the man's legs crumbled, sending him down. The men at his sides caught him. A faint murmuring could be heard. The old man was led back into the crowd.

The villagers seemed a little disappointed, but not greatly bothered. Everything continued as it had been—greetings and handshakes and smiles. Someone brought out steaming cups of chai for us. Jedd walked off by himself. Things were spinning around in his head. His face felt hot, feverish. "Lord, please heal this man," he uttered. "You said faith as small as a mustard seed could cast a mountain into the ocean. I *know* we had at least that much faith tonight. Why didn't You heal him?"

Eventually, Anil led us to the Jeep. The crowd pressed around us, smiling and thanking us for coming until we were driving down the dirt road. Mike gazed out the small rear window, staring at the old man who leaned upon his staff.

It was several miles down the road that Mike finally spoke. "Did that bother you guys as much as it did me?"

"I don't know," replied Trey. "I guess it disappointed me a little, but, you know . . . God sometimes says no to our requests."

233

"Yes, but tonight I felt different. I really thought God was going to heal him. I always feel like I never ask with enough faith to see a miracle. Sometimes I see things that *might be* miracles, but I never know. But tonight . . . tonight I *had* the faith. I *knew* God was going to heal him."

"I felt the same, Mike," said Jedd almost inaudibly.

Mike's Reflections—February 8

I just can't shake what happened tonight. But why did it bother me so much? I think I felt like for once I really had the faith, and God was going to do some miracle that I could point to for the rest of my life and say, "That was an undeniable miracle."

If I'm honest, even if he did get healed, I know that after the fact I'd probably think of ways to doubt whether he was really crippled or something, but still, I felt like God was going to undeniably prove Himself once and for all.

It leaves me doubting . . .

234

The next morning at Anil's house, Mike closed his Bible and let out a deep sigh.

"What are you thinking about?" Jedd asked.

"What happened the other night at that village. I still just don't know what to think."

"I know what you mean. Is it making it hard for you to pray?"

"Kind of. I do believe we need to allow God to say no when He's decided that is what's best but—"

"But the Bible is full of invitations to pray and really *expect* things of God," Jedd continued for him.

"Exactly. I always feel like I'm sandbagging—you know, protecting my faith—when I say 'if it be Your will.'"

"Me, too. What about Bible verses with promises like, 'The prayer lifted up in faith *will* heal,' and 'Whatever you ask,' and 'Approach the throne of grace boldly,' and 'In the name of Jesus of Nazareth, get up and walk'? Is that all just for the past?"

Trey and Matt entered the room and Jedd directed a final question to them. "What are you guys thinking about last night? Why doesn't this bother you two as much as Mike and I?"

Trey smiled. "I guess different things affect our faith differently. I just figure there must have been good reasons for God to deny our request. As C. S. Lewis says, when God does a miracle, He is setting aside the laws He designed to rule nature. Sometimes He may set the rules aside, but most of the time not. We should be thrilled to experience miracles when they happen, but not base our faith upon them."

Matt added, "Remember when Jesus said that the Holy Spirit is like the wind? Sometimes we feel a little breeze, other times we see the wind blowing houses over. But we can't decide when it blows or demand that it produce a certain effect. We just need to recognize its work and be thankful for it, not try to control it according to our whims."

Jedd's Reflections—February 9

Just for once, I would like to see an irrefutable miracle.

Perhaps, though, there is no such thing. Even some of the people who saw Lazarus raised from the dead found a way to doubt. I've heard someone say that if we did see a miracle we could not possibly disbelieve, our freedom of choice would be lost. We would have to believe. The Bible seems to indicate that even in God's greatest miracles, He always allows room for us to disbelieve. He does not use miracles to create faith. When it is according to His will, He allows faith to see the miraculous.

I still struggle with this, but it is important for me to see that belief is a choice. It is—and always has been—in my hands. I have reasons to doubt, but also many solid reasons to believe. I must choose. I have seen many things in my life that I really do think reveal God's amazing work on my behalf, even on this trip. When it comes down to it, though, miracles would never be enough to make me follow Christ. What makes me want to commit myself to Him is that I have found Jesus and His words to be the only source of true life. There is simply no other place to go if I desire to truly live.

I've tried to capture some of my thoughts in a poem:

Doubt

My faith lies like a broken man.
Yesterday, I praised Him with palm branches, but something in me today cries out, "Crucify your foolish hope; you only thought

you saw the leper cleansed and that lame man click his heals."

I writhe in my unsurity.

Christ never used the coercion of a miracle one must believe. "Why," I shout with the Inquisitor, "do You not make belief compulsory? Show Your hand!"

But finally, my rage spent, I crumple down upon the dusty road, and in my mind sift through a desert.

Some see God as shackles, and in doubt they glimpse a liberating key. But I see better than that. For even if the skeptics were right, and heaven did not exist, hell most certainly would. For whether or not there is a God, hell is to live without Him.

Life alone is meaningless, a chasing after the wind. A moment of joy, a taste of pleasure . . . "the early leaf's a flower, but only so an hour." Hope is false, peace an illusion, and happiness, at best, is fleeting. Indeed, if Christ is not raised from the dead, we are all most miserable men . . .

And invading my thoughts, the soft slap of sandals upon the path. I do not raise my head, for fear of seeing no one. But still, a voice speaks deep and gentle, "You, too, will not leave Me?"

And I reply, "Whence shall I go, Lord?"

Following a late lunch, we found ourselves lying on our mattresses in the upstairs room at Anil and Annie's. The day was hot and humid, and the breeze from the ceiling fan was welcome as we digested another meal of rice and curry.

Trey set down his copy of the *Rough Guide to India*. "Guys, I think we'd better decide whether we are going to go directly to Calcutta from here or whether we're going to visit some other places."

"What were you thinking, Trey?" asked Jedd.

"I was scanning the guidebook and it doesn't look too hard to make it to Nepal. I think we could swing a trek up into the Himalayas, and still have time to work with the Sisters of Charity in Calcutta."

"That would be incredible," Jedd said. "I've always dreamed of seeing Mount Everest."

Mike broke his silence. "What about Samuel? He really wanted us to come. Don't you think that since we have a few days free, we should spend time with him instead of heading off to Nepal?"

"Mike, we planned to do some tourist stuff during this week all along," Jedd said in a defensive tone. "I'm not exactly planning on coming to India again, and . . ."

"Look, I'd love to go to Everest, too, but I really feel like God might want us to visit Samuel. This trip is about loving people for Christ, not just some adventure tour. What's the priority here? God is giving us an awesome opportunity to encourage some believers. To be honest, I don't see how you could feel okay about passing it up."

Jedd looked over at Matt. "What do you want to do?" he asked somewhat tersely.

"I'd like visiting Nepal, but I agree with Mike. It's not every day God presents an opportunity like this."

Jedd's eyes narrowed. "What makes you think that would be worth the time? If we went with every random Indian off the street who wanted us to visit his home, we'd spend the rest of our lives here. Samuel may want us to come, but do you really think he'll have any real ministry opportunities we wouldn't have anywhere else?"

"I don't know," answered Mike, "but I am pretty sure that us running into him on the train wasn't just a coincidence."

The conversation ran late into the night. When the dust settled, we had agreed to split up. Jedd and Trey would leave for Nepal; Matt and Mike would go to the town of Chirala to spend time with Samuel. We would meet in Calcutta at the end of the week.

237

seventeen

A Change of Plans
Chirala, India

"M ike, Mike!" shouted Samuel. He waved and broke into a run through the train station. Samuel gripped Matt and then Mike in a hug. "It is such a blessing to have you come. Thank you, thank you!"

Matt saw an elderly man who followed a few steps behind Samuel. "Who's this?" he inquired.

"My father, Muthali-Roy. He is pastor of the church here in Chirala. Father, this is Matt and Mike."

As he greeted the pair with a handshake, a smile as big as Samuel's broke on the old man's face. Any lingering doubts Matt and Mike had felt about coming to Chirala quickly vanished as they soaked in the delight their arrival had so clearly brought.

Matt hopped on the backseat of Samuel's moped, his large backpack protruding precariously behind it. Mike climbed onto a bicycle rickshaw with Samuel's father. Even in the small town, people seemed to be everywhere. Vendors lined the streets, spilling out onto the dirt paths used as roads. In the recesses of one of the shops, Mike saw a blacksmith hammering at a glowing piece of metal. A few shops down, men gathered in a garagelike café and drank their afternoon chai. A cow roamed on the main roadway, while hordes of bicycle rickshaws swerved around him.

"I'm glad you received our message, Samuel," said Matt. "Mike and I weren't sure what we'd do if you weren't here to meet us."

"Oh, we knew you were coming. We were gathered in the church praying that you would come when your telegraph arrived."

Message from the Areopagus

Next to the church stood a small parsonage. Matt pushed the door open and felt for a light switch. A simple kitchen and table completed the front room. Several cots filled the back.

"Not a bad little place," remarked Mike.

Samuel excused himself for a moment, promising to return soon.

"I wonder how long ago the missionaries that started this church left," Matt said, thinking out loud.

"I hadn't heard Samuel mention missionaries," responded Mike.

"I guess I haven't, either, but I would be surprised if the townspeople here could have afforded a place like this."

The pair had just set their bags near their cots and stretched out with hopes of a brief nap when Samuel's father entered. Mike smiled at him, secretly hoping Muthali-Roy would not try to speak to them. Like many in India, Muthali-Roy had learned to read and write English well, but knew little of how to pronounce the words. The resulting rapid-fire sound might as well have been Hindi.

"Da sayvis veet stat aht seben tuhnaht."

Mike shot Matt a quizzical glance. "What's that?" he queried.

It added to the difficulty of discerning Muthali-Roy's words that he bobbled his head rapidly from side to side as he spoke. The picture was a bit like that of a turtle's head protruding from its shell.

"Yih wih spihk tonaht at da sayvis aht seben. Mney indoo eepel weel com."

"You're having a church service tonight?"

Muthali-Roy's head bounced in a slightly different direction, perhaps indicating an affirmative.

It took several more repetitions to piece together the message.

"I think they want us to speak tonight at a church service at seven o'clock," suggested Matt.

"I caught that part."

"Did you pick up the rest?"

"I don't think so."

"Samuel mentioned something to me at the train station, but I think I missed what he was saying. As best I can tell, they've told everyone in town that two American evangelists are here. It's going to be a mostly Hindu audience. Muthali-Roy and Samuel are thinking we'll speak for two hours, each night."

Mike laughed slightly, realizing Matt's translation was entirely serious.

Matt responded, "Um, Muthali-Roy, we would be very glad to . . . um, speak . . . but I don't think we can speak for two hours tonight. Since we only have a little while to prepare, I think we can speak for about an hour. Would that be okay?"

Muthali-Roy rolled his eyes. It was not a sarcastic motion, but simply showed he was thinking. Finally, he bobbled his head in a way that seemed to say, "That will be fine if that is how it must be."

When Muthali-Roy had disappeared through the doorway, Matt turned to Mike. "Can you believe this?"

"I know! I had no idea Samuel intended for us to speak at all, let alone lead an evangelistic crusade."

"We've had a few surprise speaking engagements before on the trip, but they never asked for two hours, cold turkey . . ."

"And we always had Jedd around. He's more comfortable with this stuff than I am."

Matt stood up and walked back and forth between the cots. "I feel like I know so little about Hinduism in general. How are we going to know what to say?"

Matt's Reflections—February 12

Lord, I feel like I don't know how to fill five minutes tonight, let alone an hour. And these people—I hardly know their lives, their problems, their needs.

As You reminded Moses, though, You gave man his mouth in the first place. You can equip me to do whatever You want me to do.

I may not know these people in particular, but I know that You made them and love them, and that whatever their temporary needs are, their greatest need is to know You. Even if they can't put this need into words, I know that everyone on this earth has a deep longing within them. They may resist this need, but I know they need You. Help me to simply share about You and the life You offer—that's the need that cuts across every language and culture.

In the church's open sanctuary, square plastered columns held up a metal roof from which were suspended fluorescent lights, two speakers, and several ceiling fans. On the cement floor was a podium and hand-woven mats. The lone wall at the front was decorated with Bible verses in Hindi along with the English words "The Good Shepherd."

"Who built this church, Samuel?" queried Matt.

"Many years ago, a missionary man came to Chirala and shared Jesus. A number of us accepted the Lord, and soon we decided that we would build a church."

"So did the missionary pay for the building?"

Samuel smiled. "No. All of the new believers pooled our jewelry and Hindu idols. We melted them down, sold the raw gold and precious stones, and built the church."

Matt might have felt a little embarrassed over assuming an outsider had paid for the church had Samuel not seemed so proud to correct him. "That's great," Matt said. "It sounds like something out of the New Testament."

Mike questioned, "What happened to the missionary?"

"After some time with us, he left, but he came back often to visit us and encourage us. We were very sad when he died. We will see him in heaven."

The sun was disappearing when the townspeople began to appear. The evening was still quite warm, and a breeze, blowing in between the pillars, provided a welcome cool. Mike noticed that the armpits of the men's shirts were soaked with sweat.

"I guess that's what life was like before deodorant," he whispered to Matt.

Matt leaned toward Mike. "Even with deodorant, you're not smelling so good. The people here must wash themselves every half-hour to stay as clean as they do."

As seven o'clock approached, the sanctuary neared half-full. A sea of colorful saris filled the women's side of the sanctuary; on the other side, hardly a dozen men.

Mike's Reflection—February 12

As in many of the countries we've been to, the women in the church tonight outnumber the men by a significant margin. I wonder why this is.

I can't help but think it might be the male ego, ashamed to admit need, constantly striving for self-sufficiency. Like Alexander back in Russia, they see God as a last-ditch life preserver for people who can't stay afloat on their own.

I have to admit, though, religion is often just that. In many American churches, "Christianity" is just another self-help program full of positive psychobabble with the words God and Jesus thrown in for good measure. I also know plenty of cases where faith is little more than an object on which to pin hopes of seeing dead loved ones again.

I wish more men could see how faith in Jesus—if we truly seek to follow Him—demands the utmost strength, endurance, and bravery. The disciples who followed Christ had to have been among the most courageous people to ever walk the earth. I don't know many today who withstand the threat of dying, let alone deaths like stoning, the cross, or lions for the sake of truth. There was no weakness there.

After a short time of singing led by Samuel, Matt shared about his own story and relationship with Jesus. Mike then began the central message from the book of Acts, reading the same words that had been offered to another crowd of polytheists nearly two thousand years before:

> Paul then stood up in the meeting of the Areopagus and said: "Men of Athens! I see that in every way you are very religious. For as I walked around and looked carefully at your objects of worship, I even found an altar with this inscription:
>
> TO AN UNKNOWN GOD.
>
> "Now what you worship as something unknown I am going to proclaim to you.

"The God who made the world and everything in it is the Lord of heaven and earth and does not live in temples built by hands. And he is not served by human hands, as if he needed anything, because he himself gives all men life and breath and everything else . . . God did this so that men would seek him and perhaps reach out for him and find him, though he is not far from each one of us . . ." (17:22–25, 27)

At the close of the evening, Mike asked if anyone would like to commit their lives to the One and only true God. A hand slipped up in back, then another, and another . . . That night seven people committed themselves to following Jesus.

Meanwhile, in Nepal

Jedd and Trey lay atop their beds in their room in the small trekker's lodge deep in the Himalayas. With the sun down, they wrote in their journals by candlelight.

Trey's Reflections—February 14

Today we ventured by Jeep farther up and farther into Nepal—past Buddhist temples, multicolored prayer flags, and small wooden villages huddled on the mountainsides. When snow finally made our narrow stone road impassable, we covered the final miles to this trekker's lodge on foot. What a journey!

Before going to bed, Jedd and I went outside for a bit. All was totally silent, except the sound of a distant cowbell. A full moon blazed down, turning the expanse of clouds that stretched out below us to a milky sea. Beyond them we could see the great peaks rising out of the mist, glowing white—K2 and the mighty Everest.

Jedd and Trey in the Himalayas
(Mount Everest in Background)

I feel I could write forever, but I am sleepy, and my candle is giving its last flickers . . .

Jedd's Reflections—February 14

This side trip has been great—the scenes and the people, and especially the time with Trey. As always seems to be the case, time out in God's creation has refreshed my faith as well. Part of me has wondered if we should have stuck with Mike and Matt, but this is where we are, and I am enjoying it a great deal. Perhaps it was God's purpose that we split up for a time.

I've had a chance to reflect about the issue of prayer and what happened the other night in the village. I feel like I see it all a lot more clearly now.

For one thing, I see that so much of the problem lay in the fact that when I prayed the words, "If it be Your will . . ." I really didn't mean them.

Jesus Himself prayed those words, acknowledging that God might not answer His request in the affirmative. Saying the right words or having more faith is not always the issue—God often has good reasons for saying no.

And even though we won't know all those reasons until we get to heaven, it's not hard to conceive of at least a few purposes He might have had for denying our request the other night. Maybe a miraculous healing that night would have turned the villagers' focus away from Jesus and onto "healings" (as the message of some televangelists does). It could have done that to me also—gotten me all hyped on supernaturally healing people instead of on helping people to come to know Jesus.

Jesus did many miracles, but of far greater importance to Him was changing hearts and lives. Even someone who has been raised from the dead will eventually die again. But a person who gives their life to Christ

Jedd Journaling

enters true, rich, incomparable life that will only grow more complete when physical death occurs.

This is why miracles were never the centerpiece of Christ's ministry. He hated the effects of evil like blindness, sickness, and death. He wept at the pain evil caused. At times, He proved His dominance over it supernaturally. Often, though, He did not. His purpose for coming to earth was not to dazzle people with miracles. The miracles were primarily "signs" that affirmed the validity of His message of redemption. Many times, He refused to do miracles at all because the people requesting them just wanted a show.

My focus must be on living—and offering to others—the abundant life Jesus provides. On this earth, there will always be times when God will grant requests to suspend the effects of evil, and others when He will not. I will not always understand the reasons, but it is something I must accept, just as His Son did.

Men from the Dream

Mike and Matt split up the following day to visit some of Chirala's other believers. Late in the afternoon, after visiting a half-dozen homes, the rickshaw carrying Samuel and Mike halted before a small hovel near the edge of town. Samuel slipped some change into the rickshaw driver's hand and dismissed him, then turned and rapped against the cement doorframe as best he could. Hearing no reply, he peered into the dark entrance. A crackly voice sounded from inside; words of welcome, Mike guessed. Mike ducked to clear the tattered edges of the thatch roof as he followed Samuel through the doorway. Mike's eyes were still adjusting to the half-light as Samuel began introducing him to a hunched shape; he could just make out the prunelike head of an old woman poking up through a red-and-yellow sari. The woman scrutinized Mike for a moment, drawing her face quite close to his. As she did, she seemed to grow agitated—whether angry or excited, Mike could not tell. She rattled at Samuel for nearly a minute before he quieted her and turned to Mike.

"This woman has something to tell you, Mike. I will translate."

Samuel said something to the woman and she began again.

"These have been very hard times in Chirala. For many months I have been very discouraged. But three weeks ago, God encouraged me in a dream. In my dream, two men from far away came to our town to give us words from our Lord. When I saw you, I knew that you were the man. I saw you in my dream just as you are. You are like the olive branch that the dove brought to Noah. You are the promise that God has given to me that He has not abandoned me. Thank you so much for coming."

A tear trickled down Mike's cheek. All he could do was nod humbly as the woman took his hands and pressed them to her forehead. "Thank you for telling me," he said.

Mike's Reflections—February 15

It is hard to understand how or why I get to be such an encouragement to the people here. And is it really possible that God even gave that lady a dream about us before she'd seen us or knew we were coming? What an incredible thing.

Living like this, led not by any knowledge or expertise of my own, I am completely dependent on God's action and guidance. This is especially true here in Chirala. It is intimidating, but what amazing things we are getting to experience.

Back at the church, Samuel and his father left Mike and Matt alone to allow them to prepare for the night's talks. Matt was fascinated by Mike's retelling of the old lady's dream.

"No one told me about any dreams, but it was kind of like that for me, too, in just about every house," Matt agreed. "The believers here are so thankful we've come."

Mike shook his head in wonder. "I don't fully understand it, but it's an awesome experience to get to be such an encouragement."

A concerned look crossed Matt's face for a moment. "One thing I've been wondering, Mike, is if Samuel and his father are going to be able to help teach and disciple the people who received Jesus last night. I would hate to think that these Hindus might come to believe but then have no support and fall away."

"Samuel told me that he knows each one of the people that raised their hand. In fact, we visited two of them today. I don't think they'll have any problem following through with discipleship."

"I'm glad to hear that."

Matt's Reflections—February 13

I tend to question the value of short-term evangelism in foreign countries, especially when there is no one left behind to encourage and instruct the new believers.

Leading a person to faith in Jesus and then leaving them without someone to guide them is like leaving a newborn puppy alone in the middle of a forest. Unless someone finds them, they likely won't last long.

I understand that we each have different roles in the Church—some till the soil, some plant seeds, some tend them as they grow. But every one of us needs to know that evangelism is not just to convert people to accept certain ideas about Christ, but to make disciples of Christ. The last verse of the Great Commission is often overlooked—it says we must make disciples by "teaching them to obey everything I have commanded you" (Matt. 28:20). Disciples are not people who merely believe things about their master; they are students of him, continual learners. They seek with all their hearts to become like him and to follow his teachings.

It seems to me that evangelism that merely tries to get people to pray the "Sinner's Prayer" can hardly be called evangelism at all.

247

Twice as many people attended the second night's meeting, well over one hundred. The third night, even more came to listen to the out-of-town evangelists. Each night, a scattering of raised hands declared intent to follow Jesus. After the final meeting, Matt and Mike sat on the roof of the parsonage. The church grounds were silent now. Though nearly midnight, the air was balmy and completely still. To both of them, the stars this night seemed unnaturally bright.

Finally, almost reverently, Mike spoke. "I still feel like I'm wondering exactly what's happened these last few nights."

"I know. I don't think I've ever experienced anything quite like it."

Mike Gets Swept into a Political Rally in Chirala

"We've gone in feeling so inadequate. Even tonight, I felt like I had no idea what to say."

"But all of the right words seemed to come out . . . or, I don't know if they were the right words, but somehow God used them to draw people to Himself *despite* what we said."

Matt slowly shook his head, unable to distill the feelings that ricocheted inside. Finally, he tried. "I've never had such a strong sense of my weakness being swallowed up by God's strength. It's incredible."

"I know. I honestly can't think of anything better than being used by God like this . . ."

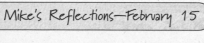

Mike's Reflections—February 15

Even on our third night of speaking, we felt completely inadequate. Maybe that's the way God works best. Perhaps only when there is less of us can there be more of God.

We sure are going to have a lot to tell Jedd and Trey when we get to Calcutta. I wonder if they actually made it to see Everest . . .

More than a year later, back in the United States, Mike received a letter from Samuel. Besides relating certain events from the prior year and telling how Samuel's father and family were doing, it also read, ". . . I know you will be happy to hear, brother, that almost all of the Hindu people who accepted Jesus the nights you and Matt spoke to our city are still with us. Many of them have grown much. We thank God greatly for them and also for you . . ."

Sisters of Charity
Calcutta, India

According to our guidebook, Mother Teresa's Sisters of Charity house was just three blocks from our hotel in Calcutta. Friends back in the States had informed us that anyone could volunteer with the Sisters.

Mother Teresa had started as an instructor at a parochial school for the children of Calcutta's wealthiest citizens. Her heart ached, though, for the poor and destitute, and the words of Christ weighed heavy upon her, "If you have done it unto the least of these, you have done it unto Me." Abandoning her safe, well-provided-for life, she set out to love and serve the poorest of the poor in any way she could. For decades, she and the group of Sisters who slowly grew around her served quietly, known to few but those they served. Over the years, this radical love offered in the name of Jesus made Teresa an international heroine. At her death the summer before our visit, the world—especially the Hindu nation of India—wept.

Sisters of Charity

Jedd pushed against the heavy wooden door. It opened onto a small courtyard, encircled by the high walls of the buildings. In the middle of the courtyard, a silver-haired woman sat behind a desk, dressed in the simple blue-and-white habit adopted by the Sisters of Charity. Several bohemian-looking Westerners were standing nearby, waiting.

"You are here to volunteer?" the Sister questioned.

"We are," Matt replied. "There are four of us who would like to begin work tomorrow, but just two of us were able to come today."

"Mass begins at five-thirty and work a little after six," the Sister explained. "Tomorrow morning you can pick which of the homes you would like to work at. If you would like to get an introduction to our work today, Sister Helen can take you around the Mother House here."

Sister Helen, a young Indian woman dressed in the same garb, nodded at us with a pleasant smile. "We can begin our visit now," she announced, loud enough for the others in the courtyard to hear.

She led us all toward a doorway at the far side of the courtyard and directed us through an enormous laundry area. Several Sisters and volunteers labored over large vats of water—washing, rinsing, hanging to dry. Helen explained, "Part of the commitment the Sisters make is a vow of poverty. Throughout our lives, we will not own anything, except for two sets of clothing. And we do not use machines to do our work for us."

The final stop on the tour was the doorway to the third-floor ward. "You are welcome to come in for a time if you wish," offered Helen. "I need to talk with some of the Sisters here for a moment."

The room suggested something of a warehouse, set with long, even rows of bedded cribs. A dozen Sisters moved from bed to bed, tending the children's needs as best they could, often simply holding them, rocking them, or singing softly. Despite the resemblance to a hospital ward, the room had none of the sterile feel most hospitals seem to have. It was clean, but not impersonal or stifling. Part of this may have been the variety in the donated blankets and wooden cribs, but it seemed to go deeper than that. The room held a hushed, peaceful aura.

This place feels so unlike any hospital I've ever seen. It may be that hospitals in America are concerned almost exclusively with repairing physical ailments. Here, they can't do much for these kids' problems. They focus instead on helping these deformed, abandoned children feel loved and wanted. That is an entirely different sort of healing. It seems to affect every inch of this place.

Timidly, Matt began to walk among the rows. Most of the children sat or lay silently, eyes half-open, squirming slightly in search of a hug or tender touch. A boy with only small stumps of limbs poking out from a bent body roused as Matt passed his crib and cried out once. Opposite him, a fine-haired girl stared blankly over the top of the bars of her crib with unseeing eyes. In a third crib, a head as large as that of a normal twelve-year-old lay on a pillow, connected to the body of an infant.

Jedd looked toward Helen. She noticed and nodded her head gently. "Yes, the children need all the love and touch that we can give them. If you would like, they would love for you to hold them."

He reached his arms into the crib of a small girl who appeared to be blind and lacking digits on her feet and hands. As he lifted her, the girl's touch-starved limbs clamped around his neck. She seemed to hold him with all the strength her feeble body could muster, hoping her grip would prevent him from setting her back down.

Matt glanced around at the Sisters and novices who moved about the room. Most of the children did not wear diapers, and some of the women were kept busy cleaning the cribs and their inhabitants. One was on her hands and knees, wiping up a mess that had leaked to the floor. Several others moved from crib to crib, caressing the children or lifting them for a time to hold them or even sing to them.

Matt turned to the crib next to him. The eyes of a small boy, his legs twisted like pretzels, grew wide and his breathing quickened. A soft moan—yearning mixed with excitement—prevented Matt from simply looking any longer. As he leaned into the crib, the child clamored into his arms and fastened himself tightly around his neck. Immediately, the boy's body relaxed and his breathing slowed, like a lost, scared child who had just found his father.

After twenty minutes, Sister Helen announced, "It is time to go. They'll be serving the children dinner soon."

As Matt walked back toward the boy's bed, the child began to squeeze tighter. Matt leaned over the crib and tried to set him down, but the boy's arms gained the strength of desperation.

"Here, little buddy. I'm sorry I have to put you down, but they say it's time for dinner."

The boy would not release his grip, and Matt was forced to try prying off one arm at a time. As he did, the boy's crooked legs and other arm groped wildly for a better grip. Finally, Matt was able to release him into the crib. As he did so, the boy scooted his body to the bars of the crib, his legs dragging behind him. He pulled himself up partway and let out a wail of abandonment that made Matt's heart race.

He looked into the crib for a moment longer, his eyes moist. "I'm sorry, buddy. I'm real sorry."

Back in the courtyard, Jedd turned to Matt, his voice almost a whisper, "Did that tear you apart like it did me? I just didn't want to let go of that little girl."

Matt just nodded.

° ° °

Five-thirty the next morning came early. Mass was a series of songs, recitations, and a brief homily from the head priest. The volunteers who had opted to attend sat in their own section, and were asked to take Communion only if they confessed Jesus as their Lord and Savior. After the service, the Sisters served a simple breakfast of bananas and slices of bread. The fifty or so volunteers formed a rather motley bunch, milling around in the courtyard. Longhaired English hippies conversed with conservative Canadian evangelicals; an old Chinese man sat chatting with a young South African girl.

Mike talked with an American couple who were heading in the same direction we were. The middle-aged pair looked a bit contrived in their Indian garb—she in a sari, he decked in a long robe and small, Muslim-looking cap. They both had grown up wealthy, but apparently had come to despise their materialistic forebears. Now they spent their days living off inheritance, drifting from spiritual quest to spiritual quest.

"We knew there would be a lot of positive energy in a place like this," the man explained. "And we were right, you really can feel it."

Mike nodded slightly, not quite sure how to respond.

"Energy," the man repeated slowly.

"Where do you think it comes from?" questioned Mike.

"The good karma, you know, people doing good things."

"You're Hindu?"

The man shot a glance at his woman-partner and gave a faint, possibly condescending laugh. "Oh, no. We're not locked into any religious schemata. After all, no religion is perfect. We take the best from each."

"What if you make mistakes in deciding what the best is?" Mike probed.

"We may, but at least we will never stop seeking. That's a trap that many religious people fall into."

"Do you expect to find what you are looking for?"

"For us, I'd have to say that the seeking is the finding . . ."

Mike's Reflections—February 17

The spiritual-seeker types always mystify me.

Of course, seeking truth is a noble goal. God certainly desires that humanity seek Him. As in the passage from Acts I read the other night, "God did this so that men would seek him and perhaps reach out for him and find him" (17:27).

In some sense, I'm a seeker, too. I hope to keep learning all my life, and even then, I know I'll never have all the answers.

So often, though, these so-called seekers view "seeking" as the end in itself. I get the feeling that if real truth dropped in their laps, they'd scoop it away as if it were hot coals.

The word seek implies there is something to be found. If there isn't, or if a person would refuse to accept the Thing they are seeking if they did find it, it doesn't seem like there is much point in "seeking." They might as well quit playing games and just grab for all the pleasure they can before they die.

The Sick and the Dying

For our volunteer work, we went to Primdan, the Home for the Sick and Dying. Before us spread at least an acre of interconnected concrete buildings. Grass, flowers, and palm trees grew in lightly tended gardens to our left and right.

"This place isn't anything fancy, but it sure is a peaceful escape from the city," commented Trey.

"I think that's the intent," suggested Matt. "None of the people that get brought here have long to live. The missionaries of charity want them to die loved, in as peaceful a place as possible."

It was before 7:00 A.M., but the complex was already a hive of activity. Catholic Sisters and Brothers were already about their daily tasks: sweeping, cooking, washing bedclothes, and tending to the dying men and women who had been found on the streets and brought in to Primdan. Many of the "residents" were outside as well—hobbling about the gardens, sitting on benches, or lying on cots that had been set on the grass. The marks of pain, disease, and death were everywhere: missing limbs, bandaged heads, raspy breathing, skeletal frames, mucus-blocked coughs.

Mike noticed a man sitting on the cement edge of a large planter. His legs ended at the shins, gauze covering both stumps, soaked through with splotches of crimson. The man's neck was so small that the opening of his ragged T-shirt hung down to reveal his collarbones, which stuck out like door handles on an old car. Mike acted as if he had been studying the planter when the man caught him staring.

"Can you believe this place?" whispered Trey. "All these people all around on the verge of death. It's like some sort of nether world or something."

"Or a war zone," followed Matt.

"Before this trip, I don't know if I'd ever seen one person as terrible-looking as just about every patient in here."

A red-haired Sister with a cheery Irish accent interrupted our thoughts. "Men, this way to care for the gents; and women, you'll be over there. Don't be shy, now. Pick a job you see someone else doing and start doing it with them. Ask questions if you need directions . . . you'll figure it out."

We discovered quickly there were only a few tasks the new volunteers could do without getting in the way, all of them unpleasant. Trey quickly found himself helping a feeble man toward the makeshift shower, his scabby legs dragging behind him. The open wounds on his chest oozed onto Trey's shirt as the man clung to him with all his might. Many of the patients could not stand or even sit up, so Trey worked with another volunteer—one supporting the patient, the other cleaning him.

Mike and Jedd washed soiled blankets with at least a dozen other volunteers. Each blanket went through a series of pools—one for a general rinsing first, a second for washing, finally another for rinsing. Once a blanket was clean, a pair would need to tax their muscles to twist it between them to dry it as much as possible before taking it to the roof to hang in the sun. Mike used a long pole to stir the blankets around in the second washing pool. His eyes watered from the strongly chemical steam.

"Potent stuff," he commented with a cough.

"I can smell it from over here," replied Jedd from the rinsing vat. He continued as Mike stepped over to help him wring out a blanket. "You know, it is not that I mind this work, but I can't help wondering a little about the Sisters' vow of poverty. Their work would be so much more efficient if they used modern conveniences."

"I've been thinking about that, too. They don't see efficiency as that high of a value."

"I can respect that, I guess," Jedd continued. "I know I get too caught up in wanting to be efficient sometimes. Still, it would just seem logical to use whatever tools you could to love the greatest number of people."

"They probably see it as quality over quantity."

"I don't see how those two are mutually exclusive."

"They aren't always, but I don't think our responsibility as Christians is necessarily to love the greatest number of people possible. We just need to do a good job loving the people we are supposed to love, whether that's a big number or a small number."

Jedd's Reflections—February 17

The Sisters of Charity epitomize the opposite of what most would consider efficiency. They could care for so many more people if they would use things like washing machines, dishwashers, and other modern conveniences. I know they'd have no trouble getting those things donated. I'm still not sure what to think of that.

What is more significant is that the Sisters' service is poured into what some might consider "black holes." All but a few of the people they care for here will never be healed. This goes for the Sisters' other homes as well, like the AIDS home.

Very little "functional" value will come of the Sisters' work. It's just love poured out in the name of Jesus. It will not produce anything in most of those being served except for occasional smiles or thank-yous. Some might say it is pointless.

But it all comes down to this: If we are eternal beings, loved by God, then there is reason to show love to each and every one, no matter what their state. If we are no more than meaningless links in an evolutionary ladder, though, then the strongest and smartest might as well look out for themselves.

The Sisters' work here, just like Jesus' work and teachings, resoundingly affirms the former.

Jesus didn't operate on a "maximum effectiveness rule." His concern was not even to heal the greatest number of people or to feed everyone. He sought simply to love those around Him and to do the work He had been called to do.

As hard as it is for me to think in terms other than "maximum efficiency," I need to realize that sometimes—maybe even more often than not—"inefficiency" is the path love takes.

It was on the taxi ride back to our hotel that we had a chance to talk together again.

"What'd you guys think about today?" asked Trey.

"What struck me was the difference between the permanent workers and the temporary volunteers," said Mike.

"How so?"

"The nuns and the permanent staff seemed so full of love for the people. I got a very different sense from the volunteers. Maybe I am just a cynic, but I felt like a lot of them were volunteering because it was hip and gave them something to brag about when they got home. They seemed to think there was something cool about saying that they worked with Mother Teresa's Sisters of Charity."

Jedd thought for a moment. "I can't say I noticed that, but I do agree that it is incredible what the Sisters do there. They're just continually doing things I would find so repulsive."

Trey remarked, "That's true. Their work is the most undesirable I've ever seen. And yet they seem to enjoy it . . . not as if it's fun, but because they wouldn't want to be doing anything else."

"What really hit me," said Jedd, "was this sense that all the evil and suffering we've seen all along this trip was distilled into this one place."

"You had an evil feeling in there?" questioned Trey.

"No. The opposite. It was like evil was in its most concentrated form with all the death and suffering you could see, but the goodness of Christ's love was so much more powerful."

"I guess I had that sense, too," noted Trey, "but there was just so much pain also . . . they were both pretty potent."

"I know what you mean. I don't want to diminish how bad the badness is. I know we'll be dealing with it as long as we're on earth. But the way Christ's love was poured out there . . . *that* is the antidote. Things won't ever be totally right until we get to heaven, but wherever people are really living out Jesus' love, there is just incredible goodness and peace."

"I agree, except on one point," stated Trey. "I don't think evil was any more concentrated in there than anywhere else in the world. The world is full of evil. In there it was just less disguised. Most places, badness is more subtle—things like greed, hatred, pride, and stuff."

Jedd nodded. "You're right. In fact, subtle evil is probably a lot worse. The root disease is the same everywhere, though. So is the antidote."

Matt, as usual, had been listening and forming his thoughts. "What's sad is that even though people see that the Sisters of Charity are onto something, most would define 'success' just the opposite of how the Sisters live."

 Matt's Reflections—February 17

The lives of the Sisters are just the opposite of what the world defines as success. It will not provide the least bit of power, fame, wealth, or prestige. They are just a bunch of unknown women caring for deformed children and dying people who will likely never even get well enough to thank them.

But there is something powerful there, more powerful than I can put into words. So much of it, I know, is the incredible beauty of sacrificial, selfless love.

There is something else, too. Comparing the Sisters' lives to the lives the world declares "successful," I think of Jesus' words, "Whoever finds his life will lose it, and whoever loses his life for my sake will find it" (Matt. 10:39).

You can see that so many of the people whom the world views as having "found life"—from celebrities to CEO's to star athletes—actually lose it. There may be bright lights for a while, but the honest biographies often reveal tragic realities: broken marriage after broken marriage, years spent without purpose or hope, the squandering of vast resources, desperation to hold on to fame or position, and frantic attempts to fill the emptiness with drugs, alcohol, and sex.

I'm sure the Sisters here have plenty of difficulties as well, but it seems they also have a deep sense of contentment and purpose. They "lose" their lives in the world's eyes every day that they do their unnoticed, insignificant tasks. Yet it seems to me that they have found much more than the rich and famous ever find. And they are confident of an even greater eternal reward as well.

I know it would be incredibly hard to live as they do, but I hope I can live by the same principle—finding my life by losing it for the sake of Jesus.

258

Trey looked out the window. "Tomorrow it's on to Bangladesh!"

"Do you think it's going to be as bad as it sounds?" asked Matt. "The few people I've talked to who have been to Bangladesh say the culture shock there is worse than any other place in the world."

"Culture shock is for wimps," said Mike with a grin. "Besides, how could it be any crazier than India?"

The taxi driver, not quite following our conversation, interjected a question of his own, "You like India?"

We smiled at each other. Trey took it upon himself to fill the silence. "I'll tell you one thing for sure, sir: There's no other place in the world quite like it."

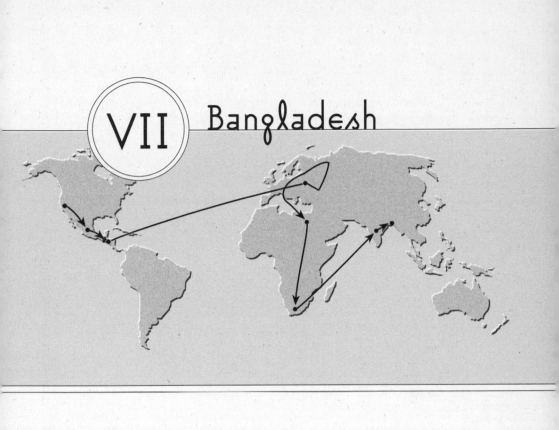

VII Bangladesh

nineteen

The End of Our Rope

Bangladesh? Cyclones, floods, famine, unstable governments and people everywhere . . . it is hardly surprising that Bangladesh doesn't rate highly on traveler's itineraries.

—*Lonely Planet* GUIDEBOOK

Come to Bangladesh before the tourists do.

—BANGLADESHI DEPARTMENT OF TOURISM

We had little idea where we were—just somewhere in the heart of Dhaka, capital city of Bangladesh. Our drive through the teeming streets and alleys had left even Trey's sense of direction spinning. After a half-dozen flights of stairs on the crumbling cement building, we were wheezing. The air tasted like lead.

The Bangladeshi man who had met us at the airport unlocked a door and motioned us through with a tilt of his head. His name was Ihan, his dark eyes, almond skin, and boyish face suggesting he was younger than his thirty-something years.

"Eight of us who work for Bangladesh Christian Service live here," he explained. "We call it our dorm."

The unpainted cement walls and glassless, barred windows had little resemblance to any dorms we had ever lived in. We expected to spend only a day or two in the dorms. Our goal for the next six weeks was to aid the work of Bangladesh Christian Service, the local branch of the worldwide JESUS Film International. For the first time on our trip, we would work separately, each joining a separate "team" on a month-long mission to show the *JESUS* film in villages far from Dhaka.

"Is this a kitchen?" wondered Mike, entering the first room. A sink crafted from sheet metal took up one corner. Next to it stood a large plastic barrel of water; most likely, it was filled during the few hours each day when the city's pipes flowed. A propane tank with some sort of burner attachment lay on the floor—apparently the stove.

Three large gunnysacks leaned against the wall. Matt peeked into one. "Now that's a lot of rice," he remarked. "It looks like this is about the only food in the kitchen." Matt recoiled as three large cockroaches bolted from the folds of the sack. He stifled a reaction as our host reentered the room.

262

We had been warned Bangladesh could be difficult. With more than 120 million people crammed into an area the size of Wisconsin, Bangladesh is three times as densely populated as India. In fact, Bangladesh is the most densely populated country on the globe. This demographic reality impacts every facet of life. Jobs and food are scarce. The average person makes less than $400 per year. Eighty percent of the people do not get enough nutrition to meet what food experts say is needed to subsist. How do they survive? God only knows.

"You can put your bags back here," Ihan directed, leading deeper into the apartment.

A bedroom held four pairs of metal bunk beds and a ceiling fan; the bathroom connected to it. Since there was no running water, the sink and shower fixtures seemed to be little more than decorations. The squat toilet—a hole in the ground with a footpad on either side— apparently could be flushed with a cup of water from the kitchen.

"You can share this room with me and some of the others until you go out to the villages," Ihan

Matt and Trey in a Rickshaw in Dhaka

explained. "I'll cook some rice in a short time for dinner. Before that, who will tell me more about America?"

We looked at one another, hoping one of us would volunteer. Already we had been asked 101 questions about America on the way home from the airport. As in so many countries, America represented a golden, almost mythical land across the sea.

Reluctant Messengers

Ihan had kept us up after dinner with more questions about America until our eyelids gave out. When we reached our beds, however, a combination of humid heat, noise, and mosquitoes kept sleep just out of reach. An hour after lights out, Mike lay sweating, stripped down to his boxers. The beads of moisture made him feel as if he were glued to the top of his nylon bag. Sounds of traffic poured through the open windows. He heard Trey tossing restlessly in the bunk below.

Mike stared at the unmoving fan above. "Why don't they turn on the fan!" he grumbled, just loud enough to be heard. He knew our hosts would not hear, though; their breathing had grown deep and steady within minutes of the lights turning out.

"That's just what I was thinking," said a voice from the darkness.

"You're awake, too, Jedd?"

"What else would I be doing," came a grunted reply.

"I think we all are," joined Matt.

Ihan had insisted that sleeping with the fan on was unhealthy. "We'll all catch colds if you turn that on," he had warned as he climbed under several layers of blankets. He informed us it was still the "cool" season in Bangladesh. Maybe it was. It sure would not have passed for "cool" with anyone we knew, though.

o o o

The smell of curry and fish, mixed with wafts of exhaust fumes, permeated the bedroom. Morning sunlight sifted through the barred windows, painting stripes of light on the walls. Trey lifted an eyelid. Two men wearing what looked like colorful skirts and undershirt tank tops stood in the middle of the room, speaking and laughing out loud as if it were the middle of the day. Trey felt under his bunk for his glasses and slid them on.

263

He glanced at his watch. 5:30. He wondered to himself, *Why are they talking so loudly? Don't they know what time it is?*

Jedd pulled his pillow over his head. Matt slid out from under his mosquito net and climbed down to the floor. His face felt puffy and his eyes stung.

"Time to get up. Breakfast is ready now," Ihan announced with a smile, his head bobbling from side to side.

We roused ourselves as quickly as possible. After downing a mound of rice topped with sprinkles of fish curry, we were on our way to the Bangladesh Christian Service office.

Dennis Sammadar, director of Bangladesh Christian Service, was waiting for us at his desk. An American employee of the JESUS Film International had put us in contact with Director Sammadar nearly a year before.

"Please come, sit down," the small man invited, returning his glasses to his face. His English was flawless but heavily accented. "I am glad that you have finally arrived. I must talk to you about the work we have planned for you. As we discussed in e-mail, you will be going to villages tomorrow. Tonight, we thought it would be good if you went to show the *JESUS* film with us in a region near Dhaka city."

The four of us exchanged glances in silence.

Jedd finally responded, "Director Sammadar, we're looking forward to beginning work, but we are not feeling very well today. We think it might be best if we rested this evening before we separate and go out to the villages."

Director Sammadar glanced at the checkered tile floor, then raised his eyes. "I'm sorry. Normally I would encourage you to rest, but we have informed the government chairman of the region that four Americans would come with us tonight."

"Is there any way you could tell them that we were not able to make it?" asked Mike.

"No. That would not do. We have been trying to show the film in this fundamentalist Muslim area for many years. Tonight is our first opportunity to do so. We got permission because we said we were bringing Americans. I think if you don't come, it would not be good."

Trey mustered a smile. "In that case, we're very willing to join you. We didn't understand how important it was."

The sun had dropped below the earth's edge by the time our Jeep reached the regional chairman's office. Fading baby-blue walls surrounded a large wooden desk. As we entered, the well-fed, graying man behind it stood, shook our hands, and motioned us toward the chairs directly in front of him. Behind the chairs, a wall of men—apparently lower-level regional officials—stood looking on. Forty pairs of eyes followed with interest as we took our seats.

"The way they're looking at us, I wonder if they have ever seen a white person before," Mike whispered.

The chairman leaned back confidently in his chair, gripping both arm-rests firmly. On either side of him stood assistants dressed in traditional white Muslim garb. They inclined their heads slightly toward the chair-man; it seemed they would be quite ready to clean his bellybutton with Q-Tips should he demand it. An awkward silence fell on the room for a moment. Overhead, an out-of-balance ceiling fan *click-click-clicked,* provid-ing little respite from the night's moist heat. Finally, the chairman barked, "Give these men refreshments—fruit and snacks!"

The servile assistants rushed to obey, laying a plateful of pretzels, fruit, and other less recognizable goodies before us. Mr. Sammadar stated loudly, "The chairman would like to explain his plan to increase the region's literacy rate. He would like your help in implementing his pro-gram. I will translate for you."

We nibbled hesitantly at the snacks, trying not to betray our bewilder-ment. The chairman appeared pleased that we seemed to enjoy his delica-cies and began popping pretzels into his mouth. Every few bites, he held out a pretzel or bit of fruit in an open hand, allowing his assistants to clamor like monkeys to retrieve a treat from their benevolent leader.

He launched his first question. "Should the first priority in a literacy program be to teach the old or to teach the young?"

We glanced at one another with a tinge of fear. We knew absolutely nothing about literacy programs.

"There . . . are many theories . . . in regard to this matter," began Jedd, speaking slowly. "I tend to think it might be best to . . . begin instruction with the group that can learn most easily, and then allow them to teach the others."

The chairman nodded, apparently pleased with the answer. He contin-ued, "And should this be done in schools or in homes?"

Another difficult moment of silence. Matt spoke directly to Director Sammadar, trying to convey our dilemma. "We do not know this location very well yet. Do *you* have a suggestion, Mr. Sammadar?"

Mr. Sammadar's response to the chairman was long enough to suggest he had answered the question himself.

Mike leaned over to Matt. "It's funny the chairman is asking us this stuff. We have no clue. I guess just the fact that Americans are here gives Mr. Sammadar a lot of credibility."

Matt whispered back, "It's crazy how much deference they show us—we're just a bunch of nobodies."

The questions continued, but Mike had successfully guessed our role. Somewhere in the middle of the conversation, Mr. Sammadar stopped translating the chairman's questions into English altogether. Somehow, our presence had accomplished its purpose. A relationship had been built that would allow Mr. Sammadar to aid with the local literacy program. Better yet—even before our meeting finished—the *JESUS* film was allowed to proceed outside. As the meeting concluded, we were ushered to a soccer field where the film was being shown on a fifteen-foot portable screen. Several hundred Muslims sat on the ground, watching intently. We joined them, listening to a Jesus who spoke Bengali.

266

Matt's Reflections—February 19

I had no idea tonight would be such a remarkable evening.

As weary as I felt coming out here, it was exhilarating to witness hundreds of Muslims being presented with the truth of who Jesus Christ is and what He did for us. It seems almost laughable that I, just because I am an American in Bangladesh, could be so key in opening the opportunity for the film to be shown here.

I'm thankful the Lord allowed us to be a part of His work even when I really just wanted to rest tonight. I do want to serve Him in the way He desires of me, not just in the way I wish to serve.

We spoke little most of the way home, scrunched four across the backseat of a compact car. Finally, Mike pulled his forehead off the seat in front of him. "You know, guys, I think the craziness of India took more out of me than I realized," he announced, his voice vibrating with the bouncing of the car.

"Is this Mr. Culture-Shock-Is-for-Wimps speaking?" poked Matt.

"Four and a half months of travel has probably taken a little toll on all of us," said Jedd.

Matt nodded. "All except Trey."

"To be honest, I'm feeling a little worn down, too," admitted Trey.

"I'm starting to wonder if it is best to go off on our own for five weeks when we're feeling like this," remarked Matt.

"I'd vote for staying together if we weren't already pretty committed to this," said Trey. "I think Mr. Sammadar is really counting on us to help his teams make headway into new areas, just like tonight."

The others had to agree.

With morning, we would depart for the provinces, each accompanied by a Bangladesh Christian Service translator. Once in the provinces, we would join up with local believers. Director Sammadar explained that our teams would travel from village to village by day, visiting with what Christians there were and inviting everyone to the nightly showings. Beyond that, we had little idea what to expect.

Matt would be traveling to the northwestern Thurkagon region with a BCS worker named Kinjapur. Jedd would journey to a small village several hours north of Dhaka. Trey's venture would take him to the southern Ganges River delta region with a man named Ajonni. Mike and his partner would head in a northeasterly direction, although he still does not know exactly where they ended up.

Matt—Northwestern Thurkagon Region

Kinjapur, the BCS worker who would serve as Matt's translator, had roused him from his bunk before six that morning. Now—an hour later—Matt was still trying to wake up. The depot was chaos. Matt sat in the bus, waiting for it to fill. Regardless of schedule, it would not depart until every seat was taken. The entire scene seemed surreal. It felt almost as if he were outside his body, watching himself from a distance in a strange land.

He looked down at the crowd that churned around the buses. The shifting colors—especially the women's brilliant saris—made him think of a spinning kaleidoscope. Individuals shouted to each other to be heard over the din of bus horns. Brightly painted bicycle rickshaws pressed through the mix as well, their drivers forced to walk alongside their carts and push. The air was thick with noise and diesel, making his head feel empty.

Matt's Reflections—February 18

I am officially starting to feel a little homesick for the first time on the trip. I feel like I just want America and comfort. I want to be home. Instead, I have Bangladesh, alone, for five weeks.

Part of me wonders why and how I got here. But then, I remember: I followed my Lord Jesus' voice that told me to step out in faith. I stepped out and found solid ground beneath my feet. And even when the ground seems to quake, my faith continues to grow firmer the farther I go. After all, what does a little shaky ground matter when you know you're in the loving hands of the living God?

268

The bus barreled down a narrow, potholed lane. As the largest vehicle on the road, it had unquestioned right of way. As it roared past, other traffic squeezed onto the road's narrow shoulders—women carrying market supplies, bicycle rickshaws, rusted trucks, ox-drawn carts. The bus driver honked incessantly, seeming to say, "I'm not stopping for anything, so you'd better get out of the way!"

Matt winced as the open door of the bus nearly clipped a woman with a large bucket balanced on her head. She steadied her cargo, but her eyes held little anger as she stared after the bus. Matt glanced at the driver. It seemed he had not even noticed the woman.

Matt's Reflections—February 18

Roads seem to personify the rules in Third World countries: Right of way goes to the biggest and strongest. The only "right" of the small guy is to get out of the way of those bigger than him.

As Americans, we have the sense that each individual has inalienable rights, regardless of their status in society. These rights apply everywhere. We believe you shouldn't be able to send someone to jail or take their property just because they are poor. You shouldn't be able to deny someone the right to vote, even if they have little education. Whoever gets in line first should get served first, even if someone more important comes in.

This is part of our Judeo-Christian heritage, which places law and justice above any man, no matter how powerful he might be. Of course, it *doesn't always get worked out perfectly, but we still expect that things should be this way, and we get mad when they aren't. That's not the case here. Everyone seems to accept that rights are merely a product of size and power—even on the road.*

Some time later, the bus began to slow. The wind, which had been whistling through the windows, became a breeze and then stopped all together. Little pearls of sweat quickly took shape on Matt's forehead. Sticking his head out the window, he saw a long line of vehicles stopped where the road disappeared into a coffee-colored river.

"What are we doing?" Matt asked.

Kinjapur responded, "We must wait for the ferry. Our government is too poor to build bridges, so we have to use ferries to cross rivers."

"No road bridges at all?" The way the map looked, Bangladesh was crisscrossed by hundreds, if not thousands, of rivers.

"Very few. That is why it can take several days to drive across the country even though Bangladesh is a small country. Ferries are not rapid."

"Not rapid" was an understatement. A full three hours later, the bus finally lurched forward onto the bed of the ferry. Nineteen other vehicles packed on, mostly buses, all parked within inches of each other. It took four hours of winding down the rain-starved river to reach the road on the other side.

o o o

Kinjapur had obtained the key for a small, brick building in the center of the village. Besides the school next door, it was the only brick building in sight. The rest of the homes and shops lining the dirt pathways had thatch roofs and walls of mud. Matt glanced up from his book as Kinjapur and two local JESUS Film Project workers entered their temporary residence. Although the room was windowless and its cement floors unfurnished, Matt was beginning to prefer it to the alternative. Whenever he went outside, crowds gathered around him, peering in wonder at the tall, white Westerner.

"You are well, Matt?" asked Kinjapur for the eighth time that morning.

"Just fine." As politely as possible, he questioned, "Why do you keep asking me that?" Matt was finding elements of life in rural Bangladesh difficult, but still manageable. Kinjapur and the other JESUS Film Project brothers, however, seemed to fear he was going to wilt and whither or something worse.

Kinjapur did not seem embarrassed by the question. "We've never had Americans come with us out this far—only to Dhaka sometimes. This is not a very good place, I think, for American people's bodies."

Matt was not quite sure what Kinjapur meant, but tried to assure him. "I'll be just fine. You know, Mr. Sammadar wanted us to call to let him know we had reached the region safely. Can we do that now?"

Kinjapur nodded. "The nearest phone is in a town a short distance from here. We will take a rickshaw."

Matt looked down to finish the page he was reading when a knock came at the door. One of the JESUS Film Project workers opened it. A small crowd of men in long robes flowed in. Traditional Muslim prayer caps covered their heads, and tangled beards draped down from their faces. They spoke rapidly at the man who had opened the door.

As Matt stood, Kinjapur whispered to him, "These are teachers from the *Madresse*. Be very respectful."

"What is the *Madresse?*"

"A fundamentalist Muslim school known for its strict obedience to the Koran."

The men moved past the local JESUS Film Project workers. They seemed most interested in Matt. Kinjapur translated their greeting and the questions that followed. They did not smile, but did not seem angry, either.

Kinjapur explained, "They ask where you are from."

"I am from America."

Kinjapur translated, then followed with the next question, "And why have you come to visit Bangladesh?"

"I am traveling all around the world. I am learning much about the people and country of Bangladesh."

"The teachers say you must be Muslim to have such a fine beard as you do."

Matt smiled. "No, I am a Christian. Tell them they have much finer beards than I."

The men seemed to enjoy Matt's answer; one even let out a chuckle.

Several more questions came before what seemed to be the grand finale. "The teachers want to know if you are willing to donate money for their school."

Matt smiled, but glanced at Kinjapur. "What do you think?"

Kinjapur smiled back in a slightly strained manner. "I think it would be a good idea."

Matt pulled two fifty-*taka* notes from his wallet. The teachers seemed quite pleased as he handed it to them, the equivalent of just over two dollars.

They shook Matt's hand once again as they filed out.

When the door was shut, Matt asked, "Did they come and ask all those questions about me just so they could get a donation?"

"No. They liked the donation, but I think they just wanted to check us out and see if we're safe. I think they also were just curious about you." Kinjapur opened the door once more. "Are you ready to go make your phone call?"

Kinjapur's description of the trip to the nearest phone as a "short distance" was another understatement. Matt wondered where their slight, wiry rickshaw driver got the strength to continue straining against the peddles for an entire hour, and even well into a second. The path led through rice fields, over bridges, and down semipaved roads for at least a dozen miles.

Finally, they came to a stop before a two-story cement building in a town significantly larger than the one they had left. On the second floor, a lone man sat at a desk, pulling plugs in and out of a wooden box and turning a crank. The device seemed to be a turn-of-the-century British switchboard.

"We wish to call Dhaka," requested Kinjapur when the man had set his listening device down.

The number, however, did not go through on the first try. Nor on the second, nor the third. Half an hour later, Kinjapur turned to Matt and shrugged. "I do not think we will able to get through today. Perhaps we will send a letter to Mr. Sammadar to inform him all is well."

Before they left town, they obtained permission from the region's government chairman to show the *JESUS* film in local villages. The chairman was a Muslim, of course, but a film about a man he accepted as a great prophet was not necessarily a negative thing. The presence of an American, Kinjapur told Matt, also helped a great deal.

It was late in the afternoon when they made it back to their simple residence. "We need to hurry," directed Kinjapur as he slid a key into the door. He grabbed the projector and screen. Matt followed with the generator.

The rickshaw Kinjapur engaged had no passenger seat, only a four-by-five-foot flatbed of wood. They placed their loads on the flatbed, then climbed aboard. The rickshaw driver got a long running start, pushing on the handlebars to gain momentum before jumping on. Dusk was fast approaching as the rickshaw neared its destination. A long, earthen path ventured through the rice fields on a levy, three or four feet above the flooded fields. Set among coconut and eucalyptus trees at the path's end were a dozen or so mud huts with thatched roofs. As the rickshaw bumped to a halt, a crowd of children ran out to greet the visitors. Kinjapur explained something in Bengali, and all but a few of the children shot off in every direction. Matt could hear their little voices crying, "Publicity! Publicity!" as they ran among the huts and out along other paths to neighboring villages. He wondered where they had heard that word.

The two local JESUS Film Project team members arrived a few minutes later. Matt aided as they set up the screen and the projector, then primed the generator. Glancing up from his work, Matt was surprised to notice a Hindu temple rising a short distance from the open area where the film would show. He gazed at the twenty-foot pyramidal structure. Its yellow and sky-blue paint was chipped and faded, but the cement seemed quite solid. Intricately carved faces and animals peered back at him. He could see a woman draped in an indigo sari lighting candles and incense sticks near the entrance.

"This is a Hindu village," explained Kinjapur. "Most of the country is Muslim, but there are . . ."

He was cut short as a piercing scream rang out from the temple.

Matt peered toward the temple. "What was that!?"

Kinjapur gave a half-smile. "They scream to chase away evil spirits before they go into the temple. Here, can you give me a hand with this cord?"

A large crowd had gathered by the time the film began; where they had come from, Matt could only wonder. He sat in the stiff wooden chair that had been presented to him by one of the village elders. Around him in the darkness, Matt could make out perhaps two hundred faces in the colored light reflecting from the screen. The crowd extended behind him as well, and a group of men even leaned against his chair and on his shoulders.

Matt's Reflections—February 20

What a remarkable day in such a strange and foreign place.

I spent most of it trying to make a single phone call that I ended up not being able to complete. From a productivity standpoint, most of my hours were a total waste. Reflecting back on it though, I have to say that it was relationally rich. I spent over four hours talking with Kinjapur on the back of a bicycle rickshaw. I didn't accomplish the one task I set out to do today, but perhaps I accomplished something even more valuable through my time with a friend.

I would have thought that living without the conveniences of electricity, running water, or a car would give one less time for relationships. Surprisingly, I have found the opposite to be true. Wealth and material things so often detract from time for relationships. The complexities that come with more possessions—even while making life more convenient— often bind people to having bad relationships rather than free them to have good ones.

Mike—A Village Somewhere Northeast of Dhaka

Mike could not help shaking his head as he emerged from the hut he had slept in. *I've never felt so far from home,* he thought.

Rice paddies stretched off in every direction. Most had been flooded by farmers, their waters reflecting silver from the predawn sky. In some, tender shoots of rice poked up through the water. The village, with its twenty or so huts, stood on a levy of hard-packed earth a few feet above the surrounding fields. The purpose of the levy was to hold the village above the yearly floods that cover more than 70 percent of Bangladesh's surface area during the rainy season; the few feet of elevation also allow for an extensive view of the countryside in a land that is essentially flat.

Not far off, wearing only a loin cloth, a man bent over in a field. He seemed to be plucking individual stalks of rice out of the ground and bunching them in his hand. Apparently, the shoots needed a certain amount of space to grow initially, but could be relocated closer together once they reached a certain height. It looked like painstaking work.

Mike glanced over as a small boy emerged from a hut and placed a pile of banana peels before a bony cow. As he worked, the boy never took his eyes from Mike. His mother squatted before a small fire in front of their hut, boiling rice. Every minute or two, she stuck another piece of dried dung into the fire and blew on it softly. The boy who had fed the cow disappeared back into his hut. A moment later, several more children emerged, moving toward Mike, but stopping a short distance away, their clothes tattered but clean. The girls all had enormous brown eyes and rings in their noses. Two carried their infant siblings—hefty loads for the girls' size.

"Good morning," offered Mike.

Giggling and moving behind one another shyly, they followed as he moved to the village well and doused his head with several pumps of the handle. Mike next headed in the direction of the small bamboo enclosure that housed the village's single pit toilet, glancing back at the trail of children.

"You can't follow me in here," he said.

At least he could latch the door. From the moment he had arrived in the village, the children watched him as if he were a moving TV set. Even when Mike and his BCS partner, Isali, bedded down for the night in their hut, they could hear children scurrying around outside, peeking through the thatch for a glimpse of him. The adults were not much better. Although the women were generally shy and deferent, and at least tried to appear as if they were not continually staring, the men gathered around him in groups and stared unabashedly. Some introduced themselves, but most simply gazed at him silently, emotionless, as if they were watching a zoo animal. It was understandable. Most of the people in the remote villages he was visiting had never seen a foreigner before. Even so, he was beginning to wonder how much more of it he could handle.

Mike's Reflections—February 23

There are things I enjoy about being in the village here, but this is also a very difficult time. The challenge goes much deeper than the mosquitoes and the heat, the absence of modern conveniences, or even the stomachaches I'm getting. It is that I feel stripped of all the things I enjoy most. I have no access to the things that give me my "sustenance" for living: meaningful relationships, good books, good conversations, activities like surfing, or even a sense of being an important part of a purposeful ministry.

I wonder if this is the "desert experience" Christians often speak of. Perhaps a "desert experience" is not merely a difficult series of events. It is a time when all of our sources of sustenance, except God Himself, have dried up. In this, we discover how much of our sustenance we have drawn from sources other than God. In this place, I am seeing how much of my joy for life actually comes from things other than my relationship with God. I know that God does want me to enjoy His good gifts, but ulti-mately, He desires to be my source of final joy and purpose.

As I think about it, I realize that all the people God has used in pow-erful ways have gone through significant desert experiences in their lives, often in literal deserts. Moses, David, Paul, and even Jesus Himself spent significant time in the wilderness before beginning more public work. Knowing this may not make the desert times of my life any less difficult, but it can make it a little easier to embrace them if I know they are a necessary part of becoming the man God wants me to be.

"Please, Mike, I think you should share the four spiritual laws with him," Isali advised.

Mike did not respond. His attention had been drawn to his stomach for a moment. It seemed to be protesting eighteen straight meals of little but rice. The slight ache was getting worse. "What did you say, Isali?"

"Give him the four spiritual laws."

Mike glanced at Isali and the two other JESUS Film Project brothers. They watched expectantly, waiting for him to produce the "magical" Christian tract. Mike's hand moved across his chest with noticeable hesi-tation as he reached for the pamphlet that lay in his shirt pocket. The old Muslim man on whose dirt porch they sat continued to offer his near toothless grin. For several minutes, the man had listened with fascination as Mike explained faith in Jesus. Now Isali wanted Mike to cut to the evan-gelistic chase with the tract.

"Use the booklet and ask him to pray the prayer," came the next suggestion.

"Isali, do you think he understands who Jesus is?" questioned Mike.

"I think maybe . . . I don't know . . ." Isali seemed taken aback that someone would question the formula for making Christians.

Mike shook his head. "I want him to come to know Jesus, Isali, but I don't think it's right to ask him to commit his life to Christ if he doesn't know what he's getting into."

Isali looked at the ground thoughtfully. The other two Bengalis, sensing their American counterpart was not going to proceed as they had hoped, produced their own copies of *The Four Spiritual Laws*. Fifteen minutes later, they were on their way to the next village. The old Muslim had remained polite throughout the conversation, but declined to "pray the prayer."

275

I greatly respect the evangelistic zeal of the BCS workers. It highlights how often I let opportunities to share about Jesus slip by. I also admire their commitment to serving God under persecution and some of the roughest of circumstances I can imagine. I just don't know what to think about the focus of the methods some of them use sometimes.

It seems that the goal is often just to get people to "pray the prayer," whether they understand what they are doing or not. It's like a rushed, assembly-line mentality.

I know we are commanded to spread the good news of Jesus, but the Great Commission is a command to make disciples. "Conversion" that is nothing more than repeating a formulaic prayer for getting in to heaven without a decision to give one's life totally to Jesus bears little similarity to the invitations Jesus offered to those He met up with.

276

Trey—Jhalakhati Region, Southern Bangladesh

The roosters began crowing a good while before dawn. By the end of the first week, Trey had learned that getting back to sleep was unlikely. With a grunt, he submitted to another early morning. The usual crowd of locals stood at the door and window, staring in at him. He wearily returned a smile and climbed out from under the mosquito net. Apparently, his BCS partner, Ajonni, had a long journey planned for the day. A local woman who helped with cooking brought in a tin plate piled high with breakfast—another mound of rice, this one topped with a potato. Trey washed the starchy taste down with a few swigs from the well.

"I'll be ready in a second, Ajonni," he promised, splashing water on his head and combing at the tangled mass as best he could. His decision to not cut his hair on the trip was becoming a bit cumbersome.

A muddy river flowed on the outskirts of town. Trey nodded at the turbaned beanpole of a man who balanced on the far end of the boat as he and Ajonni boarded. The ancient wooden craft creaked as the old driver used a long staff to push off.

"What are we going to do today, Ajonni?" Trey queried.

"Oh, it is down many rivers." Trey nodded, waiting for Ajonni to continue, but the Bangladeshi seemed to think he had answered Trey's inquiry fully. Ajonni's imperfect English often meant questions had to be repeated.

"Why, Ajonni? Why are we going down many rivers?"

Ajonni seemed to understand. "Today, we visit a Christian village. They saw *JESUS* film some years ago. Now they all Christian. They will like to see you very much. No American Christian ever visit before."

Several miles downstream, Ajonni directed the old boatman toward a concrete dock on the edge of a good-sized town. Not far down the river, Trey could see it joining a second river and widening considerably. "This is beginning of Ganges River delta," Ajonni explained. "We will switch here to a boat with motor."

Ajonni paid the boatman and set off in search of a motorboat for hire. A merchant who was going their way finally agreed to take them on. Trey settled in as best he could beside the merchant's cargo—a load of fresh coconuts—beneath a broad bamboo awning. With the day as warm and humid as it was, he was thankful for the shade. As they moved deeper into the delta, the air grew noticeably warmer and the buzz of insects louder. Two hours later, Trey noticed the first building he had seen for some time. It seemed to be growing right out of the water. He noticed a second, then another.

"This is town of Pirojpur," Ajonni announced. "We walk from here. You know the Sundarban jungle? They beginning only few miles from here. That is where Bengali tiger lives."

For one with an imagination like Trey's, Pirojpur seemed an Asian Venice with its homes and shops poised high above the water on stilts. Bridges made of bamboo and woven reeds linked individual homes with one another and with the mainland.

"It's amazing how they build everything up on stilts like this," remarked Trey as he and Ajonni debarked onto a bamboo platform.

Ajonni tilted his head slightly, as if pondering the thought that there might be something interesting about building houses on stilts. He asked, "You want chai before we start hike?"

Trey had little desire for a hot drink, but he nodded anyway. He knew Ajonni would insist that he ought to have some until he gave in. They stopped at a small café on the way out of town and sipped hot chai from dirty cups. Dish soap has yet to make its appearance in rural Bangladesh.

The hike led along the levies that crisscrossed the rice paddies. Occasional stretches of unbroken water suggested that certain areas of the delta remained flooded almost year-round. Trey had been watching a man plow with a large black ox when he felt Ajonni's hand close around his. He started and pulled back slightly, but Ajonni's fingers were already interlaced with his own.

Ajonni acted like nothing had happened. "The village is two miles more from here, I think," he remarked nonchalantly.

Trey had noticed that male Bangladeshis appeared completely comfortable holding hands as they walked or sat talking. It was merely a mark of friendship. Even so, it felt quite unnerving. Noticing that a farmer was watching them, Trey unconsciously pulled his hand back again. Ajonni did not let go. *I'll just have to get used to this,* Trey decided, smiling at the thought of what friends back home would think if they could see him stroll across the rice fields hand in hand with a Bangladeshi man.

A patch of trees grew out of the horizon as they approached. It took nearly half an hour to become life-size. Entering the grove, Trey caught sight of small huts set among the trees. Although not built above water, these homes also were balanced on stilts.

"This area will flood every year," explained Ajonni. "Often even with the stilts they have to spend several weeks a year living on their roof."

Ajonni and Trey emerged into a clearing in the middle of the village. Women and young girls were about their daily chores, sweeping, washing clothes, and cooking. Children played at their mothers' feet and under the houses. Several old men sat talking to boys, apparently teaching them. No one seemed to notice Trey or Ajonni.

Suddenly, one of the boys cried out something in Bengali. Faces turned toward the visitors. Several men in traditional *longi* skirts crowded around, shaking hands with Ajonni and eagerly pointing at Trey. Children squeezed in between them to get a good look at the tall white man. Women, decked in their bright saris, watched and whispered from a distance. Into the swirl of welcome, an aged man with untypically long hair stepped forward. As the others quieted to a low buzz, Ajonni translated for the village elder.

Trey in a Rural Hindu Village

"We welcome you, our brother, to our simple village. We are blessed to have you here."

He grasped Trey's hands firmly for a moment, then pulled him into a welcoming embrace.

"Thank you," said Trey, a bit overwhelmed.

The elder nodded. "Understand, brother, our love for Jesus is our love for you."

Trey's Reflections—February 24

I can tell these people want to emulate their Lord in everything. Ajonni says he thinks the elder even grew his long hair so that he could be like the Jesus in the movie.

With Muslims on every side and the only other minority villages being Hindu, these believers are a virtual island of Christian faith. Somehow, the simple fact of my presence here is an incredible encouragement to them. It seems that a visit from an American Christian to those who often feel so isolated is refreshing and encouraging—even validating—in a way I could never fully understand.

Darkness was nearly complete when one of the villagers brought out an old oil lantern. Its flame cast flickering light over the congregated faces—large, eager eyes of children; gold glinting in the noses of the women; time-carved foreheads of the old. Trey, Ajonni, and the old men sat in chairs. The others stood or sat on the ground, the old men conferring with one another in hushed tones before launching a question on behalf of the group.

"How many days did it take you to walk here from America?"

"Actually, I did not walk, I flew . . ." Trey could not hold back a smile.

He stopped, realizing how little his words would mean. His eyes fell on a piece of sheet metal that lay against one hut. Picking it up, he tried for several minutes to demonstrate how a man-made bird could be made of metal. The crowd had not lost their quizzical looks when Trey decided to ask if they had any other questions.

After more conferring, "What color is the dirt in America?"

Trey's response that dirt was pretty much the same in America as in Bangladesh brought roars of laughter from the crowd.

Another man spoke up, "But do you have stars in America?"

Trey nodded, trying to hold back a laugh. "Oh yes, we see the very same stars in the sky from America that we see here in Bangladesh."

The man seemed somewhat relieved. Perhaps it made the mythical land of America not all that far off after all. Trey glanced around at the circle of faces once again. *What a strange thing,* he thought, *that I am here on the far side of the world with people who have absolutely no clue about America—and yet, we worship the same Lord!*

○ ○ ○

A letter waited for Trey upon his return to Ajonni's house. He could not decipher the return address, but it appeared to be from Dhaka. He tore back the flap and pulled out a single sheet of paper that read:

Dear Trey,

Greetings in the name of our Lord Jesus Christ. Mike is sick. Come to Dhaka immediately. Hope you are doing well. See you soon.

Sincerely,
Dennis Sammadar, Director of Bangladesh Christian Service

Jedd—Village of Borkali

Along the horizon, the lights of distant villages twinkled. Jedd stood between two JESUS Film Project workers, just beyond the glow reflecting from the film screen. Before them, seventy-five people watched transfixed as Jesus laid His hands on the eyes of blind Bartimaeus and declared in Bengali, "Receive your sight, your faith has healed you."

Jedd breathed a faint sigh. This was the first time all day the attention of the crowds had not been utterly focused on him. His translator had returned to Dhaka nearly a week before, but although he could exchange only a handful of words in Bengali, everyone he encountered was constantly watching, following, and trying to interact with him.

A gangly shape shuffled up next to Jedd in the darkness. *"Shomosha,* brother? *Shomosha?"* It was Swapan, the local pastor in whose church building Jedd was staying. Once again, he was asking if Jedd was doing okay, if there was any "problem."

Jedd shook his head. *"Nah,* Thank you, brother, *Shomosha nah."* As

Swapan melted back into the darkness, Jedd silently breathed, "I just need some time alone." As touching as their care and concern were, the constant attention was wearing on him.

One of the film workers noticed he was standing and brought the village chair from the place Jedd had left it only a few minutes before. He placed it behind Jedd and indicated for him to sit. "Thank you, brother," said Jedd, sitting, although he had no desire to do so.

For a moment, everyone's attention returned to the film. Jedd quietly rose from the chair and stole in the direction opposite the film, glancing over his shoulder to make sure he had not been seen. Past the village's dark huts he moved, past a bony cow that was tethered to a tall eucalyptus tree, then down off the levy on which the village stood and into a drained rice field. The film continued to play—now a small, colorful square a few hundred yards off. Only faintly could he hear the deep voice of the Bengali Jesus explaining the kingdom of heaven. All around him stretched the rice fields, some dry, others glimmering with stars reflected from above. Jedd plopped down on the cracked earth of an empty field, placed his head between his knees, and breathed deeply for a moment.

"Oh God, please lift this weight. I love Your people, Lord, but I am really pretty tired of them right now."

Looking up, it seemed to Jedd that the expanse of stars above him was blazing brighter than he had ever seen. It felt as if the psychological weight of always being watched, of never having a moment to himself, was beginning to dissolve. A smile creased his lips. He began to sing a hymn, "Praise God from whom all blessings flow, praise Him all . . ." Refreshment began to pour over him. The solitude felt rich and velvety. He began another song; "Be Thou my vision, O Lord of my heart. Not be . . ."

With a start, he noticed that the *JESUS* film had suddenly stopped. The screen had gone dark, disappearing into the night. All was silent for a moment, and then, over the bullhorn used earlier to invite villagers to the film, the voice of one of the workers crackled, "Mister Jedd, Mister Jedd! Please come to home of Swapan Das. Please come to home of Swapan Das."

Jedd sank his face into his hands and let out a long, desperate breath. "No! No, no, no! I can't believe this!"

Slowly, Jedd rose to his feet and began plodding back toward the village. As he walked, the bullhorn sounded again and again. "Mister Jedd, Mister Jedd, please come to home of Swapan Das."

281

He entered the ring of light cast by an oil lamp that sat next to the projector. Several of the JESUS Film Project workers ran up to him, their faces creased with worry. "*Shomosha*, brother? *Shomosha?*"

Jedd swallowed hard before replying. Something close to anger welled up. "*Shomosha nah! Shomosha nah!*" The brothers looked at him with a blend of relief and concern. Jedd's anger melted into weariness. He could not feel mad, but a stifling desperation pushed upon him, even seemed to fill his throat. Tears crept into his eyes. The workers were staring at him. He knew they would not understand what he was saying, but he said it anyway, "I just need some time alone. You understand? Time alone, by myself."

Jedd's Reflections—February 25

282

I feel tired, desperate, almost claustrophobic. The people here are good, kind, and so loving to me, but I feel my love for them is wearing thin.

I need time alone. They seem to have no concept of such a need. Their lives are crowded shoulder to shoulder from birth. They are surprised, even worried whenever I indicate a desire to be by myself. But I need it. I feel like I need it now as much as I need air.

Jedd's belly churned like the inside of a volcano. He had not felt right for several days and seemed to be getting worse. Placing his hand on his forehead, he felt the clammy skin, disconcertingly warm.

I hope I can make it back to Swapan's village, he thought, forcing himself to place one foot in front of the other.

"*Shomosha,* brother?" Swapan asked.

"I do not feel well," replied Jedd in Bengali with a faint smile.

Swapan gazed at him with his wide, bulbous eyes for a moment, concerned. "Rest here?"

"No. Go to village. Rest there. I am fine." Jedd did not want to give Swapan too much cause for worry. Swapan was always anxious over Jedd's comfort, even when nothing was wrong. For a moment, the world seemed to roll before Jedd. He closed his eyes, and the dizziness passed. "I will be fine, Swapan. I will rest at the village."

Their path led through the vast expanses of rice fields and into a small town. As always, the people stopped whatever they were doing to watch Jedd pass. He did not smile at them as he usually did. The pathway was a bit muddy from a recent downpour. Brightly clad women sat on bamboo mats along the side, their small piles of rice, guavas, eggs, or fish set in front of them for sale.

Swapan paused for a moment to bargain for some eggs. Suddenly, Jedd felt the contents of his stomach rushing up to his mouth. There was nowhere he could go. He erupted onto the muddy road: half-digested rice, a little fish, and part of an egg. He placed his hands on his knees, bent over, and threw up again. A crowd began to form to watch as he wretched several more times, coughing, breathing hard. Swapan ran to his side and placed his hands on Jedd's stooped shoulders, "Oh, brother, brother!" Swapan seemed on the verge of tears.

Jedd glanced up at the flock of onlookers. "Stare if you want. I don't even care," he muttered. He gagged again, but nothing came out. A dog crept out from between two buildings and began lapping up the vomit.

Swapan signaled a rickshaw driver. "Will you take us to the village of Boruka?"

"There is no road there. You know it is hard to go along the levies."

"Yes or no?"

"I will take you."

° ° °

Throughout the night, Jedd slipped in and out of consciousness, sometimes miserably awake, sometimes twisting in a feverish sleep. The rickshaw had taken them to Swapan's village, and Swapan brought Jedd into his family's hut and laid him on his own bed—a low table covered with two blankets. After getting Jedd's mosquito net from the church and setting it up over him, Swapan sat cross-legged on the bed at Jedd's feet. Whenever Jedd drifted into consciousness, he could hear Swapan praying quietly, fervently for his American brother. Whenever Jedd moved, his feet poked out from below the not-quite-big-enough mosquito net. Swapan would pause in his prayers, pull Jedd's socks up as high as they would go to protect his ankles from the mosquitoes, and then work to pull the netting as close to covering Jedd's feet as he could.

Even in the midst of delirious dreams, Jedd wondered, *What amazing love this brother has for me! I never would've appreciated him if I hadn't gotten sick.*

○ ○ ○

Jedd woke in the morning. He must have fallen into a deeper sleep some hours before. The small room was full of villagers. Swapan talked with them in hushed tones. When Jedd stirred, he came and sat on the edge of the bed. "You are better, brother?"

Jedd managed a faint smile. "I am not bad." Although his stomach still ached, his head felt much clearer. Relief poured over Swapan's face.

"You like rice?"

Jedd shook his head, but seeing the concern creep back into Swapan's tired eyes, he replied, "I would like a little rice, please."

An hour later, he vomited the rice on the side of the hut when no one but a group of children was watching. Jedd walked around the hut to where Swapan was crouching next to his wife as she prepared lunch over a dung fire. "Swapan, I need to go to Dhaka. I will see a doctor."

"Yes. I think so also."

Bidding good-bye to all of the villagers, he and Swapan departed for Dhaka. On the side of the road where the bus for Dhaka would pass, Swapan looked at Jedd one last time. His wide eyes were sad, loving. "We"—he placed his hands together, as if in prayer—"for you," he finished, pointing to Jedd.

"And I . . . will pray . . . for you," said Jedd, repeating the pantomime.

Tears began to fill Swapan's eyes and he leaned forward, wrapping Jedd in a bony embrace. Jedd could feel tears dripping on his neck. "Thank you, brother, thank you," whispered Swapan as he finally released Jedd. "Thank you for coming to Bangladesh."

twenty

100,000 Rickshaws
Dhaka, Bangladesh

dhaka's smog made for brilliant sunrises. Matt might have noticed had he not felt so weary. Screaming babies, incessant honking, and a cage of distraught roosters had not allowed him much sleep on the twenty-four-hour bus ride back to the city. Questions as to why Mr. Sammadar had summoned him back gnawed at his mind the entire trip. The letter had explained nothing; it simply directed him to return to Dhaka immediately. Had something bad happened to one of the other guys?

The road was already crowded. Matt and Kinjapur's rickshaw driver, calf muscles straining, pushed forward, deftly negotiating the traffic. Thousands of bicycle rickshaws flowed every which way, somehow managing to dodge the charging buses and other large motor vehicles. Hundreds more rickshaws waited along the roadsides, their drivers hoping the day's labor would bring in enough to feed a family for a day. Matt glanced off a bridge at one of Dhaka's sludgy, trash-filled rivers. Several women had already begun doing their laundry. They lofted each piece of clothing into the air to catch what little breeze there was before floating it down to the lumpy water. He could not help wondering if the clothes would come out dirtier than before they were washed.

Kinjapur paid the driver at a busy corner and led off down an alleyway toward the BCS dorm. Matt made it to the door first. He pushed it open and headed straight for the bedroom. It took a moment for his eyes to adjust to the dim light. On an upper bunk, Mike stirred slightly. From the other side of the room, the sound of deep, methodic breathing came

Rickshaw Lineup in Dhaka

from under Jedd's mosquito net. Trey sat against the wall, writing in his journal. A feeling of relief passed over Matt. Everyone seemed to be okay.

In Search of Plan B

At the sound of footsteps, Trey looked up. "I'm glad you're back," he whispered as he stood and welcomed Matt with a big hug. "How are you?"

"Pretty tired, but I'm doing fine. I've just been worried about how everyone else is here. Do you know why they had us all come back?"

A faint moaning came from Jedd's bunk.

"Here, let's go talk on the roof so we won't wake up the guys."

Up two flights of stairs, they emerged into the blinding morning light. A waist-high wall of cement block surrounded the flat roof. Up here, the sounds and smells from the streets below were less overpowering.

Trey looked at Matt and smiled. "Man, it's *really* good to see you. I'm glad you're okay. Mike and Jedd are pretty sick. Out in the villages, both of them came down with some kind of dysentery or something."

"How bad are they?"

"Not good. They've got constant diarrhea and are throwing up any-

286

thing they eat. The doctor can't seem to figure out what's wrong. Mike has been talking a lot about trying to leave the country."

"Hey," came a weak voice from the stairwell. It was Mike. Matt would have been tempted to laugh if it had not been so pitiful how much like an old man Mike moved across the roof. To see the always rough-and-ready Mike so feeble was disconcerting.

Mike noticed the concern in Matt's face and turned his lips up in a faint smile. "So, Matt, you made it back all right?"

"Better than you, I guess."

"That's not saying much," Mike replied. "Did you get sick at all?"

"Not really. I had a few stomachaches and stuff, but nothing real bad."

"I'm glad to hear it. Jedd and I both got worked. I wasn't in the village for more than a week before it hit me. I think someone served me some water out of a pond they use to wash and go to the bathroom in. I've never been so sick in all my life."

287

A pained look crossed Mike's face, and his hands went to his belly. He waddled quickly toward the wall and leaned over, dry heaves, nothing came out. He offered Matt a faint smile. "I haven't been eating much."

"You going to be okay?"

Mike nodded. "Yeah. But I don't know how much longer I can handle Bangladesh."

"Trey told me you're thinking about trying to get out of the country."

"I don't know if I can last four more weeks here. I probably sound like a wimp, but I am just totally miserable."

"What about Mr. Sammadar and the other BCS guys?"

"Maybe I should care what they think, but I honestly don't. To tell you the truth, I didn't feel like I was doing anyone out there in the villages any good anyway. Did you?"

Matt thought for a moment. "Actually, I did. Obviously, there was a language barrier, but I felt like my presence made it possible to show the film in regions they'd never been allowed to before, and having an American helped with publicity. It also seemed like the local Christians were really encouraged just by the fact that I was there."

Mike was nodding but did not seem to hear what Matt had said. His voice held a faint tremor, "I guess what I'm saying is that I don't think I can handle it here anymore. I think we should leave as soon as possible. It doesn't seem like there's any point to us being here if all we're doing is feeling sick and miserable in this place they call a dorm."

Matt looked at Mike with surprise. Mike was the last person in the world to complain, let alone talk of cutting out on a job before it was done. *He must be a total wreck,* thought Matt. "What do you suggest?" he asked gently.

"I have some friends in Australia who work with Young Life, and I'm going to have my sister send me their contact information. We could go work with them."

"Australia?" Matt was a bit taken aback. "Plane tickets would probably cost at least a few hundred dollars from here."

Mike stared blankly at Matt as if prepared for a showdown.

Matt continued, "Look, Mike. Whatever we need to do to get you well we should do. But it seems to me that we should at least talk to Mr. Sammadar and . . ." Matt stopped as he noticed tears were filling Mike's eyes.

"I'm sorry," sputtered Mike after a moment. "I know I'm being a total wimp. I just don't know if I can stand to be in this place for another month . . ."

o o o

Mr. Sammadar's overhead fan whirred quietly. We sat in four chairs in front of his desk as he asked about Jedd's and Mike's conditions and our thoughts about what to do now.

He ran his fingers through his black hair, thinking. "I believe you should not return to the villages. You must take time to rest."

"Would there be work for us to do here in Dhaka?" followed Matt.

"Oh yes. There is much we would like you to do. You can teach English classes here at BCS headquarters and many Muslims and Hindus will come. You can also visit the Dhaka University and speak with students. Other things, too. There is much to do."

Mike glanced at the others before responding. "Thank you for that offer, Mr. Sammadar. We need a few days to rest and think about it, but we'll give you a call."

"Yes, take some time to think and pray about it," he said, pausing for a moment to adjust his glasses. "It would also be good if you found another place to stay—Dhaka has several reasonable guesthouses. The BCS dorm is not a very good place for an American to get well. Please let me know when you decide."

We shuffled out and moved into an unoccupied room in the BCS office.

"What do you think, Mike?" asked Jedd.

"I still want to go to Australia," he stated flatly.

No one dared respond for a long minute. Jedd let out a long breath. "I was thinking the same thing, Mike, until we talked with Mr. Sammadar. If they can really use us in Dhaka, I'm starting to feel like maybe we should stay."

Matt and Trey remained quiet, apparently viewing their generally good health as disqualifying them from offering an opinion. Finally Mike responded, "All right, guys. I'll try to stick it out. Let's see if we can find a decent place to stay and if they can really use us. If not, I may just go to Australia with whoever will come with me."

o o o

"Who would like to read the next section in English?" asked Trey, looking around the circle of Bangladeshi men and women.

Ihan, the young man who had first welcomed us to the BCS dorm, was waving his hand again. He and several other BCS workers had joined our classes, both to build their English skills and to spend time with us. Trey looked for any other takers. Ihan had read too many times already. A young Hindu woman raised her hand, the crimson dot in the middle of her forehead matching the deep red of her sari. Trey nodded at her and smiled.

"Okay, verse 16," he directed.

She read slowly, mouthing the words carefully. "'For God so . . . loved the . . . world that He gave His only be . . . beg . . .'"

"Begotten," pronounced Trey. "It means, 'to be born of.' Go ahead, you're doing well."

English Class

"'He gave his only begotten son. That who . . . who . . . whosoever . . . believes in Him will not . . . perish but have et . . . et . . . eternal life.'"

"Excellent!" affirmed Trey. "You're doing great. Now who wants to try answering the next question—I want you to answer only in English: What did those words mean?"

We had begun our English classes several days before with little publicity. Already, our two classes had more than twenty students each. Jedd and Mike taught a two-hour session in the morning; Matt and Trey led a second in the afternoon. Although few people in Bangladesh speak English well, young people—particularly university students—are eager to learn. When one pair was teaching, the other ventured out to Dhaka University, seeking recruits for our classes and talking with the groups that inevitably gathered round. In the meantime, we also had discovered a decent guesthouse. It was not much by American standards, but it was clean and relatively bug-free. Mike still saw the whole situation as somewhat probationary, but we were all feeling generally better about life.

Trey looked around the circle and repeated his question, "So, who wants to try explaining to me in English what the verse means?"

Welcome to the American Club

Mike tapped the rickshaw driver on the shoulder. "Turn here," he said, directing with his hand.

"Are you going to tell me where we're going?" asked Matt.

"Just wait, you'll find out."

Large, leafy trees reached out to touch one another over a quiet lane. The pollution-stained apartments and high-rises that dominated most of Dhaka were nowhere to be seen—only individual homes, many of them encircled by high walls. As we moved along, the gates grew larger and the houses less visible.

"Stop here, please," instructed Mike before an eight-foot whitewashed wall, topped with barbed wire. Trey and Jedd's rickshaw followed suit.

Jedd handed several bills to each driver as Mike proceeded to a gatehouse set within the wall and spoke briefly with the Bangladeshi guard. A moment later, a steel door beside the gatehouse swung open.

"Matt, why don't you lead the way," offered Mike with a grin.

Matt looked around in wonder as he passed through the wall. He could hardly believe what he was seeing. Before him spread manicured tropical gardens, tennis courts, a sparkling swimming pool, and a large white building that looked like the clubhouse at a country club.

"Where are we? What is this place?" asked Jedd.

"Welcome to the American Club!" Mike announced, gesturing forward as if to his own plot of land. "I stumbled on it when I visited the U.S. Embassy."

"This is unbelievable. I almost feel like I've been transported back to the good ol' U.S. of A.," sighed Trey.

Mike was obviously quite proud of his discovery. "As nice as it looks here, the best thing is the food. I think they serve just about anything—cheeseburgers, fries, salads, even milkshakes." We would have been embarrassed to admit it, but each of us had had lengthy daydreams about American food over the past several weeks.

"How in the world did you find this place?" asked Matt.

"See, I went by the American embassy. It's not much to speak of. There weren't even any Americans working there that I could see. When I was there though, I noticed a flier for something called the American Club.

"I got on a rickshaw and said 'Ammerriccann Cluuub' very slowly to the driver, and this is where he brought me. I guess the club is usually restricted to Americans that are attached to the embassy, but I pleaded with the administration and they were kind enough to give us all passes."

"Cheeseburgers . . .," Trey said slowly, shaking his head.

Mike nodded toward the large white building. "So, you guys ready for lunch?"

Matt looked at Jedd. "Is your stomach going to be able to handle it?"

Jedd shrugged. "It will probably end up hurting pretty good, but right now I don't care."

o o o

As he had been doing for more than two weeks now, Matt spent the morning on a patch of lawn at Dhaka University. He never sat alone for long because a student or two—often a large group—soon descended upon him. Talking with Bangladesh's best and brightest made for fascinating conversation. This morning, a slender young man sat across from him, black goatee protruding from his narrow chin, head set back proudly, but his gaze respectful and thirsty for knowledge. Zaki had been plying Matt with questions for nearly an hour.

"I am so intrigued by what you say," continued Zaki. "I like what you tell me about Jesus and what He teaches. I have spoken little with Christians before. That is why I ask so many things."

"I don't mind at all," replied Matt. "Ask anything." Already, Matt had spent some time explaining how Jesus' death and all He taught through His life opened the way for man to be reconciled to his Creator.

"So then, what I want to ask," said Zaki, "is if I can be a follower of Jesus but not a Christian?" He leaned forward with anticipation as Matt pondered the unexpected question.

Matt began slowly, "In some sense, I suppose you can. My definition of a true Christian, though, *is* a person who follows Jesus. I see them as the same thing."

"But does a person have to call themselves a Christian to follow Jesus?"

"A person who truly wants to follow Jesus would accept Him completely, including everything He said about Himself. They wouldn't just view Him as 'some nice teacher.' They would want to make Him their Master and Lord."

"If I wanted to do that, would I have to be a Christian?"

After another pause, Matt responded, "I know there are plenty of people who call themselves Christians, but really don't follow Jesus. I guess it would be possible to do it vice versa."

Matt guessed he might be beginning to understand what Zaki was driving at. For Zaki, being a Christian, a Muslim, or a Hindu was almost like being a certain ethnicity or culture. It was something you were born into, like your skin color, and was not necessarily tied to what you believed.

"So being called 'Christian' is not the important thing?" Zaki continued.

"Whether or not you call yourself a Christian, the most important issue is whether or not you are truly placing your faith in Jesus—whether you are giving Him your life and seeking to live it as He would want you to. The word *Christian* really just means someone who has committed their life to Christ Jesus, but sometimes the word gets diluted into something else. The thing that really matters to God is what your heart is committed to."

Zaki nodded but appeared to be deep in thought. Matt was about to ask a question when a voice shouted from across the lawn. "Zaki! Time for class."

Zaki stood slowly, still thoughtful. "The things we have talked about will be on my mind." He shook Matt's hand and jogged off across the grass. "It was good to meet you," he called over his shoulder.

Matt's Reflections—March 11

I wonder if I responded correctly to Zaki's question. Can a person be a follower of Jesus without being a Christian?

I wouldn't blame someone for not wanting to be linked to all the evil things that have been carried out by people who have called themselves Christians. I also know a lot of the cultural aspects associated with "being a Christian" (whether it's seeing alcohol as a sin in America or women not being allowed to wear makeup in Russia) really have little to do with following Jesus. After all, what really matters anyway? As Paul put it, "The only thing that counts is faith expressing itself through love."

At the same time, I know that a central part of the faith taught in the Bible is a community of believers who love and serve together. I don't know that a person needs to call themselves a Christian to follow Jesus, but it does seem that if they were really interested in doing so, they would soon want to join with others who were seeking to do the same thing.

293

Mike's Reflections—March 12

I can't believe how differently I feel now from just a few weeks back. Bangladesh seems an entirely different place. A short time ago, I would have given anything to leave. Now, I can even see myself coming back someday.

A lot of it is just that I'm feeling better. There is still something weird going on in my stomach, but the medicine has definitely helped. It has also been so nice having a haven from the madness of the streets at our guesthouse and the American Club.

A big part of the change, though, is the amazing difference it makes when you feel like you are truly accomplishing something meaningful. I love spending time with the students in the English class, teaching them and sharing Jesus with them. Several have even had us over to their homes for meals. And the college kids I'm meeting at the university seem so eager to learn about anything I share.

I feel like I'm realizing more every day that the heart of this epic life we are seeking is, more than anything else, living with true purpose—not just some "random acts of kindness" mentality, but a deep sense that what you are doing in the ordinary moments of your life has eternal significance.

Answering the "Call"

Trey's neck popped as he rolled it slowly to the left, then back to the right. "You sore?" asked Matt.

"Kind of. Having to share that double mattress with you, I always end up sleeping squinched up on the side of the bed. For some reason, it leaves me sore sometimes."

"Just be thankful you don't share a bed with Mike or Jedd. You can tell their medicine hasn't totally fixed 'em yet by the way the room smells every morning."

The first series of tests run by the local doctor had not been able to discover what was wrong with Jedd and Mike. When they requested a repeat of the tests, the diagnosis suggested that giardia or a similar parasite was the culprit. The medicine prescribed, however, had little effect. Only when Jedd acquired the drugs suggested by our guidebook at a roadside stand did they begin to show signs of recovery.

Trey turned his attention back to their surroundings—the outdoor dining area in which they sat, the freshly cut lawn, the flowers hanging from the fences around the tennis courts, the clear waters of the swimming pool. They had made a morning trip out to the American Club for a luxury breakfast—fresh orange juice, toast, and two slices of bacon. Life felt so much better than it had just a few weeks before. He was especially enjoying the students in his and Matt's English class. The relationships they were forming were great, and it was almost embarrassing how the young men and women lavished them with appreciation after every session. Best of all, each of the students—Muslims, Hindus, and Christians— were spending time every day in the Bible, getting to know Jesus better as they learned English.

Trey jumped as a low voice whispered just inches from his ear. "You were at the international church service yesterday, right?"

He shot a surprised glance at a stout man in his late twenties. "Uh, yeah, we were."

"When you introduced yourself, you said you were working with the . . ." The man paused briefly as a Bangladeshi waiter walked by, then continued more softly, ". . . the *JESUS* film."

"Yes, Matt here and I and our two friends are showing the film with Bangladesh Christian Service. We've been here about four weeks, and we'll be here for another two or so. How long have you been here?"

"Nine months now. I'll be here indefinitely."

"And what is it that brings you here?"

The man took a quick look behind him—as if he thought someone might be eavesdropping—and replied in a hushed tone, "The Call."

Trey shook his head. "The what?"

"You know," he repeated slowly, "The Call."

"Oh, I get it. You mean you were called to the mission fie—"

"Shh, shh, shh!" he said almost frantically. "You never know when any of the M.'s or F. M.'s might be around."

"Hmm," said Trey, trying not to reveal that he had no idea what the man was talking about. "So, what organization are you here working with?"

"I can't tell you."

"Okay."

A moment of awkward silence passed before the man spoke again. "Have you run into any problems with the F.M.'s while you've been here?"

"The what?" interjected Matt. "Oh . . . do you mean fundamentalist Muslims?"

The man nodded, a grave look on his face.

"No, no problems at all."

The man hmmed, then put on his conspiratorial look once again, glancing back and forth for any spies. "May God bless your work."

He left as stealthily as he came. We never saw him again.

Trey's Reflections—March 13

That secret agent missionary guy this morning seemed a little bit weird to me. It was like he thought danger was lurking everywhere.

It does make me wonder, though. Maybe we are a little too casual in how we talk about our faith. Just because we haven't faced any opposition doesn't mean it does not exist. After all, it is officially illegal to share Jesus in this country—something we've been doing every day.

Jedd also told me just last night how one of the men he spent time with in the villages had been beaten by a mob of angry Muslims when he showed the JESUS film just a few months ago. They broke both his kneecaps and left him to die out in a rice field.

We should probably be more careful. I'm thankful God has kept us so entirely safe through our time here—we shouldn't push it.

° ° °

The night before our departure, we were up until nearly 2:00 A.M. with students who stopped by our guesthouse with thank-you gifts. It was the first time we had been given flowers, piling them, eight bouquets deep, next to our packed backpacks.

Our clocks had not yet hit six in the morning when a rapping came from the door of our room. The sound was repeated several times before Mike untangled himself from his mosquito net and stumbled to the door, pulling it back a crack and glaring through. All he could make out was a single eye and a large smile.

"Ihan? What are you doing here so early?"

"I wanted to make sure you did not leave before I could say good-bye."

"We don't leave until this afternoon," replied Mike flatly.

"I know, but I feared I might miss you." Ihan squeezed past Mike into the room. He did not notice that we were still trying to sleep; rather, he seemed overcome with relief. "I was awake all night. I worried I would come to your guesthouse and you would no longer be here. Then I would never see you again."

Mike was beginning to soften. "Well, thank you for coming, Ihan. We definitely wanted to say good-bye, too."

"I also brought you some presents. Here, open this."

Mike untied the twine and peered into the brown bag. Four plaid shirts lay piled neatly inside.

"One for each of you," explained Ihan, grinning.

The Guys
Display Their
Parting Gifts

Matt lifted his head from his pillow, his eyes only partially open. "Thanks, Ihan."

Matt, Trey, and Jedd never did fully awaken. The half-aware smiles and nods were apparently enough for Ihan. It was an hour before he left. "I will be back this afternoon to go with you to the airport," he promised.

Mike glanced at our pile of flowers as he moved back to his bed. "You know, getting woken up like that was annoying . . . but really, how can you not appreciate that guy."

"That sums up how I've come to feel about Bangladesh," said Trey.

297

8 Thailand

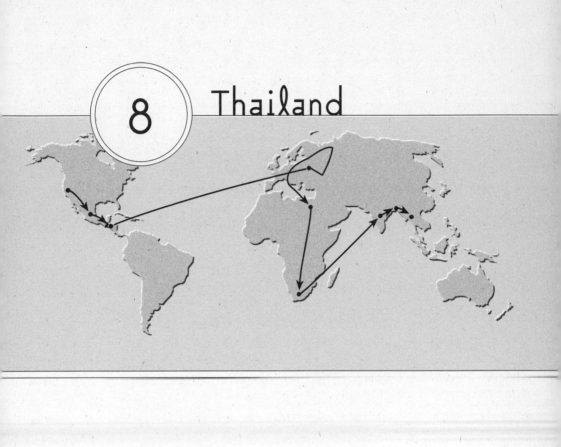

twenty-
one

From Mosquito Nets to Marble Tile
Bangkok, Thailand

trey did not notice that the line in front of him had moved. He was staring at the pile of golden fries beneath the heat lamp.

"Perfectly prepared," he concluded. "Big Macs, too."

He could see hands moving rapidly, loading the sesame-seed bun with
lettuce, tomato, pickles.

"I've never liked McDonald's," remarked Jedd. "Now I'm dying for it."

Matt warned, "Paul says we'll be going to Pizza Hut for dinner. We
probably shouldn't eat too much here."

"They have a Pizza Hut here, too?" Jedd asked with mock wonder.

Trey bulged his eyes. "Don't worry, I'll have plenty of room for pizza."

Earlier that afternoon, a Westmont alum had picked us up at the
Bangkok airport. We had never met Paul Honeyman. One of our professors
had suggested him as someone who might know people who could use our
help in Thailand. He sometimes worked with the local branch of the

Christian aid organization World Vision and said he would be glad to plug us into the many volunteer needs they had as well as find us a place to stay.

Bangkok, with its glass skyscrapers, Western restaurants, and orderly streets had us almost giddy. It felt as if we were rediscovering the modern world.

Mike glanced around the dining area. "It is amazing how clean and shiny everything seems—like it's all brand-new or something."

Jedd nodded. "That was my first impression in the airport, too. I thought it must just be a new airport, but then on the streets . . . *everything* was like that. I already love this place."

"The sidewalks seemed so clean you almost wouldn't mind eating off them," added Trey.

"You wouldn't mind eating off *any* sidewalk, Trey," joked Mike.

Paul waved Trey over to where he sat saving us a table. "It's pretty crowded in here, Trey. If you want, we could just go now and get an early dinner at Pizza Hut."

"Is it far from here?"

"Less than five minutes."

"Let's go! I'd rather have pizza anyway."

On the way to the exit, a young Thai woman in the corner of the restaurant caught Jedd's eye. Her slight figure and long, dark hair made for a pretty picture, despite the fact that her makeup was a bit too heavy. There was something else about her, though, something slightly odd.

Mike's New Pet

Jedd glanced toward the girl again, trying to figure out what it was. He could not quite get a good look because every time he turned his eyes in her direction, she seemed to be looking back at him. He pretended to be looking at a painting above her head, but she was not fooled. She smiled demurely.

"Looks like you've got yourself a friend," remarked Paul, holding the door open for Jedd.

"Uh . . . yeah."

"You've got to avoid eye contact. He'll think you want to spend some time with him."

Jedd looked at Paul, a bit taken aback.

"That was a man, you know."

"I thought she looked kinda weird, but . . ." The others snickered.

"That's Thailand for you, or at least, part of it," began Paul. "The people here are great. I really love them. But it's a very permissive society. At least as far as sex goes, just about anything is acceptable. Bangkok is considered the sex capital of the East—pretty much everything is for sale."

"I'd heard there's a lot of prostitution," remarked Mike.

"There is, but that's just the tip of the iceberg. There's a lot of really weird stuff, and a lot of it involves children. In Bangkok alone there are thousands and thousands of little kids being used for sex. When men want a total license to do anything they want, they come here."

"Why do you think that is?" queried Matt.

"It is hard to know exactly, but in some ways it is just the overextension of the natural Thai mentality—'live and let live.' I guess you'd call it an extreme tolerance. As long as you're not outright hurting anyone, no one seems to care what anyone else does."

Mike shook his head. "You can't say it doesn't hurt the kids involved."

"Stuff like that hurts *everyone* involved," remarked Jedd tersely.

"It definitely baffles me," agreed Paul. "Like I said, the majority of the people here are some of the friendliest you'd ever meet. And I wouldn't say many engage in that kind of activity. But unless it's some sort of outright crime, no one wants to stick their nose in anyone else's business."

Jedd's Reflections—March 26

Tolerance is a strange word. These days it is being lifted up in America like it is the highest of all values. The only sin in the postmodern world is intolerance.

Tolerance, though, really doesn't offer all that much. It requires no love or concern for others, no compassion or benevolence. You just have to be able to ignore.

Of course, if a society doesn't have any higher virtues, tolerance is the best you can hope for. At least it allows people to coexist without killing one another just because they don't like the other person's appearance, beliefs, or habits.

But there's a time for intolerance, too. When I think about what they do with little children here—and many other places, too—it makes me want to really lay into someone. In circumstances like this, tolerance is not a value at all. In fact, if you have the ability to stop something like that, but instead choose to be "tolerant"—that's straight-out evil.

We swung into a supermarket before proceeding to Pizza Hut. Mike and Jedd needed to pick up another dose of medicine. Both were feeling much better than they had several weeks before, but most meals still brought on stomachaches.

"I hope this finishes the parasite off," groaned Mike. "That last medicine we took helped, but I'm ready to be done with this once and for all."

Paul empathized. "I've had a few trips down that road. If this medicine doesn't work, maybe I can suggest a few things." He had lived most of the seven years since his graduation in locations overseas—Guatemala, Romania, and elsewhere—working on economic development projects for World Vision.

We waited at a crosswalk, stopped not by a light but by a traffic cop who directed the flow by hand. The policeman, sensing the right moment had come, waved his black-and-white stick at the cross traffic. It quickly came to a halt in a neat line; then he turned and waved us on.

"Why is that cop wearing a surgical mask?" asked Trey.

"I've seen other people on motorcycles wearing the same things," added Mike.

Paul explained, "They're to filter the air—there's so much exhaust on the streets down here."

Matt chuckled. "I'd just been thinking how incredibly clean the air is."

"It almost tastes sweet to me," remarked Jedd, not entirely joking.

"It's all perspective," stated Mike. "After Dhaka, I bet any air would seem clean."

"I guess that goes for everything else here, too," suggested Matt. "On the bus from the airport, I was amazed how smooth the bus ride was, and the air conditioning was so cool. I couldn't believe that people were staying in their own lanes and not honking all the time. Then I talked with this American guy. He was complaining about the bus and how dirty everything was."

"Yeah," agreed Trey. "When Paul said we might want to leave McDonald's because it was so crowded, I was thinking, *There's hardly anyone in here. Everything feels so open and spacious.*"

Jedd followed, "Did you notice that flight that arrived just after ours? It was a bunch of Americans coming straight from San Francisco. Some of them looked like they thought they were walking out onto the surface of the moon. And we were feeling like we were almost back in America."

Mike's Reflections—March 26

Rich or poor, fat or skinny, short or tall, clean or dirty—they are all comparative terms. How a person views their life is so much a product of their perspective. Our conclusions about what we "are" are mostly just products of what we compare ourselves to.

On this trip, we have seen many a man who sleeps on the floor of his home and toils in the fields from morning to night, but he considers himself rich because his family does not lack for food to eat.

I hope the perspective this trip is giving me will help me be more content—especially as I remember the poverty and struggles so many face and contrast it to my life as an American.

The way we feel about life depends not on the way things actually are so much as on how we view them. A thankful, positive attitude—like Trey has most of the time—continually shapes the world we see into something good. I hope I can become more that way.

305

The Royal Treatment

Click! The doorman's heels snapped together. As he opened the bronze-and-glass door, his gloved right hand shot up in salute. Smartly dressed tenants acknowledged our entry with polite smiles, apparently not noticing our grubby clothes and soiled backpacks. We gazed in wonder at the subtly lit foyer, which contained sculptures, paintings, oriental rugs, and leather couches. After five months of the unexpected, we had given in to a continual state of bewilderment.

"This place is called Oak Park," explained Paul. "It is one of the nicest complexes in Bangkok. My fiancée's parents are letting me live in a penthouse they own here until we get married."

Paul had met his Thai fiancée, Yeewa, during his work on an MBA in South Carolina. They would be married the following year. Until then, at least, Paul was working for the company owned in part by her father and helping a ministry called Opportunity International on the side.

A distinguished-looking man in a tweed sport coat nodded as he passed. Paul leaned toward us and noted, "That's the Hungarian ambassador to Thailand. He lives in the suite above me."

We followed Paul up a half-flight of marble steps and into an elevator, wary of touching even the gleaming handrail. *Ding, ding, ding!* The elevator raced up the tower.

"Forty-second floor," the voice from the ceiling stated matter-of-factly as it came to a halt.

Paul led to the left and, with a twist of his key, pushed open the double mahogany doors.

"In Asia, it's always necessary to take your shoes off at the entrance," he directed, removing his sandals.

We walked in slowly, almost reverently, our socks sliding on the hardwood floors. The front room looked like a presidential suite, sporting the finest décor. Mahogany woodwork surrounded a state-of-the-art entertainment center. Across the living room lay the gleaming lights of Bangkok, framed by an expansive window that covered the far wall from floor to ceiling.

Paul could tell we were impressed. "Not a bad place, huh? I'm blessed to get to live here. This will be your home as long as you're in Bangkok."

Jedd sneaked an excited glance at the others. We had not expected to stay with Paul. We imagined that we would sleep on the floor of a church or have to find a cheap hotel room.

"You can sleep here," offered Paul, opening a door. This room also offered a view of the twinkling expanse of Bangkok. Best of all, bracing air poured from several air-conditioning vents near the floor. "I'm sorry I don't have beds for you all. Do you mind sleeping on the carpet?"

We could not help but laugh at the thought. Matt assured him, "Not at all. This is the nicest room we've had in six months."

"One of the nicer rooms I've *ever* slept in," remarked Jedd.

"I knew you guys would be worn pretty thin by the time you got to Bangkok. I want your time here to be some good R and R." Paul indicated a piece of paper stuck to a bulletin board. "I've got you guys guest memberships to Oak Park's athletic club downstairs. It's pretty posh. You'll be able to use it as long as you're here."

What's next? thought Trey. *Is he going to bring out silk robes for us?*

Again and again and again, God's blessings have been poured out to us through the generosity of others.

When we left Bangladesh, I assumed our time in Bangkok would be more of the same—long, sweaty days and mosquito-bitten nights. And now look at this!

Christians sometimes talk about the way God "provides," but it is just amazing to really experience it. All my life, even though I thanked God for my blessings, they came so easily that it usually just seemed like they were just "there" or that I somehow obtained them on my own.

It's incredible to see how God takes care of us when we are more dependent on Him for whatever comes next. Sometimes it's a little mud hut and sometimes it's a forty-second-floor penthouse, but whatever He provides is always everything we need, and often a lot more than that.

I remember a thought from C. S. Lewis: "The best fruits are plucked for each by some hand that is not his own." I totally agree. It is so much more enjoyable to receive the incredible gifts we've been given, rather than to live a life where we are just trying to grasp good things for ourselves. And besides, no matter how hard we might have tried, we would never have been able to secure blessings this great on our own.

307

"To the Royal Palace," Trey directed the taxi driver.

Mike looked out the window and released something of a sigh. "It's funny. Here we are in the exotic city of Bangkok, and I don't feel like doing much besides hanging out at Paul's apartment."

Matt laughed. "You just want to keep telephoning Brittney."

"It has been great to talk with her, but seriously, I just don't have the desire to do any exploring these days."

"Well, I'm glad we're finally visiting a few places, but I know what you mean," followed Trey. "Maybe we're all just a little burned out."

"If Trey Sklar says he's burned out, then you *know* we're burned out."

Trey grinned. "Yeah, maybe. I'm hoping this relaxing we're doing will rev us up for the last month of the trip."

It was not looking like we would be of much use to anyone in Thailand. Celebrations leading up to the year's biggest holiday, Thai New Year, had already begun. The Christian groups were all on vacation. Events like the Thai Water Festival—which sounded like nothing more than several days of nationwide water fights—would be everyone's focus for several weeks.

Deep down, we were not entirely disappointed. Coupled with Paul's generosity, the turn of events made for a life of ease. We lounged by the Oak Park pools, lifted weights, e-mailed from Paul's computer, caught American movies at a theater, wandered nearby malls, and ate like royalty on Paul's hospitality. After nearly a week in Thailand, we were finally venturing out to visit a few popular tourist sites.

Mike's Reflections—April 1

I've always wanted to visit strange places and experience crazy things. That was probably my biggest reason for deciding to go on this trip. I saw the travel and adventure as the way to really experience life.

This trip has been an incredible adventure, and, aside from a few rough spots, I've enjoyed just about every aspect of the travel. Still, more and more I'm realizing that the heart of real "epic life" is not mostly about globetrotting adventures after all.

You could pour out a fortune going from one place to the next your entire life, always in search of "the next big buzz." That would be fun for a while, but even the most extraordinary activities lose a lot of their excitement if you do them enough times.

As fun as the travel adventures have been, the parts that have been most meaningful have been the relationships with the guys and the people we're meeting, and learning to serve and growing in my faith. Those things aren't as flashy, but I'm really starting to see them as the truly epic aspects of life.

Questions in Paradise

A high whitewashed wall several stories high surrounded the palace grounds, the main entrance jammed with sightseers.

"Welcome to Disneyland," Matt stated dryly.

Despite the fact that we had been traveling for five months, we had not encountered many tourists thus far. Of course, we definitely did not think of *ourselves* as tourists. Few travelers do.

"Do we have to do this?" lamented Mike.

Trey ignored the complaint. "Have you guys ever seen the musical *The King and I?* This palace is where a lot of it is supposed to be set."

"Wasn't that in Siam?" questioned Matt.

"Thailand used to be called Siam. Did you know this is the only country in Southeast Asia that was never colonized by a European country? That is why they still have a king."

"That guy we saw yesterday?"

"Right."

The day before, we had gone to the movies. Just after the previews, everyone in the theater stood in unison. We joined them, trying to figure out what was going on. For the next several minutes, we watched as a pictorial history of the life of the current king of Thailand paraded across the screen, accompanied by triumphant music.

"The king seemed like a nice enough guy, but he looked like a middle-aged dad on vacation," commented Mike.

309

"Don't say that too loud. Paul was telling me this king guy is the national hero. He doesn't have much of an official function, but everyone totally loves him."

"He's got a nice house here," Matt declared as we passed through the gates and into the palace.

What struck us most as we wandered among the grounds was the intricacy of the workmanship. In Europe, palace walls housed paintings, sculptures, and other works of art. In this palace, the walls *were* art. Every inch of wall, gate, and tower was carved with geometric shapes, miniature faces, or intricate flowers. Others had been inlaid with brilliantly patterned mosaics. Worked into it all was gold, everywhere—even in the temple areas where Buddhist priests lived out their vows of poverty.

Mike glanced over at Jedd, who was staring up at the monster face of a thirty-foot statue. Jedd had been uncharacteristically quiet all day. Mike guessed it had to do with a conflict from the prior evening, one that had carried reconciliation time out until well past midnight.

Ornate Temple Statuary

The disagreement began over whether or not to act on a friend's suggestion of a welcome home party for our return. Somewhere along the line, it became a revisitation of an issue that had come up several times during the trip: the aggressiveness with which Jedd promoted his opinions. The conflict ended well, but Jedd still seemed to be a little stung.

Mike walked up next to him. "These statues are pretty wild, huh?"

Jedd's smile was halfhearted. "Yeah. If this guy came to life, it'd be pretty scary."

"So what's up, Jedd? You haven't talked much today."

Jedd was quiet for a moment. "I don't know. Probably just a little down."

"Is it about last night?"

"I'm not holding on to what we were arguing about. As late as we had to stay up to resolve it, I'm glad we did."

"You're just tired?"

"I am a little tired, but it's not that. I guess I feel like our reconciliation time keeps focusing on me. Like I'm always at the middle of every problem. I want to be able to take criticism, but I guess I'm getting kind of sick of it."

"Jedd, you're *not* at the middle of every problem." Mike thought for a moment before posing the question "Do you feel like we're being too nitpicky?"

"I don't know. I always learn from the issues we work through, but I just feel like I'm always the one who has some area he needs to 'grow' in. I felt that way in Russia, too."

Mike showed part of a smile. "You know why? It's because you're so intense about everything. When there's a lot of energy, even if most of it is good, there's going to be more friction there."

"Maybe, but that doesn't exactly help when I'm getting criticized all the time."

"Seriously, Jedd, you know how much we respect you—your discipline, your focus, your speaking ability, your passion for the Lord. I know some of the reconciliation times have been harder on you than the rest of us, but I already see you growing through it, and I know the end result will be even better."

"Thanks, Mike. I appreciate your saying that," said Jedd quietly. "Not to be touchy-feely, but I do think it would be good if we all did a little better job of affirming one another every now and then. Reconciliation pretty much just focuses on working out frustrations. That's fine, but it would be good to have a reminder every once in a while that we appreciate one another."

Jedd's Reflections—April 1

Some of the reconciliation times recently have been pretty hard for me.

I try to learn from the conflicts and from the things the other guys are saying. I know a person's ability to grow through criticism says a lot about their character. Sometimes, though, I just feel like I have had too much. (I guess that shows how far I still have to grow.)

As hard as it is sometimes, though, I do feel like I'm growing through it. Being together so intensely for so long makes it impossible to hide the real you—both the good and bad. That has created some struggles, especially for me, but with our commitment to reconciliation and to one another, it can produce growth we just couldn't get anywhere else.

311

For part of the ride home from the palace, we took a water taxi, a narrow craft that looked like a long banana, its ends raised well above the center where we sat on cross-boards while an outboard motor, directed by the driver, pushed us through the brown waters.

Canal-like river ways connected many sections of Bangkok to the central river that passed through the city. The quiet canals, like alleys, ran mostly along the back porches of personal residences. Some of the homes were upscale, even manorlike. Most, though, were simple affairs of wood and corrugated metal built up on piers. In other areas, only dense undergrowth lined the banks, sometimes forming a leafy canopy overhead.

Floating BBQ

A group of boys waved and shrieked as we buzzed by their swimming spot. One clambered out and performed a flip off the cement embankment.

"Nice trick!" called Jedd over his shoulder, giving him a thumbs-up.

As our canal joined with the main river, its width of forty feet became two hundred. The shapes lining the edges made for incongruous neighbors. Western-style office buildings shimmered in the sun next to multi-tiered shacks. Ornate Buddhist temples from ages long past stood alongside massive billboards that proclaimed the glories of Coca-Cola and Apple computers. Thailand was like a man dressed in a suit coat and tie above the waist, but wearing only ragged shorts and sandals below. Modern and ancient, poverty and opulence, East and West were blended together in an unpredictable cocktail.

"I wonder what people here think of all the Western influence and change," mused Trey.

"Paul told me most of the young people embrace it, but some of the old people really don't like it," Mike answered.

"That's usually the case."

"Yes, although here I'd bet the rate of change has been some of the most radical the world's ever seen, especially with the economic growth of the last decade. Some people probably feel like they woke up one morning and found the future had taken over their city."

The "Asian financial miracle" of the 1990s brought to Thailand a time of incredible transformation. Wealth poured in with international investment. Development was both rapid and awkward, like a boy's adolescent growth spurts. Paul's residence was an example: The towering Oak Park complex shot up quickly, its owners eager to cash in on increasing demands for luxury from Thailand's new rich.

But the speedy pace had consequences. Oak Park's builders lined its elevators with marble. The elevators' machinery, however, was incapable of carrying more than one or two people along with the weight of the stone. They broke down constantly until the elevators' marble was replaced with wood paneling. Paul's bathroom was another example. Although full of gleaming brass and modern appliances, his toilet plugged up at every other use.

° ° °

"That was the fanciest shower I've ever been in!" said Trey with wonder. "There was a nozzle coming from every direction and even a digital control for the water temperature."

"I know; mine was the same," said Matt. He lay on his back on a black leather recliner. The chair's vibrations slowly rolled from under his feet up to his head.

Trey opened the locker room's minifreezer and took out two wash-cloths. They had been soaked in menthol, neatly rolled, and frozen. He lay back on a chair similar to Matt's and turned it on, then placed one of the cloths over his face. He breathed deeply. "Ahhhh. So refreshing!"

After passing the morning reading on lounge chairs by Oak Park's swimming pools, Trey and Matt had headed to the gym for a workout. They spent two hours scaling routes on the club's climbing wall, lifting free weights, and watching TV while jogging on the treadmills. Following a sit in the sauna and a visit to the high-tech showers, they donned the club's thick bathrobes and settled in for a chair-massage in the men's locker room.

"What a place, huh?" remarked Matt.

Trey smiled beneath his menthol cloth. "It's like one of those elite clubs you see on *Lifestyles of the Rich and Famous*."

"So do you feel fully recovered yet?"

"I felt recovered last week. Now I'm starting to feel a little indulgent."

"It's funny how quickly you can get tired of being pampered."

Trey peeled the towel off his face and rested on one elbow. "I've been thinking about that. I don't want to complain in the least, but as nice as all this luxury is, it doesn't take long before you start wanting something more than late breakfasts and reading by the pool."

"That's probably why God gave us six days to work and one to rest," Matt commented. His voice shook slightly from the chair's vibrations. "Taking time off is great, but you can only fully enjoy it when it is really a *rest from* something and not just a continuing self-indulgence."

"Definitely. Which is why I'm glad you were able to get in contact with that missionary."

Since our original plans to work in Bangkok had fallen through, Matt had tried the phone number of a missionary in eastern Thailand, who encouraged us to visit, affirming he would appreciate our help on a few projects.

Matt followed, "I'll be glad for the chance to work. In the meantime, there's no reason not to enjoy these blessings. It really is one of the nicest places I've ever been."

Trey nodded. "What a far cry from the mud huts we were in just a few weeks ago. It almost feels like that was just a dream."

"I know. When I was in Bangladesh, I promised myself I wouldn't forget the struggles the people live with every day there. As sad as it is, I feel like I already am," Matt admitted.

"I don't think we'll ever completely overlook them, but I know what you mean. The reality starts to fade. You find yourself getting irritated when your toast is a little burned or when a restaurant doesn't have air conditioning. Then you catch yourself and think, *What a spoiled brat I am.*"

"So how do we remember when we get back home?"

"Good question. Maybe it's not entirely possible to just 'remember.' Maybe you just have to keep experiencing things to keep them as part of your perspective," responded Trey.

Matt's Reflections—April 3

314

I believe this trip will impact my life as long as I live. But still, even before it's over, I see how quickly I can forget things I've seen and lessons I've learned.

When living in the lap of luxury, it is really hard to retain a full sense of how most of the world actually lives. I want to hold on to what I've seen. I want it to make me thankful at all times. I want it to keep me from complaining.

But it is so difficult to keep seeing their lives and faces. If I really want to remember, I need to choose to remember. I must do things that keep bringing these things to mind: continue service to the needy, make real sacrifice at times, and continue to pray for my struggling brothers and sisters around the world.

Brave Girl

Our train flowed smoothly across the Thai countryside, swaying slightly from side to side, the tracks leading straight ahead, straight behind, splitting the plain in two. Despite the lushness of orchards, palm trees, and rice fields that spread off in all directions, the soil itself appeared dry and dusty. The rainy season wouldn't arrive for several months. A smattering of buildings appeared on the left, but the train did not slow. Only the town's steep-roofed Buddhist temple—gleaming with red and gold—had escaped the decay that marked almost every other structure. Despite the peeling paint and crumbling concrete, the town's inhabitants appeared to value tidiness. Even dirt streets appeared to have been swept free of debris.

We were headed to the missionary's home in a town on the Cambodian border. Mike had remained in Bangkok to help a small ministry group with a brief project. Jedd, tired of reading, stared out his window at a vast mango grove. Matt brought out his journal, but returned to his book when it became clear that the train's rocking made legible writing impossible. Trey sat a few seats away, conversing with a pretty young woman. She had Asian features and long black hair. Her name was Kathy—ethnically Filipino, but a resident of the Netherlands since the age of three, she spoke perfect English, along with Dutch, Tagalog, and Spanish.

"I graduated last spring from a university in the Netherlands," she explained to Trey. "I plan to travel for about eight months, mostly here in Asia."

"You're traveling for fun?"

"I spent a couple months in the Philippines to visit relatives and things like that, but I've been to a lot of places. I enjoy the freedom. What about you guys?"

"We graduated last spring, too. We worked for the summer to make some money and then took off in October. We've been in a number of different places; we stay with local Christians and join them in whatever work they are doing."

Jedd slid onto the bench seat next to Trey and introduced himself to Kathy. Conversation shifted into the usual exchange of travel stories.

Kathy had picked up some sort of intestinal parasite in Myanmar. In desperation, she ventured to neighboring Bangladesh, hoping to acquire medicine. "The guidebook said Bangladesh was a little more open to the West and that I'd be more likely to find the drugs there," she explained. "If I would've known what Bangladesh was like, though, I think it's the last place I would have gone."

Trey and Jedd just smiled at each other.

In a lull in conversation, Kathy indicated the book on the seat next to Jedd. "That is an interesting title—*Knowing God*. Any good?"

Jedd picked up the book and fanned the pages. "I'm enjoying it. It's a biblical view of how we can enter relationship with God and come to walk with Him in our day-to-day lives."

"How do you mean?"

"It would take me a bit to explain," replied Jedd, "but if you don't mind, I'll try."

"Go ahead," she encouraged.

"As the Bible explains it, God created man in His own image. God intended that we live in perfect relationship with Him as our Creator and Friend, and also with one another. Of course, God had the power to force man to do anything He wanted, but He chose to give us freedom, that is, the choice to accept or reject the life God intended for us. We rejected it because we wanted to be in charge, rebelling against God and His purposes for us."

"That's the Adam and Eve story, right?"

"Yes—*and* it's what we do every day. What the Bible calls 'sin' is basically our choices that reject the good God wants for us. We think it will give us more happiness, more pleasure, more control. That actually might be the case in the short run. But the net effect of sin in the end is always destruction of relationship, both between us and God and between us and one another."

Kathy nodded, indicating for Jedd to continue.

"So, in essence, our sin separated us from God. And from that point on, selfishness and brokenness became the dominant marks of our relationships with others also. At that point, God could have just let us go and left us to bear the consequences of our decisions. But the Bible says that God loved us so much that instead of allowing us to remain separated from Him for eternity, He sent His Son to become a man to take upon Himself the pain and punishment for our choices. That is why Jesus came. With His life and His teachings, Jesus showed us the type of life God wants us to live. With His death, He paid the price for our rebellion. If we accept that gift and commit our lives to Him, we reenter relationship with God and someday will go to spend eternity with Him in heaven."

Kathy continued to listen intently, her right eyebrow slightly lowered. "My parents are Catholic," she said. "We never took it too seriously, though. I didn't really know much of what the Bible said."

"We're still learning as we go, Kathy," inserted Trey. "But the more we discover about life and about Jesus, the more we're convinced that what He taught was the truth."

"I guess my experience has been the opposite," she said. "Most of the religious people I know don't seem all that much better off than anyone else. Maybe worse."

"We've seen that, too," Trey agreed. "We really have no interest in being 'religious people,' either. Most of religion is man's creation anyway, not God's. True Christian faith is not about being religious or doing rituals or ceremonies or anything like that. It is about living in a relationship with your Creator. It is about living as we were designed to live."

"But there are still a lot of things you can't do," Kathy asserted.

"You mean moral decisions?" asked Jedd.

"Yeah—lifestyle choices, things Christians aren't supposed to do."

Trey answered, "There are certain things we choose not to do; but if those things are ultimately destructive to your relationship with God and with others, why would you *want* to do them? God fully intends us to enjoy all the good gifts He has given us. We only need to avoid distorted forms of those gifts because they end up destroying relationships. Besides, they aren't anywhere near as good as the *real* gifts."

"I don't totally understand."

317

"A simple example might be food. God equipped us with taste buds to enjoy it. Think about it—isn't it awesome that the process of getting energy into our bodies is not just a functional activity, but actually can provide pleasure? That shows God wants us to have pleasure. He wired us for it."

"So what's the problem?"

"When we take His gift and use it in a way He did not design it for, we ruin it and create all kinds of problems. Food is great, but look what happens when a person thinks he can get more out of food than was intended and becomes gluttonous. And that principle is just as true of drugs, sex outside marriage . . ."

"You guys are virgins?"

Trey nodded.

"No way! You're serious?" She did not seem disdainful, just surprised.

"Yes. But not just because we want to 'keep the rules.' As we see it, God designed us and He knows how we work best. He's given us instructions. If we follow them, our lives are better."

Kathy nodded faintly, not accepting, but not disagreeing either.

Jedd continued. "It is not that sex is a bad thing. We believe sex once we are married will be one of the greatest gifts God's given us . . ."

Trey agreed with a slightly overloud "Yep!" Jedd glanced at him and grinned.

Trey began, "See, a big part of the reason God gave us sex is to bond two people together at the deepest level. You may have heard the analogy—sex is like two pieces of paper being glued together. If you pull them apart, both pieces are going to tear, and you leave part of yourself behind."

"Yeah, I think that is true," Kathy acknowledged.

"You probably know people—especially girls, but guys, too—who are just torn apart when they've been in a sexual relationship and then things don't work out."

"I do. But really . . . there are dangers to everything."

"That's true," Jedd followed. "We definitely can choose to risk the hurt and emotional tearing, the STDs, single motherhood, and the other dangers. But why? And look at the other side of the coin. The best argument for saving sex for marriage—or for any other aspect of Christian morality—is not the bad things that might happen if you don't obey; it is the beauty of how things work when you do them the way God intended. Two people who love each other and have saved themselves for each other, and who are committed to each other for life in marriage . . . there is almost nothing more beautiful in the world."

"I respect you for thinking that. I wish there were more guys like you," she confessed. "I guess I'd still have to say that it seems kind of confining to me, though."

"With all respect, Kathy, the way I see it is totally opposite," offered Trey. "A writer named G. K. Chesterton gave a good analogy. Imagine a group of children playing on the top of a high plateau with steep cliffs on all sides. They try to play games, but the cliffs are so dangerous that some of the kids just huddle in the middle, and some of the ones who do run around end up falling off the sides. Christian morality is like putting up a fence around the edges of the plateau. You *could* say that the fence is a limitation, but what it really does is free the kids to play fearlessly within its boundaries. Now they can run freely over the entire plateau. When people follow God's directions, they are free to enjoy sex and all the other good things God has given us within the fence that He's put up for our own good. We never have to worry about falling over cliffs like STDs, AIDS, unwanted pregnancies, or the psychological pain of seeing someone you've been sexually bonded with walk away from you."

Kathy smiled faintly. "That's an interesting way to see it. So you actually think you are freer when you follow Christian morality?"

"Definitely," said Jedd. "Here's another way to see it: If I sit down at a piano, I have no constraints at all because I don't know a thing about notes or scales or music in general. I obey no rules at all. I just hit any key I want.

But if a master pianist sits down to play, he *does* have constraints. He doesn't just hit any key that catches his eye. He knows the 'rules' of music and chooses to operate within them. But this self-limitation isn't an impediment to his freedom. Working within the rules, he is infinitely more free than I am. Just compare his music with the terrible sound I would make and you can see the beauty found in obedience."

Trey started to say something further, but an indiscernible sound crackled over the intercom, cutting him off.

"Did you hear what stop this is?" asked Kathy.

"I couldn't even tell if he was speaking English or Thai," said Trey.

Kathy leaned against the window to get a better view of the approaching station. "I think this might be our stop."

"This is your stop," confirmed the ticket-taker who had just entered the car.

Trey tore a scrap of paper from his small organizer and scribbled out Paul Honeyman's phone number. "We'll be back in Bangkok by the end of the week," he said. "Give us a call if you end up coming back to the city. We'd love to hang out."

The train screeched to a halt, and we all piled out of the car onto a dusty cement platform.

"I've really enjoyed talking with you guys," said Kathy a bit soberly.

"We have, too," responded Trey.

"I'll give you a call if I'm in Bangkok next week," she promised. She waved as she struck off down the town's slightly paved road. "See ya."

"She's a brave girl," remarked Trey. "Traveling the world by herself like that."

Trey's Reflections—April 4

I really don't know what Kathy thinks of everything we said, but she appeared so surprised by it all, even moved. Something in our conviction and our commitment to Jesus seemed almost shocking to her. Now that I think about it, it should be that way. Christ's "life to the full" is more interesting and rewarding than living by the world's insipid rules. Goodness is the exciting thing; vices get old after a while. It reminds me of a C. S. Lewis quote from "The Weight of Glory":

If there lurks in most modern minds the notion that to desire

our own good and earnestly hope for the enjoyment of it is a bad
thing, I submit that this notion . . . is no part of the Christian faith.
Indeed, if we consider the unblushing promises of reward and the
staggering nature of the rewards promised in the Gospels, it would
seem that Our Lord finds our desires, not too strong, but too weak.
We are half-hearted creatures, fooling about with drink and sex
and ambition when infinite joy is offered us, like an ignorant child
who wants to go on making mud pies in a slum because he cannot
imagine what is meant by the offer of a holiday at the sea. We are
far too easily pleased.

Our transport for the final thirty miles to the missionary's town was a
tuk-tuk—something of a cross between a Harley-Davidson and a rickshaw.
Matt and Jedd lounged comfortably on the wide seat between the two rear
tires; Trey balanced on a platform above the motorcycle's engine, just
behind the driver. Once in the village, we would ask for the home of the
farang—the white man. Anyone would be glad to show us to the house.

"Just over on that side of the road there—that's Cambodia. We'll be
to the town real soon," Trey shouted to be heard above the roar of the
motor.

"This should be nice," said Jedd. "I'm looking forward to the chance to
be useful again . . ."

Together Again in Bangkok

Matt carried two water balloons in each hand, several more bulging in
his hip pack. Mike heaved along a bucket, full to the brim, an orange-and-
green squirt gun protruding from his belt. Trey and Jedd were similarly
armed. We had arrived back in Bangkok just in time for Thai Water Day.

"Up there," hissed Trey. "Let's get those guys on the steps."

We edged along the sidewalk, backs against a large department store
window. Ten yards beyond the vegetation of a large planter, a half-dozen
Thai businessmen sat talking on a set of broad cement steps. The afternoon was heavy and warm, and none of the men wore suit coats, only
white shirts and ties. One sucked air through a cigarette. The others talked
and laughed.

"You ready?" whispered Jedd, glancing back.

"Let's get 'em," urged Mike.

The men looked up, eyes wide, as we emerged from behind the bushes, whooping. Two balloons missed high and crashed into the glass door behind them. A third found its mark, soaking the shirt of a middle-aged man. The men, however, were not unprepared. Large squirt guns seemed to appear from nowhere. A heavy blast of water caught Matt in the head, and the young man wielding the super-soaker exulted with a shout. Mike returned the favor, dousing the fellow with a slosh from his bucket. Trying to conserve balloons, we began to fire with our water guns, slowly backing up the street. An old flatbed truck rumbled toward us from the opposite direction. As it sputtered past, shouting sounded from the truck's bed. Trey looked up in time to catch a bucket of water across the face. He blinked, eyes stinging.

"Oh yeah?" retorted Jedd. He launched a pair of balloons at the company of water-warriors in the back of the truck. He then reached for his pistol. Before he had it out, a small wave crashed over him, leaving him as wide-eyed as Trey.

321

The crowd in the back of the truck erupted with laughter. Our businessmen opponents cheered also, but only for a moment. A volley of balloons from the truck left several of them dripping as well. The truck stopped completely, and the occupants continued to attack both us and the businessmen, supplying themselves from two large barrels in the center of the truck bed. A motorcycle pulled up behind the truck and honked. Two balloons broke against the rider's helmet in response. He pulled a squirt gun from beneath his jacket and fired futilely into the back of the truck as he drove around it and roared off down the street. Ammo low, the truck finally began to roll on. We had nothing left, either, and began a retreat in the direction we had come.

"We've got to spend our balloons slower next time," advised Mike.

The businessmen waved as they returned to the steps where they had been sitting.

"Good fighting!" one called as we waved back.

"I love this," said Trey, beaming. "It is like a little kid's dream—everyone in the whole country having a water fight on the same day."

"I can't see Thai Water Day flying in downtown L.A.," remarked Mike. "You'd probably get shot."

Jedd glanced ahead at a small band of bucket-toting young people who seemed to be watching us carefully from the other side of the street. "Let's get back to Paul's place and reload. We're out of ammo and I think those guys up there have got us in their sights . . ."

° ° °

Mike grunted and pushed the barbell off his chest one last time.

"Good set, Mike," affirmed Jedd.

Mike sat up on the bench and draped his towel over his neck. "You know, I've gained back just about all the weight I lost in Bangladesh."

"I've still got a little ways to go," replied Jedd as he headed for the lat pull machine. He changed the subject. "What exactly was this work you were doing here in Bangkok while we were gone?"

"The place I was working at helps poor people start little businesses out of their homes. It's called a microcredit project. They provide instruction and know-how from day one—everything the person needs to get going, including a small start-up loan of fifty to a few hundred bucks."

"Sounds like your kind of ministry."

Mike smiled. He frequently expressed his thoughts on what constituted *real* help for the poor. His opinions had only become stronger throughout the trip. "I liked their vision a lot. Some aid groups out there think they're solving problems by passing out food and money. Most of the time as soon as they leave, the people are as bad off as they were before—maybe worse because they're used to the handouts. These microcredit guys are teaching people how to provide for themselves."

"So what were you doing for them?"

"It was just a little office with a couple of people. I was doing a bunch of things. I spent one whole day just trying to fix their computer."

"You? Mr. I-Break-Every-Computer-I-Touch?"

"Yeah, I even kind of got it working. The main thing, though, was just trying to help them sort through their accounting and stuff. They had a guy working for them for a couple years who embezzled most of their small-business-loan fund. They're starting again from scratch."

"Bummer."

"Yeah. So what were you guys doing?"

"A lot of odd jobs—sanding, painting, building shelves. Nothing too exciting, but I think the missionary guy we were helping really appreciated it."

"Was he a good guy?"

Jedd indicated he wanted to finish his set of lat pulls before replying.

"Yeah. He was a great guy—from New Zealand. It's just him and his family and one partner. What a different mind-set a guy like that has: no sense of climbing the ladder or keeping up with any Joneses. He just does his projects to help the people out there and shares about Jesus and takes care of his family. Seems really content."

"So could you live that way?"

"I thought about that while we were there. I don't know. I've never thought I'd like being a missionary, but there's definitely some things about his life that I want to be in mine: peace, contentment, and purpose. After all, what else really matters? It'd still be a hard life, though. They live without a lot of things we see as necessities."

"Like air conditioning?"

"That was one. It was so hot at night I had a hard time sleeping."

"It would take some adjusting, but . . ." Mike paused for a moment, thinking. "The more I compare life in this fancy place here to all the other places we've been on this trip, I really can't say that this is all that much better."

323

"It's easy to say that while we're here."

"Of course. But think about it. Where have we really been happiest on this trip? In fact, as much as we needed the R and R, I've probably felt less content here at times than anywhere."

"That's true, I guess, but you can't say you haven't totally enjoyed yourself here."

"No, I have. But it just kind of hit me how all the benefits of wealth here, as nice as they are, are so insignificant compared to the experiences we've had in so many situations that were much less comfortable."

Jedd's Reflections—April 11

I love the way Mike gets me thinking sometimes. Comparing this time of living in luxury to the other experiences of the trip, I see yet another strong validation of the truth of Jesus' instructions for life: "A man's life does not consist in the abundance of his possessions."

It makes me think of the book of Ecclesiastes in the Bible. The most powerful king in Israel's history was looking back on his life. He had acquired more wealth, achieved greater accomplishments, and amassed more knowledge than any ruler before him. But at the end of it all, he concluded that it all amounted to nothing but a "chasing after the wind."

What a terrible thing to come to your final days and realize that. But I can't help but believe that it's true: All of the things the world uses as its measures of success—although we can enjoy them in their proper place—really matter little in the long run. Neither do they bring the deep joy and purpose we desire.

I remember how this really struck me the summer I interned at Price-Waterhouse. As "successful" as everyone was, there just didn't seem to be a whole lot of purpose in many of their lives. That was difficult for me. It was almost suffocating when I first realized that even if I were to make it to the very top of the business world, I wouldn't necessarily be any happier for it.

As hard as it was to come to grips with this, I'm glad I was forced to. I know I would never follow Jesus with abandon if I believed in my heart of hearts that what the world has to offer is better than what He has to offer. Thankfully, He keeps reminding me that this isn't the case.

It's great to begin learning these lessons while I'm young, while I still have the majority of my life ahead of me to give to those things that really matter.

° ° °

In the final days of our stay in Bangkok, we made contact with the local branch of the Bible League, a Christian organization committed to putting Bibles into the hands of people around the globe. Before the trip, Jedd called the group's Southeast Asia coordinator, who promised we would be able to acquire Vietnamese Bibles at their Bangkok office. The man also suggested we could get information on good contacts within Vietnam from the local Bible League.

Trey and Mike stood in a quiet courtyard. "I think this is the right place," stated Trey, leading toward a whitewashed door on the far side.

He pushed on the door and it opened into a clean, airy room that whirred with ceiling fans. Banana trees stood outside the slatted windows, their long, frayed leaves coloring the sunlight green as it streamed into the room. The place smelled of adventure. A tall American with a kind, weathered face rose from his desk.

"Good afternoon, gentlemen. You must be the ones from California."

"I'm Trey, the one you talked to on the phone. This is Mike. We're glad you had time in your schedule."

His handshake was so firm it hurt. "I'm Jack. And no problem at all. We jump at any opportunity to get Bibles into Vietnam. With young, single guys like you, we'll send as many as we can. What exactly are your plans?"

"We don't really have any at this point. We just want to get Bibles into the hands of Christians," said Mike.

"Anything else you're planning to do?"

"We'd been hoping to do some work with a World Vision worker, but apparently he's out of the country right now. We've got the number of one Christian lady—a friend of a friend. That's it."

"Listen. Just in case this lady doesn't work out, I'll give you the number of another good contact who'd be able to distribute the Bibles. If you use him, though, you gotta know what he's risking. One hint to the government that a Vietnamese national is trafficking Bibles and he's off to the cage."

Trey whistled. "Wow. What happens to Americans who are caught?"

"It's not so bad if you're caught at the airport. At worst, they'll just have you deported immediately with no jail time. But if you get caught with Vietnamese Christians on the inside, the stakes are higher."

Trey leaned closer as Jack took a sip of his water and continued, "First of all, the Vietnamese Christians will be off to prison for a long, long time. They'll keep them behind bars until the guards have had their fun or until they can be pumped for names of other Christians. You guys could go to the lockup, too, and I've heard it's pretty rough. Even then, though, chances are good you'd get kicked out of the country before you had enough time to get to know the jailer. Here, why don't you guys have a seat and we'll go over some details . . ."

∘ ∘ ∘

Matt and Jedd were not home when Mike and Trey returned to Paul's place where they unboxed 160 Vietnamese Bibles and began exploring creative ways to hide 40 each among the contents of their backpacks.

"You know, Trey," began Mike, "there may be some sketchy stuff once we get into Vietnam, but we've really been blessed thus far."

"I know. I'm thankful everything worked out so well with Jack."

Along with the Bibles, Jack had provided the phone number of a Vietnamese underground pastor. That made two good contacts, including the one we had received from a friend in the States. Jack also gave careful instruction on how to make the Bible exchange as safe as possible: "Call from a pay phone or a hotel. Be as vague as possible. Don't mention their name or yours or anything to do with Christianity. Just say something about gifts; these guys should figure out what you've got. They may just suggest a place for you to leave them—that'd be safest for them and for you."

We also had been fortunate enough to meet an American at church the prior Sunday who frequently traveled to Vietnam on business. He suggested the hotel he normally stayed at as cheap, clean, and safe.

"You know," said Trey as he set a stack of forty Bibles next to Matt's backpack, "maybe we shouldn't tell Matt that we could go to prison if we get caught."

"Yeah, that'd probably be better. No need to tell him anything that will make him any more nervous. We can always let him know after we deliver the Bibles."

"So are you nervous at all?"

"A little, I guess. Thinking about how little we have to lose compared to the Vietnamese believers helps to put it into perspective, though. What's a few days in prison? For them it could be life."

"That's true. All the same, I'm glad we'll have a lot of people at home praying . . ."

IX Vietnam

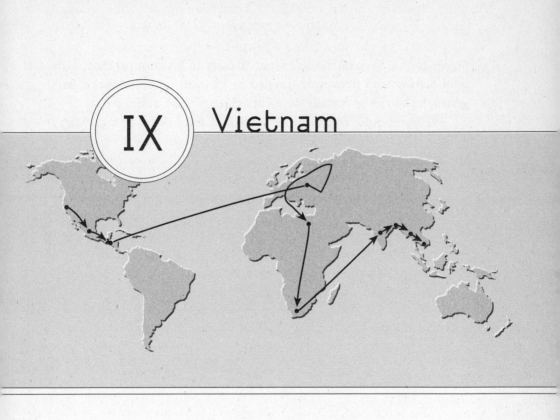

twenty-
two

Notes from the Underground

Last night, Matt suggested we ask very directly in prayer that
God do grand, visible things during this trip. I will pray specifically
for Vietnam, a place I have little desire to see, where we will be
for only nine days with few specific plans and almost no
knowledge of culture or language. It will indeed take God's
action to produce anything remarkable there, for right now I
can't imagine much happening besides getting the Bibles in.
Lord, please reveal Your work.

—JEDD'S REFLECTIONS FROM NOVEMBER 8 (IN GUATEMALA)

The wheels of our 737 collided with the landing strip, sending a jolt
through the plane and leaving in their path two streaks of sizzling rubber. Haze hovered above the concrete all around us. Rotting on the far end
of the tarmac lay the hulks of old U.S. military planes, captured following
the American evacuation from the Vietnam War.

"Saigon," said Trey, shaking his head. "It is hard to believe my dad flew
into this same airport so many times as a soldier."

"Just think about all those young guys," mused Mike. "They were
about our age, some a lot younger, living normal American lives and then
all of a sudden they got taken and plunked down in this crazy place with
a gun and a license to kill. If we had been born a little earlier, it would
have been us."

"I wonder how I would have reacted to it all."

It is almost surreal thinking about the countless American young men who stepped down from planes, just as we are about to, into the same steamy air. My dad was one of them. Unlike us, those soldiers had no choice in the matter. I wonder what they thought as they stepped out of America into a world of carnage, temptation, and mortal combat. It must have been terrible, pulse-pumping, wild, mind-changing. I know many of his friends never left alive.

As the "fasten seat belts" lights dimmed, we stood up and grabbed our carry-ons from the overhead bins. They were heavier than normal, full of contraband Bibles. Between his thumb and forefinger, Jedd twisted a section of his beard. We all were a little nervous.

"How are you feeling, Matt?" Jedd asked.

"I guess a little scared. It's good to know so many people are praying for us right now. What do you think will happen if we get caught?"

"It shouldn't be too bad. They will probably hold us and question us for a while, but eventually they will have to let us go."

"What do you think are the chances of them catching us?"

"Less than half of the people who try to smuggle Bibles in actually make it through."

"Well, then we better be praying."

Holy Contraband

Although relatively modern, the terminal was not air-conditioned. Sweat trickled down Mike's spine and left streaks on the back of his shirt. Soldiers, dressed in the ugly green so popular with Communists around the world, looked us over without interest. We moved toward the large x-ray machines through which all incoming luggage had to pass. Small crowds of officials gathered behind each machine, watching the x-ray monitors like TV-starved children.

"I guess it's now or never," breathed Trey. "Lord, blind their eyes."

His heart seemed to expand as it pounded. It pushed against his lungs and made it hard to breathe. We sauntered toward separate lines, one by one tossing our bags onto the conveyor belt, offering our best unsuspicious smiles, trying to look both nonchalant and hurried.

What is a normal look for a person going through customs? wondered Jedd. *As many times as I've done it in the past six months, I can't remember.* He started to whistle, but thought better of it.

Trey's bag went through first. Glancing at the monitors the officials were watching, we could make out the shapes of countless books packed among Trey's clothes. The watchers, though, did not even look up at him. Matt was next, then Jedd.

As Mike's bag finally passed through, two soldiers emerged from a doorway on the other side of the room and marched toward us, faces stern.

They've got him, thought Matt, his body tensing.

Mike turned his eyes toward the floor as the soldiers moved toward him. He held his breath. The men brushed by him without stopping. They continued on to the next counter. Trey's shoulders drooped and we all let out our breaths. We were in.

331

Matt's Reflections—April 16

Coming through customs was nerve-racking . . . but we made it! I am so thankful so many of our friends from home who were praying for us.

I am astonished that Trey made it through. Even though he is the most savvy traveler of us, he mistakenly ended up standing in the "Items to Declare" lane—where everyone's bags are opened—no matter what. Even so, we watched him walk right past the unseeing guards!

Strangely enough, mixed in with the fear today was a deep confidence that all would be well, even if the authorities did catch us. That is a wonderful thing about times when I am totally seeking to live for God: It is not that I can assume nothing bad or painful will happen—God made no such promise. But I do know that there will be eternal purpose and redeeming goodness even in the worst that befalls us. That doesn't keep me from fearing sometimes, but it gives me a confidence to take risks I could never otherwise take.

We were a bit surprised by how Western the city of Saigon appeared. Our guidebook explained that the city had been shaped and built, in large part, by foreign powers. A colonial French government ruled Saigon from

1859 until 1954, and large numbers of American soldiers passed through the city from the early 1960s until 1975. Paint on most buildings was peeling and the stucco cracked, but the streets seemed generally clean and well planned. Leafy trees, their thick trunks painted white, abounded along sidewalks and in the many parks. The grass that grew up in open lots and through cracks in the sidewalks added to the pleasant greenness of the city.

Even so, there were plenty of things to remind us that we were in a foreign land. Grimy canals ran throughout the city, and shanty homes piled to several levels grew haphazardly above the mucky water. Although there did not seem to be many beggars, people seemed to enjoy squatting along walkways for hours at a time, talking or just sitting. Soup sellers walked the streets, bearing pairs of large, steaming buckets hung from bamboo sticks that crossed their shoulders. Mingling with the traffic sounds was the ever-present buzz of insects.

We were even more taken aback by the noticeable presence of churches. Some were small, cross-topped buildings of brick; others were grand affairs with bells and steeples rising a hundred feet into the air. We did not know what to think.

"I had heard the underground church is so persecuted here. I sure didn't expect to find churches everywhere," remarked Jedd as a van taxi carried us through town. "You can't help wondering if things are not as bad as they say."

"Especially after taking the risk to smuggle all those Bibles in," added Matt. "Maybe they don't need them so much after all."

Cold Drinks for Sale

Once safe in our hotel room, we stacked 160 Bibles in our closet and locked it.

John, the American businessman we met in Bangkok, had recommended the hotel as clean and reasonably priced. He would be residing there during part of our stay as well.

"Well," asked Trey, sitting down on the bed, "should we try to get ahold of our contact?"

"Let's do it," replied Mike.

Matt pulled back the curtains a few inches and peered down at the street below. Nothing appeared out of the ordi-

nary. Bicycles and scooters dominated the road. Men zipped here
and there in dark slacks and
untucked cotton shirts; women
wore their single-piece silk dresses
or loose trousers with silk tops.
Many covered their heads with
round straw hats. For riding,
some women also donned elbow-
length silk gloves and covered
their faces with bandannas. The

Unloading Contraband

fact that everyone wore sandals made the scene seem quite relaxed.

Trey opened his organizer and took out the number of our Vietnamese contact. We did not know much about him. He had simply been recommended to us by Jack at the Thailand Bible League.

"Should we call from here?" asked Matt. "The line might be tapped."

"I've heard that a lot of hotel phones are," answered Trey, "but the guy in Thailand said just to be very general when we call. We can set up a meeting place and go from there."

Trey picked up the receiver and dialed—a beeping, then the sound of a phone-company recording. "Uh-oh, guys," said Trey.

"What?" questioned Mike.

Trey shook his head and redialed. The result was the same. "I think the number has been disconnected."

"I wonder if he moved," suggested Matt.

"Or *was* moved," stated Jedd. "This isn't good. That guy was our only solid contact."

Matt reminded the others, "I have the number of that friend of the missionary we spent time with in Thailand. I think her name is Suzanne. She probably has plenty of contacts in the underground church."

Trey's attempt to reach Suzanne, however, proved futile as well; she would be out of the country "for several weeks." Within a couple of hours after entering the country, our small well of contacts had run dry.

"We've got 160 Bibles into Vietnam and no one to give them to," stated Mike flatly.

Trey was still upbeat. "God will work something out."

Matt nodded. "Why don't we pray about it and then get some lunch. I'm hungry."

We all asked God to work in our situation. Jedd finished, "We know Your people here could really use these Bibles, Father, but we really don't know how to find them. Please bring us into contact with people who need these . . ."

Matt was locking the door to our room when a voice boomed in the hallway. "Jedd, Trey! Hey, guys. Looks like you made it in all right." It was John, the businessman we had met in Bangkok. "Everything work out well with the hotel? I told them that you would probably be coming." He grasped each of our hands in turn.

We thanked John for suggesting the hotel and conveyed the day's happenings, including the successful border-crossing.

"That's great," John said. "I was praying for you guys."

Trey explained, "The only problem is, our contacts have kind of fallen through. We are not sure if we are going to be able to find people to give the Bibles to."

An almost shocked look crossed John's face. "Not find anyone to give your Bibles to? I know some people who would die for them!"

"Really?"

"Yes. I'll set up a meeting here in your room tomorrow. They'll be thrilled."

"It's that simple?"

"They know they can trust me, so yeah, it's that simple."

Mike cut in. "One thing we're wondering about, John, is what is the deal with all the church buildings around here? We thought the only churches would be meeting in basements or attics or something."

"Many of them do. The churches you see are official, state-okayed ones. With a few exceptions, they are not much more than places for people to get a little dead religion—very little of any real commitment to Jesus. Some of the pastors are still good men, but a lot of them work very closely with the government."

"Hmm," said Matt. "So the underground church still needs Bibles?"

"You better believe it!"

o o o

Along with the bicycles, motorcycles, and scooters, a rickshaw variation called a *cyclo* was always available for a dollar or two. The back half of a cyclo looked like a bicycle, but a two-person bench seat sat in front of the driver between two tires. Several drivers hopped from their lounging place in the passenger seats of their cyclos and approached us as we emerged from the hotel.

"Americans? Welcome, welcome!"

"You want cyclo? I give you good rate."

"Where you want to go? I give you good tour of the city."

"No thanks, guys," Jedd said. "We are just walking over to the food places up the street."

The men smiled good-naturedly. "Okay, but if you need ride, come to me," said one.

It appeared we were in a more touristy part of Saigon. The rambling, clothesline-draped apartments did not dominate as they did in some of the residential parts of the city. Many of the buildings around us were hotels, small cafés, and shops.

As we headed up a café-lined street, a middle-aged man in an apron approached us. "Come in, come in, my friends. Vihn Ton's Café has the best food in town."

We nodded his way and smiled but said nothing.

He would not be easily put off. "Where are you young men from?"

"The United States," replied Trey.

"Ah, yes. How you like Vietnam?"

"We just got here today but we . . ."

"Ah, you arrive today. Welcome to Vietnam. Welcome, welcome!"

"Thank you , but um . . . we want to look around a little before we get food."

"Okay, but do not forget Vihn Ton's Café. It is the best."

As we strolled on, at least a half-dozen other proprietors gave us similar spiels. We eventually returned to Vihn Ton's.

"Ah, my American friends have come back. Come in, come in. May I ask what city you from?"

"We just graduated from school in Santa Barbara."

Mike Riding in a Cyclo

"Oh, I have heard of Santa Barbara. You know Chicago? I have cousin who lives in Chicago. Here, I go get you menus."

Mike glanced after him. "The people here are pretty cool—friendly, but not ingratiating. In every country we've been to, people try to sell stuff to travelers, but most of the people here also seem genuinely welcoming and interested in you as a person."

Matt nodded. "It is a neat mixture of East and West here, too—adventurous, but still with some amenities."

。 。 。

The café, like most in Vietnam, had no wall on the street side. Several large fans toward the rear kept the heat from being oppressive. Throughout the meal, street vendors wandered in among the tables, offering everything from head massages to Xeroxed copies of the Lonely Planet travelers' guide for Vietnam.

We were finishing the last of our noodles when, approaching our table from the street, came the eighth vendor of the evening, a boy of twelve or thirteen. He carried a case containing a variety of trinkets we'd already seen plenty of: key chains made with machine-gun shells, imitation Rolexes, pocketknives, and American dog tags. Most interesting were the "Zippo" cigarette lighters, made to look like the ones American soldiers had used, each bearing the insignia of an individual unit—the screaming eagle of the 101st Airborne, the Big Red "1" of the First Armored, the tank and "Hell on Wheels" slogan of the Second Armored Cavalry. Most had personal mottoes and favorite thoughts scratched into the back of them like what the soldiers once had: "One bad ___ boy," "Kill 'em all and sort 'em out on the other side," and, "Another day in hell."

As usual, the vendor boy approached Jedd first. "You want watch? Genuine Rolex. I give you good bargain."

"No thank you. We do not want . . ."

"How about lighter. I have very good lighter."

"No! Thank you, though, but we do not need one."

We were still learning that we needed to be more firm than we felt comfortable being. Finally, the boy wandered off.

Mike shook his head. "Poor Jedd, the vendors always go to you first."

"I guess they can just tell who the nice guy is."

"They can just tell who the sucker is."

"Don't look now," said Matt, "but here comes another one. I think he wants to shine our shoes."

"Good thing we're wearing sandals," said Trey.

I keep thinking about a section from the book The Brothers Karamazov, where a young man who had been born into privilege with many servants suddenly comes to question why they should wait on him rather than he upon them. To the modern mind, this seems an obvious question. Why should someone, just by virtue of being born a slave, have had no choice but to wait hand and foot on the one who happened to be born the child of a wealthy landowner?

What strikes me, though, is the similarity I see to my own situation. By virtue of the simple fact of the circumstances I was born into, I can basically "tell" people here to do whatever I want them to do. Granted, the system is now "voluntary" and based upon economics rather than race or pedigree, but still, my money essentially gives me the position of master.

I need to think more about what my response to this realization must be, but at the very least, I know the fact that I have been given this position demands of me humility, kindness, generosity, and even chosen role-reversal at times.

Priceless Books

At two the following afternoon, a knock came at the door of our hotel room. It was John with three Vietnamese men.

Once the door was locked behind them, he began. "Let me introduce you to some of my friends. This is Brother Phong. He has been a pastor for many years. He used to be a professor, but when the government found out he was a Christian, he was fired from his post within the week."

A middle-aged man with a serious face stepped forward. "It is a pleasure to meet you," he said in excellent English, shaking our hands.

"Brother Phong is a little weak right now. This past week he was taken in for questioning. They kept him awake for forty-eight hours, continuously drilling him about what his activities as a pastor were and who he's involved with. They couldn't get much out of him, so they let him go."

Brother Phong nodded slightly, but not as if what had happened to him was of any great significance. It was as if John had said, "Brother Phong gave a speech to the Rotary Club this week."

A younger man greeted us next, a wide, gentle smile creasing his face as he shook our hands. "It is very good to have you here," he said quietly with a strong accent. Inky hair lay tousled across his broad forehead, eyes sharp and intense, but radiating kindness.

"This is Brother Tran. He oversees a large number of churches here in Saigon, spending a lot of time working with tribal peoples in the hill country. His flock is over fifteen thousand people."

We were taken aback. The young man before us could not have been much older than us, yet he was responsible for shepherding thousands of believers.

John continued, "Tran's parents were able to go to America many years ago. If Tran wanted, he could go himself. But he feels that he has been called to minister here, so he stays." We knew this was quite remarkable in itself. It is rare to find a Vietnamese person who would not jump at the chance to go to America, but the young man before us sacrificed that opportunity daily for the kingdom of God.

John introduced the third man, a friend of Brother Tran's, and then suggested we show the three what we had brought. Trey brought out a key and opened the closet.

The men stared transfixed at the stacks of Bibles.

"You . . . you brought all those in?" asked Phong, a smile breaking across his serious face. We nodded. "How did you do it?"

"We each packed forty of them in between all of our clothes and things," explained Mike.

"And none of you were caught?" wondered Tran. "I can't imagine!"

It brought us joy to see the excitement on the faces of these brothers. Their eyes gleamed like those of children on Christmas morning.

Tran continued, "Just this past week, one of my churches in the mountains was raided by the government. They took our musical instruments, hymnals, and all Bibles. Here are many, many more Bibles than we had before the government took them."

We piled Bibles in duffel bags for Tran and Phong, fifty for each. For the next hour, they quizzed us on our travels and work throughout the world. Before going, Tran made a proposal, "Would you men perhaps consider leading a retreat conference for underground church leaders?"

We did not quite understand. "Retreat conference for underground church leaders?" questioned Mike. "You would want us to lead it?"

"Yes. I know many who would greatly value the opportunity to learn from men like you."

"Would that be too dangerous for you?" asked Matt. "We've heard it is always a risk for Vietnamese Christians to meet with foreigners."

"It is a risk, but it would be worth it to us. We are eager to learn. And also, there is a place on the coast that is not so dangerous. The government is less watchful in tourist places."

Brother Tran finished, "We can discuss more later. One thing before we leave: I know you are planning to attend Brother Phong's church on Sunday morning. Would you be willing to join our underground services Sunday night?"

"We would be glad to."

"Good. I will send to pick you up at 6:00 P.M. on Sunday. And again, thank you very much for the Bibles. We appreciate them more than we can say."

339

Trey's Reflections—April 17

As I witnessed the excitement of our Vietnamese brothers at the Bibles we brought, I was struck by how often I take God's Word for granted. They were gleeful, almost ecstatic. I sometimes see reading the Bible as a less-than-thrilling duty, and forget that its teachings are revolutionary enough to be forbidden by Vietnamese, Chinese, and many other government regimes.

I must never lose sight of what a wonderful thing it is that the God who set the stars in their places and carved the depths of the oceans desires to communicate with us. Whenever I choose, I can read His thoughts, gain His instruction, and learn His ways. What a wonderful privilege! May I never see the Bible just as another book, but as a life-changing opportunity to grow in relationship with God.

That night, after confession and reconciliation, we wandered down to an old pool hall just up the street from our hotel. Cracks crisscrossed the turquoise walls and the tables were worn and battered, but the atmosphere was lively. A young crowd, both foreign and Vietnamese, talked, joked, and played pool in the smoke-filled room. It felt the way it must have for the young American GIs. The Rolling Stones, Steppenwolf, and the Byrds blasted from large speakers that hung in the corners.

A Vietnamese girl with long sable hair slipped up behind Mike and put her hands on his shoulders. "What's your name?" she asked, smiling demurely.

Mike moved a step away. "Mike. What's yours?"

"My name is Tea. You like 'girlfriend' tonight?"

"No thanks. We just came here to play pool."

"No?" She seemed a bit surprised. "Let me know if you want."

o o o

"That was Brother Phong," said Matt, hanging up the phone. "I guess he talked with some of the leaders in the underground church. They would like to do the retreat, but don't think it would be best at this time."

"Why not?" questioned Trey.

"Next week is the celebration of the Communist Revolution. It sounds like during that time the government really steps up their work against the Church. If the wrong people learned about our retreat, it could be a prime target for a big hit."

"That is disappointing," said Mike. "I'll admit, though, that I was nervous about leading a retreat for leaders in the underground church. I mean, what could we do for *them*."

"Yeah, maybe it is best that it was canceled; although I was excited about the opportunity to spend time with them."

"Maybe something else will come up."

A Shifting World

Sunday morning we attended a church pastored by Brother Phong. Interestingly enough, although his congregation is not registered with the government and is therefore "underground," they met in a regular church building after the "official" government-allowed service.

Phong explained, "The pastor of this church is a friend of ours. It is a great risk for him to allow us to meet in his building because the government could use it as a reason to shut him down. It is a credit to his faith that he is willing to accept that risk."

We were still trying to figure out the interplay between the overt church, the underground church, and the government. We were beginning to see that the government did not strike at every little instance of Christianity. Government officials choose their battles carefully, preferring to wage a broad, crushing campaign of fear and repression rather than to spend all their efforts on constant attacks. At times they used raids, violence, and prison stays, but this seemed to be on a somewhat limited basis. Apparently, they knew they could never completely quench the fire; they just wanted to keep it beneath the surface.

The church service was similar to that of a more charismatic American church—a good deal of singing, a few people speaking in tongues here and there. A group of recent converts made their confession of faith before the congregation. The message, an exhortation to give all to Christ, was given by a visiting pastor from Malaysia.

After the service, we had lunch with Pastor Phong and the Malaysian pastor and several others.

"You see," the Malaysian pastor explained to Matt, motioning with his chopsticks, "we are coming to understand that the focus of our faith must always be on our relationship with Jesus Christ—coming to know Him and serve Him more intimately. The other things we have focused on, even the good things, have often kept our focus from the most important thing. But I feel that as we are making that relationship our first priority, all of the other things fall into place."

A smile crossed Matt's face. "It's exciting to hear you say that. We feel that God has been teaching us the same thing."

"It seems the Lord is helping people all over the world to understand this truth. It has had a profound impact on my church in Malaysia. As we center our faith around our relationship with Jesus, great things happen."

"If you are pastoring a church in Malaysia, what brought you to Vietnam?"

"There are dozens of people from my church all over Asia and even in the Middle East and Australia. Some are long-term missionaries. Others do it like me—we make several visits a year to one or two locations."

"So is your primary purpose evangelism?"

"Not exactly. Our first goal is to empower local congregations to be what God has called them to be. We work with pastors and the leadership of the church to help *them* to teach and minister to the people of their church. We want the local people to actually be doing the ministry; we just encourage and help equip them."

Matt's Reflections—April 19

Americans are often surprised when we learn that Westerners are not the only ones sending out missionaries. God's church, though, is vibrant in many countries throughout the world, maybe much more so than in the United States.

In some ways it makes me sad to see America losing its place as the center of world Christianity. At the same time, it is also exciting. The situation seems a bit like what happened in the fourth century. At that time, Rome was the center of world Christianity, but it was falling to barbarian raiders. Many thought Christianity would disappear, but St. Augustine knew that God would keep His church alive and well no matter what happened to the "Christian" Roman Empire. Sure enough, the barbarians became the settled people of Europe and for countless centuries served as the new center of world Christianity. As Europe's torch flickered, America picked it up, and now it seems that we may be passing it on to nations some might consider the "barbarians" of our day.

Through it all, the Church lives on . . .

Life beneath the Surface

A call came to our room at 6:00 P.M. "Mr. Sklar, sir, there are some men here to see you."

"Thank you. We will be right down."

In the lobby we quietly greeted Tran and two of his friends, then hurried out onto the street.

"Two of you get on behind these men on the motorcycles," Tran explained. "You other two, come with me in the car."

In a blink, Mike and Trey were speeding off down the street in an old white Hyundai. Jedd and Matt climbed behind the two young men on their motorcycles and shot off in the opposite direction.

The wind blowing over Jedd's and Matt's faces was refreshing in the sticky night. Moving considerably faster than the traffic, the driver wove through the sea of two-wheeled vehicles, the lights of shops and apartments gleaming crisp and bright from a distance, but blurring as they shot past.

Over his shoulder, the driver called to Jedd, "Are you comfortable enough?"

"Just fine. It's a beautiful night."

"Good. We forgot to ask you earlier: Will you preach tonight?"

"Uh . . . sure. I would be glad to." Jedd had to smile at the shortness of notice.

They were still enjoying the ride when the bikes turned suddenly from the main road into a narrow alleyway not wide enough for a Yugo.

"We must make sure no one is following us," the man explained.

"Is that a real danger?"

"Possibly. It is also important that we not drive past the police station. If they saw you riding with us, they might be suspicious."

After maneuvering through a maze of alleyways, the road ended at a narrow gate. The two pairs of riders dismounted and hurried through it, then turned from the dark passage into a doorway.

A narrow room, forty feet long and little more than an arm-span wide, appeared to have been constructed as an afterthought to the two buildings on either side of it, as if an alley had been roofed and closed at both ends. Rows of tiny chairs, six across, filled the room from front to back, a rough podium standing ready at the front below the cross that hung on the wall.

Despite several rotating fans whirring from the walls, the room was extremely hot. Even with a fan blowing directly on him, sweat began to bead on Jedd's forehead. In groups of two and three, the believers appeared. Each shook Matt's and Jedd's hands warmly before taking their seats. According to the man who drove Matt, a hospital for cancer patients operated nearby; the smiles of several attendees came from wearied faces who seemed to be losing the battle against the disease. Last to enter was a mother leading a bald girl of eight or nine who clutched a ragged teddy bear.

o o o

Trey and Mike arrived at their destination following a similarly twisty-curvy ride. When the car finally lurched to a halt in front of a tall brick building, two men emerged, pulled Mike and Trey from the vehicle, and swept them inside without a word. Trey lost count of how many flights of stairs they had climbed by the time they reached a room that appeared to be the top floor. The stairs led no farther. The room, however, was dark and empty.

"What's that sound?" asked Mike, tilting his head.

Trey peered around in the darkness. "I can't quite tell. It sounds like singing."

"Over here," directed one of the men. "Everyone is already in."

The man called out in Vietnamese, and a moment later a section seemed to drop out of the ceiling, spilling light. It took Mike a moment to realize that what had descended was a stair ladder. The man nodded and Mike placed his foot on the lowest rung. As his head emerged into the attic, Mike glanced around. A naked bulb hung from the ceiling, which angled down to connect with the floor. All windows were covered with blankets. Perhaps thirty or forty people sat on the floor. They smiled down at Mike as he climbed up and into their church. When everyone was in the room and the trapdoor pulled shut, Tran introduced the special guests.

"These are Tran's friends who brought the Bibles!" announced someone in English, creating a general hubbub. Mike and Trey faced a deluge of well-wishes and pats on the back as they moved to an open space of floor.

Then the singing struck up again.

Mike's Reflections—April 19

What a thrill to get to worship and share words with the underground church. I have heard it said regarding the Church in persecuted lands that the hotter the fire, the finer the gold. The warmth and the fervor of these believers certainly suggest that this is the case here. I don't think I've ever felt so unworthy to speak.

I think I'm also beginning to understand the Communist government's relationship to the Church a little better. They don't fear religion in the sense that I thought they did. In fact, they seem quite satisfied that people whose faith involves only Sunday morning services will never have an impact worth worrying about. What seems to terrify the government are churches where they spend time in the Bible daily, pray regularly, and where their lives are tied together in a committed community.

In a way, Marx was right. Religion that consists of only tradition, ritual, and positive sentiments is indeed little more than a drug for the masses. It rarely changes anything. However, even a small community of men and women who have truly decided to follow Jesus is enough to make tyrants tremble.

Joshuas and Calebs

We had just gotten back from breakfast when Tran strode into our room, his face barely containing his smile.

"Some of the leaders have changed their minds! They feel that God wants them to go on the retreat!"

"Are you still sure this is a good idea?" questioned Matt.

"Certain!" responded Tran, his eyes gleaming. "Besides, now it is too late to change our minds. The people who will be attending the conference are already on their way. They left on a bus at five-thirty this morning."

"How are we going to get there?" queried Trey.

"We will take a boat down the river to the ocean. It will take less time than the bus."

"Why didn't we just go with everyone else?"

"It's not wise for you to travel with them. People could be suspicious."

"When do we need to leave?"

"Soon. Let's pray for the conference before we go . . ."

o o o

Our boat reached the port of Tyon-Fahg by late morning. A small tourist city had built up around the harbor, but only a thin line of restaurants and hotels followed as a taxi carried us up the coast. Our road divided the dry, rolling hills from long stretches of empty beach.

"I never imagined places like this in Vietnam," Matt said.

"My dad says the beaches all along the coast are beautiful," noted Trey.

Tran interjected, "There is a hotel here that is owned by the army. If it is not full of soldiers, you can stay there. The police are not so likely to think to bother any of us if you are staying with the army."

"Where will you stay?"

"Not far from you in a different hotel."

"And where will we have our meetings?"

"There is a building that is safe. We can rent it out for very little cost."

o o o

Tran began the first session of the conference with prayer in Vietnamese, translated for us: "Dear Lord, we thank You for the privilege of these days we have together. May You bless our time, Father, and challenge and teach us through our American friends who will be speaking Your words. Please protect us and keep us safe from those who would wish to harm us. In the name of Your Son, Jesus, we pray. Amen."

A guitarist started playing, and worship began. Some of the tunes were familiar, translations of hymns and worship songs from the West; others were uniquely Asian. In any style or language, there is something wonderful about a heart lifted to God in song. Once again, we were reminded of the rich tapestry of music that likely will be woven in heaven from all the nations of the world.

Tran had told us we would be sharing with leaders of the underground church. We were surprised to note that many of the young men and women seated on the black-and-white-tiled floor around us were close to our own age. While we had observed people of all ages involved with the underground church, we were beginning to see that much of its energy and direction came from individuals in their late teens and twenties. Just like in the early church, God was using young people to carry out His work.

Trey's Reflections—April 20

It is exciting to realize that God often uses young people as His "green berets" when He has important work to do. Paul told Timothy, "Don't let anyone look down on you because you are young, but set an example . . ." (1 Tim. 4:12). That call is to us as well.

It is amazing to think that when Jesus left the earth, He entrusted His message and the staggering task of taking it "to the ends of the earth" to young people probably in their teens and early twenties. I'm not sure that I would have done it that way, but it worked. Those young men and women turned the world upside down. If we will seek wholeheartedly to know God and do His will—young as we are—God will do remarkable things through us as well.

Throughout the retreat's eight sessions, we built from the text of Colossians 2:2: "My purpose is that they may be encouraged in heart and united in love, so that they may have the full riches of complete understanding, in order that they may know the mystery of God, namely, Christ."

The young leaders did appear greatly "encouraged in heart" as we shared stories of their brothers and sisters from all around the world who loved them and would some day celebrate with them in heaven. We spent an entire session telling them about the people we had visited, and they prayed earnestly for each of them at the close of the session.

Mike's Reflections—April 20

I see it as a great privilege to encourage these believers. It is also fun just to hang out with them. We played a bunch of Frisbee and soccer and other games at the beach this afternoon. They thought it was so funny that Jedd and Matt were so tall. When we were playing keep-away, they'd laugh and laugh and say, "Giants, giants!" as the guys tried to climb up Jedd's back to get the Frisbee.

Tonight we ate at a simple, thatch-covered seaside restaurant. As we talked and ate fried clams, boiled mussels, squid, fresh coconuts, and lots of rice, I realized, I truly love these people. A childlikeness glows from each one of them; an eagerness to extend love to us and also to grow nearer to Jesus. They are always ready with face-splitting smiles, but in worship and prayer they are as fervent as any people I've ever met.

That evening, the group hired several vans for a drive up the coast. We stopped in a small parking lot on a quiet hillside. Everyone got out to explore a bit. Jedd joined Tran at a railing that overlooked the Vietnamese coastline. Lanterns of fishing boats flickered as they bobbed in the waves below.

"Do you miss your family, Tran?" Jedd asked.

Tran was silent for a moment before replying. "When I am very busy, sometimes I forget, but usually I miss them. I miss them very much."

"Are any of your relatives still in Vietnam?"

"My sister is in Vietnam, but she lives in the north. I do not see her much. Sometimes I ache for loneliness."

"You have many good friends in Saigon, don't you?"

"I have many people who love me and who I love, but maybe not so many that are close to me like my family. Because I have churches to help everywhere, I often travel. Sometimes I feel very alone. At times, I felt so alone I did not know how to stand it. But then God said to me, almost as if I heard a voice, '*I am your Father, Tran.*' It brought tears to my eyes."

A faint breeze came up as Tran stared out over the ocean. Jedd could see that his eyes were moist.

"It is obvious that much fruit has come from your sacrifice, Tran."

Tran turned to Jedd, and it seemed to him that in an instant the sadness in Tran's eyes was replaced by fire.

"I believe that is true, Jedd! I pray that I will be a Joshua and Caleb of a new generation. In the past generation, not a large number came to Jesus. If we do not live differently, how will we win this nation for Jesus?"

"I will be faithful to pray for you, Tran, that you really will be a Joshua and Caleb."

"And I will pray for you, Jedd. I will pray that you also will be a Joshua and Caleb for your generation."

Before we left, the group of believers presented us with plaques in thanks for our sharing with them. The message emblazoned on the marble was simple, and since they now hang in our homes, they serve as a continual reminder: "Pray for Vietnam."

Jedd's Reflections—April 21

Tran is incredible. I admire him and love him.

I feel we are learning so much more from these Vietnamese believers than they are from us, even though we are the ones speaking at this retreat. Their love for Jesus and deep commitment and willingness to sacrifice humble me. (Just the fact that they all got up this morning at 5:00 a.m. for prayer together reminds me how weak my commitment to prayer often is.)

I've been a Christian all my life, but I don't know if I've ever seen Christianity as fully as they do. It seems as if they have become Jesus' apprentices in learning how to live, just the way someone in Renaissance Italy could have become Michelangelo's apprentice in sculpting. Salomón and Mery, Steve Barrett, Anil and Annie, and many of the others we've met on this trip are this way, too. They really seek to pattern their lives as He taught. They see Him as the true expert on every aspect of life. I guess that's what becoming Jesus' disciple should always mean.

Most of us American Christians would probably say that's what we do, too. But I know that in my own life, at least, I've often seen Jesus only as a nice Savior who gets me into heaven. I've read the Bible and prayed not so much to grow closer to Him or to learn how to live, but because I've felt that I need to if I want to be a good Christian.

If Jesus is who He claimed to be, though, He is the Master of life! From what I've seen in those who really seek to follow Him, living as He taught leads to the epic life I want so badly—not necessarily life without trials, but one full of purpose even in the ordinary moments of everyday life.

Tea and Steve

The night we returned to Saigon, Jedd and Mike headed out to play some pool. In front of the little pool hall, a young woman stood provocatively in a blue silk dress. It was Tea, the prostitute we had talked with several times the previous week.

"Hello, Tea," Mike called out. "How are you?"

"Okay." She gave a slight grimace. "My stomach not feel so well tonight."

"You're sick?"

She nodded, pouting slightly.

"Why don't you go home and sleep?"

"I can't. I have work."

We entered the pool hall and were soon engaged in games on different tables. After his first game, Mike handed his cue to a young Vietnamese man. "Go ahead and take over for me. I need to go do something."

"Where you going, Mike?" Jedd called out, trying to line up a shot at the eightball.

Mike waited until Jedd took his shot, then explained, "I'm going back to the hotel room to get some money for Tea—so she can go home and sleep."

"You mind waiting for a second?"

Mike watched while Jedd finished his game and then the two moved back out to the street.

"Are you feeling any better, Tea?" asked Mike.

"No. My stomach still hurt."

"Hmm. How much do you usually make in a night?"

"Twenty or thirty thousand dong."

That would be about fifteen to twenty dollars, several times what most day laborers made. Mike and Jedd walked back to the hotel room and grabbed a few American bills and a Bible.

Back at the pool hall, though, Tea was gone. Jedd bit his lip. "Shoot. I wonder if she got picked up."

"Let's go look at that corner café just up the street. Sometimes she hangs out there."

Sure enough, Tea was standing on the sidewalk in front of the café.

"Tea, if we give you fifteen dollars, will you go home and sleep?" asked Mike.

Tea seemed surprised and a bit suspicious. "What you want?"

A young American man who had been watching the interaction from a table in the café suddenly rose from his seat and walked toward them. As he stormed by, he muttered, "Stay the ____ away from me!"

"What was wrong with him?" wondered Mike.

Jedd shook his head. "I have no idea."

Mike turned back to Tea. "We want you to go home and rest. Will you do that if we give you fifteen dollars?"

"Why?"

"We care about you, Tea. You need to sleep. You are sick."

"But . . ." Slowly the mystified look on her face began to melt. In its place grew the smile of a little girl who has been helped by a stranger. "Yes. I go home and sleep."

"We also have this for you," said Jedd, producing a Vietnamese Bible. "If you have a chance, read it. It is the best book ever written."

She nodded, taking the Bible. Mike and Jedd slowly moved off down the street. "Do you think she'll go home?" Jedd asked.

"I hope so."

o o o

Tran joined us for dinner the following evening. As we sipped on bowls of spicy soup, the conversation turned from the events of the retreat to the broader situation facing the underground church.

"What you must understand," Tran explained, setting down his spoon, "is that the Vietnamese government wants to be seen by the West as open and tolerant."

"So they do token things to make it seem like they are accepting of religion?" asked Matt.

"Yes, like last year they even allowed some Bibles to be printed in Vietnam."

"Really! So why are Bibles so difficult to get?"

"Because they allow only a small number to be printed and do not let all of them be distributed. Then, they take them away from us any chance they get."

"Would you say that things are better than they used to be?" questioned Mike.

"In some ways, yes. Now there are much fewer direct attacks and less bodily persecution, but still it happens often, especially in the north part of country."

"But they still are trying to crush the Church?"

"Oh yes. Very much so. I could tell you many stories."

"We would be interested to hear," requested Matt.

Tran nodded. "There was a very nice old man who the doctors diagnosed with cancer, saying he had less than a year to live. When government health workers visited his house and saw a Bible, they said he must renounce his faith if he did not want to lose the assistance the government always gives to people like him who are sick. He refused. So they cut off his medicine, rice, and living allowance."

"That is terrible," said Mike, shaking his head.

"It is common. Another woman I know was a hero for her work with the Vietcong during the war against America. The government built her a beautiful house to thank her for her bravery. But, when they learned that she was now a Christian, they said she could not live in the house unless she publicly declared herself atheist."

"What did she do?"

"Nothing. She now lives in a tiny apartment."

"It sounds like they get you just where it hurts."

"That is often how it happens. For example, poor Christian parents are charged more for school fees than their rich, atheist neighbors, often forcing them to choose between their faith and their child's education."

"That's rough," mused Mike. "It is a lot easier to make sacrifices that affect only yourself than to make them for people you love."

"Very true. That is why the government works as it does. When storms of hail destroyed homes of village hill people, government agents asked who was a Christian before they handed out aid. Atheists were given hotel rooms and funds to rebuild their homes. Christians received nothing, and many still live in shacks . . ."

351

The way the government works against the Church here is insidious. Yes, there are death threats, lengthy imprisonments, and mind-numbing interrogations, but the bulk of the attack is below the surface, a surface that includes plenty of nice, sedate, Sunday-morning-only churches. There may be fewer overt attacks than in the past, but what goes on now seems almost more difficult to resist than direct persecution. What terrible decisions, choosing between your faith and the well-being of your spouse, your children, or even your cancer treatment.

"I'm going out for a little walk," said Jedd later that night.

"It's after midnight," stated Matt, looking up from his book.

"Yeah, I just feel like it."

Outside, the air was warm and comfortable, the road, silent and empty. Cyclo drivers lounged on the sidewalk, talking and laughing. One called out to Jedd, "You need ride?"

"No thanks."

The man smiled. "You walk too much. Cyclo give your legs rest." His friends laughed.

Jedd turned up the main café street. The patrons were gone and the lights were all off. In the center of the street, a group of Vietnamese men sat in a circle on boxes and packing crates, gambling with dice. A young girl rode back and forth on an old bicycle with her little sister perched on the handlebars. Young boys played marbles along the gutter while cooks and merchants hunched over bowls of soup in front of their closed shops, discussing the day's business, a few already laying out bamboo mats and settling down to sleep on the sidewalk.

"Hey!" a feminine voice called out.

Jedd turned to see a girl in front of a dark café. It was Tea. Next to her was the young man who had acted so upset the previous night at the café when Jedd and Mike had given Tea money. He spoke up, "Come over here, I'd like to talk to you."

Jedd approached the pair. "I'm Steve," said the young man, offering his hand. "I wanted to apologize for last night, you know, what I said and stuff."

"No problem," replied Jedd, not sure how to respond.

"See, I've hung out in Vietnam for a while now, and Tea and I are pretty good friends. I try to look out for her. I don't want her to do any of *that* kind of work, you know? I thought she was taking a 'job' from you guys and I was angry."

"We could tell," said Jedd with a smile.

"Anyway, I wanted to thank you for what you did. I was mad, but finally I found Tea and she told me why you gave her money. Tea has had a lot of stomach trouble. I think it is because she drinks too much. She used your money to get some medicine from a doctor. I'm sure it'll help. She feels better already, don't you, Tea?"

Tea smiled and nodded.

"That was pretty cool that you gave her a Bible, too."

"Our pleasure. We think it is the most important thing anyone could read."

"Unfortunately, Tea can't read very well, but I'm trying to teach her. I think people in her family will read it, though."

"That's great."

"Why don't you have a seat," said Steve, indicating a few café chairs that remained on the sidewalk. "What can I get you to drink?"

For the next hour, Jedd, Tea, and the young American talked about life and Vietnam and work and our trip. It was after 1:00 A.M. when Jedd finally headed back to the hotel. Most of the shopkeepers now lay fast asleep, lying on mats in front of their businesses. The cyclo drivers were folded awkwardly in the passenger seats of their three-wheeled bikes, sleeping as well. One lifted an eyebrow as Jedd walked past him, "Good night, American."

"Good night, cyclo man."

Brother Hong

Matt rounded the corner and peered across the street at the café. A Vietnamese man stood against the wall to the left of the entrance. Every few seconds he glanced up the street, then down it. He appeared to be in his late twenties, with sinewy arms connected to shoulders that seemed surprisingly broad for a Vietnamese man. Matt made as if to walk past the man, but offered a "good evening" as he neared.

"Good evening," came the reply. The man stared at Matt's face for a moment before continuing, "You are Matt?"

"Yes. Are you Brother Hong?"

The man nodded and indicated the café. "Let's go inside."

Once seated, Matt waited in silence. Brother Hong turned his head slowly as he peered at the other diners. He blinked twice, almost sleepily, like a jungle cat, relaxed but always alert. Seeing nothing to arouse his suspicion, he began softly, "Thank you for meeting me. I was wanting to talk to you when I heard about you." His English was quite clear despite being a bit broken.

"I'm glad we could," answered Matt. "It's a privilege to talk with you also."

"I hear you brought Bibles to some of the pastors."

"We did."

"Thank you. We need all we can get."

"You are a pastor also?"

"Yes. I work mostly with tribal people in the mountains. That is where I am from. I have heard you are traveling very much."

For a time, Matt explained our travels and work throughout the world. Hong was excited to hear reports of the Church in other lands. "We do not always hear of our brothers and sisters in other countries," he explained. "We can sometimes feel we are small and being crushed."

Matt looked at him with understanding. "It is good for believers to know about their family in other parts of the world. I want to tell people in America about you here in Vietnam. There are a lot of people there who pray for you, but not many who really know what your lives are like here."

"We still value their prayers."

"I would be interested to . . ." Matt paused as he caught sight of Jedd entering the café. "Jedd, over here."

Jedd joined the pair at the small table and Matt introduced him to Hong. Before they could continue, a waitress approached to take their order. It was not until steaming bowls of soup had been set on the table that Matt was able to repeat his query. "I would be interested to hear your story, Hong, to hear about your life."

Hong nodded, glanced around once more, then began, "During Vietnam's war with Cambodia, my family and I ended up in a refugee camp on the Cambodian border. Missionaries who worked with the refugees told me about Jesus. I became very passionate about Him, and I poured myself into the Bible during the years I spent in that camp. When the war was over, I moved to Saigon. I liked it here, but after a time I felt called to go up to the village I had grown up in to share Jesus with my people. I was excited that God had called me to something. Soon after I arrived, though, I began to have doubts. The first two months in my village seemed totally useless. I thought, *Why did God call me here if He is not going to do anything?* I wondered if God would ever use me at all.

"But then, in one morning, eight people came to Jesus. Over the next two and a half months, thirty people in my village believed in Jesus, including my parents. I was so excited. There were also many signs and healings from the Holy Spirit."

Hong paused, and Matt turned to Jedd for a moment. "It is interesting that Hong says that about signs and healings confirming his ministry. Tran said the same thing about his ministry here in Saigon. He felt like the miracles confirmed his ministry to the other pastors of the underground church."

Jedd replied, "I feel like I understand so little of that realm. There are so many miracle-fakers in the U.S., you almost come to assume the only way God can heal today is through medicine. Maybe He chooses to heal in more overt ways in places where they don't have it."

Matt nodded thoughtfully, then turned back to Hong. "Sorry, didn't mean to cut you off there."

Hong smiled and continued. "Things went very good in my village for a while, but then the government officials learned what I was doing. They took me in and questioned me for a long time."

"What did they want?" asked Matt.

"Two things. First, to get me to renounce the name of Jesus. Second, they wanted me to tell them the names of all the people who had become Christians in my village."

"What happened?"

"I would not tell them anything, so they put me in prison. The first ten days I spent in a cell with two other men. I told them about Jesus, and both of them accepted Him."

"Wow," remarked Matt under his breath.

"So they moved me to another cell with another man. He was a government informant, and he tried to get information out of me. When this did not work, they put me in solitary confinement."

"What was it like?" asked Jedd.

"It was a very small room that was always totally black and the floor was always wet. Every few days they took me out and questioned me, telling me about all the possibilities I was missing out on in life, like an education and a job and marriage, offering to set me free immediately if I would inform on the other church members.

"This was a very difficult time for me and I . . . I . . ." Hong stopped for a moment and swallowed hard. A wave of emotion seemed to have washed over him before he was aware it was coming. He looked at the table for a moment, set his jaw, and then looked up at Matt and Jedd again.

"They just left me in there for a long time. I could not talk to anyone, read anything, even see anything. I felt like my head was turning to mush in that empty black cell. My peers were growing in knowledge, but my mind was rotting. I cried sometimes and began to pray always. God started to bring Scriptures I had read in the refugee camp to my mind. Even though I felt like I was losing my ability to think, the words kept coming to me, 'It is better to enter heaven blind than to go into hell with both eyes.' I made my decision. If my mind became dull, that would have to be okay. It would be better than to turn on God's people.

"The next time they questioned me, I said, 'I am in your hands. I cannot hand over the innocent. You must judge for yourself if I am guilty.'

"They put me back in my cell. The days stretched on forever. My sentence was five years. I had one small bowl of rice for breakfast and one for dinner. I often felt lonely, crushed. But many other times the Lord gave me great comfort. There were times when the Spirit moved me to pray in tongues and worship the Lord with words I did not know.

"Then one day, the commander of the prison came to my cell. He took me to his office and said to me, 'I am setting you free. You are more innocent than anyone in your generation.'"

Jedd leaned forward. "And they let you go, just like that?"

"Yes. So I returned to my village, where I have worked ever since."

"You have not had any more trouble with the government?"

"I have had some. Sometimes they take me in to interrogate me, and once they put me in prison for a little while again, but the work always continues . . ."

∘ ∘ ∘

Our departure was scheduled for the following afternoon. Tran came by as we were packing the last of our things.

"You are ready to go?" he asked.

Mike nodded. "Yes. But we have some things for you before we leave." He offered Tran a duffel bag that contained the last of the Bibles. Tran grinned as he peered inside.

"Also, do you think you would be able to use these?" Mike said, producing several Christian books we had read in the past few months: Lewis's *Mere Christianity*, J. I. Packer's *Knowing God*, and *The Imitation of Christ* by Thomas à Kempis.

"Books like these are sometimes more difficult to get than Bibles," Tran said with appreciation. "I can make copies of these and get them into the hands of many believers."

Finally, Trey brought out an envelope. "This money, Tran, is to help you in your ministry. Use it however you feel is best."

Tran shook his head. "From the first to the last," he said, "you have been a blessing to us. Many pray you may return."

"Thank you," Trey responded, "but you and the church here have been much more of a blessing to us."

Tran hugged each of us in turn, then helped us carry our bags out to the curb in front of the hotel. He bargained with the small crowd of taxi drivers until only one remained, and we loaded our backpacks into the trunk of a small car.

"To the airport," he said to the driver before sticking his head in the rear window. "Good-bye, my brothers. I look forward to our next meeting, whenever that may be. You will be in my prayers . . ." The car rumbled to a start and began rolling down the street. ". . . And do not forget: Pray for Vietnam!"

357

Conclusion

The Adventure Begins

We must not cease from exploration. And the end of all our exploring will be to arrive where we began and to know the place for the first time.

—T. S. Eliot

Jedd turned over and glanced at the clock on the nightstand. 3:17 A.M. Two hours lying there and sleep still eluded him.

Kind of funny, he thought. *This is the softest bed I've had in seven months, and I still can't sleep a wink.*

In Hong Kong, instead of connecting immediately to Los Angeles, we had arranged a layover so we could spend a few days with Matt's aunt and uncle who lived just inside mainland China. Their home felt like America. Although we did make a brief sojourn into Guangzhou (the city once known as Canton), we could generate little desire to do much touring. Aunt Loretta and Uncle Hank seemed to sense this. They happily allowed us to do little but lounge around the house, relaxing and playing games with Matt's two young cousins, Heidi and Tanya.

Jedd let out a sigh and pushed back the bedcovers. He stepped gingerly over Matt and Trey, who appeared to be sleeping quite soundly on the floor. The faint buzz of a television emanated from the living room.

"You're still up, Mike?"

"Yeah. Couldn't sleep."

"Me either. It is kind of funny; I think I'm just too excited about going home tomorrow."

"I'm definitely ready."

"Are you excited about seeing Brittney?"

"I've never missed anyone this much in my life."

"Uh-oh, Mike. Before we know it, you're going to go get married on us."

Mike grinned. "The way I'm feeling now, I just may." He thought for a moment, then asked, "What about you? You going to ride up to Russia's northland on a white horse anytime soon?"

"You mean Lena?" Jedd smiled faintly.

"Do you think about her much?"

"I guess I do. Even when we were there in Russia, I knew it was all kind of silly and that the feeling would fade. It has . . . at least, it's mellowed. Whether or not I ever get married, I know God's got other things for me. I guess there will always be something in the memory, though."

"Yeah, I bet there will." He allowed a respectful silence, then broke into a faint smirk. "Well, I'm going to be kissing a *real* girl tomorrow."

"If no one is there for me, I may have to kiss Brittney, too."

"One of those customs ladies might be willing to give you a smooch if you really need it."

"Yeah, well, smooch or no smooch, I'll be happy to be home. It'll be

Shekou, China

great to see my family. My mom's cancer treatment is all over and she's doing really well." Jedd glanced at the TV screen for a moment. "What's this movie you're watching?"

"I'm not sure of its name. Pretty intense, set on a college campus. There are all these groups struggling for power, different goals, some good and some evil. They all want influence and respect but call the constant fight for power 'the game' . . . we're all playing the game."

"Sounds like life as it is."

"I know. It's weird how much I've changed. I remember wanting to make it to the top so bad. I didn't think too much about why; I guess I just wanted to play, too. It really is refreshing to feel like we can live outside 'the game' if we keep living like we want to."

"I hope we don't get sucked back in when we get back into more normal lives."

"I guess that's always a danger, but I don't think we will. We've got a pretty clear sense of how meaningless it all is."

"I agree. Well, are you going to watch the rest of this?"

"Yeah. I'll sleep on the plane tomorrow."

"I never sleep on planes. I'm going to go lie down again."

"All right. See you in the morning."

"Twenty-six hours 'til America."

"Yep. We're going home."

o o o

Our ferryboat plowed through steel-gray waters. Matt and Trey leaned against the aft railing, watching the Chinese mainland disappear. A fierce wind pushed their hair out in front of their heads and made a snapping sound with the Communist banner that flew from the back of the boat.

"Your hair is sure getting long, Trey," said Matt, raising his voice to be heard above the wind.

"I know. I never let it get much longer than a crew cut growing up. Now I can put it in my mouth." Trey pulled a strand down in front of his face and held it in his teeth to prove his point.

"With as little as we've showered, that must taste really good."

"It's okay. Kind of salty."

Matt smiled and turned his gaze back to the churning wake. "So what are you looking forward to, Trey?"

"Pizza Hut."

"Me, too, but not as much as you, I think. Anything else?"

"Nothing *that* much," said Trey with a grin. "How about you?"

"I will definitely like having a little more pattern in my life for a while. And it'll be really good to see my family."

A shadow crossed Trey's face for a moment. "I think my mom and my brother will be moving back to the U.S. pretty soon. We have a lot to sort through, but it will be good to be together."

Jedd and Mike emerged from a door a short way up the deck and joined Matt and Trey against the railing. Mike's orange T-shirt, its neck stretched and frayed, seemed ready to blow off his body. "Cold out here," he remarked.

"I felt a few raindrops a minute ago," said Matt. The swollen clouds overhead appeared ready to lose their cargo at any time.

"We're just a plane ride away from sunny L.A.," remarked Trey.

Jedd slapped his hands down on the railing. The others looked over at him, but he said nothing, only shook his head slowly.

"What?" said Trey.

"I'm just thinking, what an amazing adventure we got to be a part of."

"You're just realizing that now?"

"No. It is just that I feel like we had nothing to do with creating it or making it happen. I mean, obviously we worked and organized and stuff, but more than anything, I feel like we just got to go along for a wild ride."

"I feel the same," said Mike.

"It was faith, too, though," suggested Matt. "Not that we deserved any of this or anything, but to end up in places like this, you have to go beyond what you feel totally comfortable with . . ."

"Or at least beyond what other people feel comfortable with you doing," interjected Mike. "Faith makes it possible to rebel against the expectations of the crowd."

"Rebellion isn't a value in itself, though," Jedd asserted.

"Right. I wasn't saying that. Just thrashing against the system is every bit as stupid as blindly obeying it. Real faith is different; it's the confidence in God that frees you to cut against the world's ways and values. It's rebellion, but it is guided by God and His Word. Sometimes you live in the boundaries and sometimes outside them."

We fell silent for a moment, watching a rusty scow cross through our wake just fifty yards behind. In its raised, windowless cabin, the silhouette of a sailor hunched over a large steering wheel.

361

"That'd be kind of a fun job," declared Trey.

"What, driving a scow?" Matt laughed. "That thing looks like it could sink at any moment."

"It'd still be fun. Better than pushing papers."

Mike stood up on the railing as he added another thought. "Whatever work we do when we get back, the big question now is whether or not the adventure is over."

"That *is* the question," agreed Matt.

Trey shook his head. "It's not over."

Mike glanced at him. "Why not?"

"Because—like we've been starting to see for the past couple months: What's been the real adventure of this trip anyway? The travel has been fun, but the places and experiences weren't the truly *epic* parts of the trip. What has made this all so great has been the other things . . . You know, growing deeper in our relationship with God and learning to love one another better, and getting to learn from and serve other people, too. That stuff is just as available to us at home as it is in any exotic location."

Mike chuckled. "Trey's always the optimist, but I do think you're right."

"I agree," said Jedd. "If we really are serious about living out everything we've learned, our adventure is really just beginning. Epic life isn't just going from one wild place to another. More than anything, I think, it's . . ." He paused for a moment. "It's living out ordinary life for eternal purposes."

"We just have to commit to actually *doing* it," stated Trey emphatically.

"That will be the challenge," Matt agreed. "But at least we've got a good sense of how to start. Think about Salomón and Mery, or Steve, or the Claassens, or Anil and Annie, or Tran and Hong, or so many of the others. They try to live as Jesus called them to live every day. It obviously takes sacrifices, but the quality of relationships and the depth of purpose they live with . . . *that's* real adventure. If we're able to do the same, especially together, I *know* it will be epic life."

"Look up there." Jedd pointed, turning our gaze to the front of the boat.

A quarter mile ahead, a curtain of silver-gray hung between the clouds and the water. The realm beyond appeared dark, almost black.

"Here it comes," declared Matt, pulling up his hood.

Trey paused for a moment. He glanced at the impending downpour, then at Mike, Matt, and Jedd. "Well, guys"—he smiled, the raindrops starting to pelt against his face—"our adventure is only beginning . . ."

About the Authors

During college, **Matt Kronberg** worked with the homeless in Santa Barbara and spent summers as a counselor at a camp in the Sierra. He has a double major in Philosophy and Communication Studies and is now pursuing graduate studies at North Park Theological Seminary.

Jedd Medefind grew up with his three brothers on a small farm in California's Central Valley, thriving on sports, books, and the great outdoors. He now serves as chief of staff for Assemblyman Tim Leslie in the California State Legislature.

Mike Peterson would be your run-of-the-mill beach bum had he not carved out a niche in the world of commerce with his own small business. Even so, he's still rarely happier than when riding the waves or cutting through deep powder on a snowboard.

Trey Sklar's passion has always been for lands beyond, studying at the University of Zimbabwe and working with an international corporation in Moscow. Not surprisingly, he earned a degree in International Studies from Westmont College and hopes to live a ministry of hospitality—wherever he ends up.